Cambridge English

Vocabulary
for First
Certificate

with answers

剑桥FCE

核心词汇精讲精练

BARBARA THOMAS（英）编著
LAURA MATTHEWS（英）

边卫红　李鲁闽　周珊　译

CAMBRIDGE
UNIVERSITY PRESS

西安交通大学出版社
XI'AN JIAOTONG UNIVERSITY PRESS

图书在版编目（CIP）数据

剑桥 FCE 核心词汇精讲精练 ＝ Cambridge Vocabulary
for First Certificate with answers /（英）托马斯
（Thomas，B.），（英）马修斯（Matthews，L.）编著. —
西安：西安交通大学出版社，2013.9
ISBN 978-7-5605-5720-5

Ⅰ．①剑… Ⅱ．①托… ②马… Ⅲ．①英语—词汇—
水平考试—自学参考资料 Ⅳ．①H313

中国版本图书馆 CIP 数据核字（2013）第 219446 号

版权登记：**陕版出图字 25－2009－007 号**

书　　名　剑桥 FCE 核心词汇精讲精练
编　　著　（英）Barbara Thomas，（英）Laura Matthews
译　　者　边卫红　李鲁闽　周　册
责任编辑　黄科丰　张　茜
封面设计　大愚设计
出版发行　西安交通大学出版社
地　　址　西安市兴庆南路 10 号（邮编：710049）
电　　话　（010）62605588　62605019（发行部）　（029）82668315（总编室）
读者信箱　bj62605588@163.com
印　　刷　北京鑫丰华彩印有限公司
字　　数　206 千
开　　本　787mm×1092mm　1/16
印　　张　9
版　　次　2013 年 11 月第 1 版　2013 年 11 月第 1 次印刷
书　　号　ISBN 978-7-5605-5720-5/H·1589
定　　价　30.00 元

Contents

Map of the book

Unit number	Title	Topics	Exam practice
Unit 1	Good life plan	Health and fitness, illness and treatment	Use of English Part 2 (Open cloze), Use of English Part 4 (Key word transformations), Writing Part 2 (Letter)
Unit 2	Earth, sea and sky	Geography, climate and weather	Reading Part 2 (Gapped-text sentences), Speaking Part 2 (Comparing photographs)
Unit 3	Sound waves	Music, sounds	Use of English Part 2 (Open cloze), Writing Part 1 (Email)
Unit 4	Highs and lows	Feelings, adverbs and adjectives	Listening Part 1 (Multiple choice), Use of English Part 3 (Word formation), Writing Part 2 (Story)
Unit 5	Looking back	The past, time	Use of English Part 1 (Multiple choice lexical cloze), Writing Part 2 (Article)
Unit 6	Getting the message across	Advertising, computers, telephoning	Writing Part 2 (Essay), Speaking Part 4 (Discussion)
Unit 7	The world of work	Jobs, personal qualities, employment and unemployment	Reading Part 3 (Multiple matching), Writing Part 2 (Letter)
Unit 8	Everyone's different	Physical appearance, personality	Reading Part 1 (Multiple choice), Use of English Part 4 (Key word transformations)
Unit 9	Get active	Movement, sport	Use of English Part 4 (Key word transformations), Speaking Part 2 (Comparing photographs), Writing Part 2 (Letter)
Unit 10	My world	Family and relationships, celebrations, friends	Speaking Part 1 (General conversation), Speaking Part 2 (Comparing photographs), Writing Part 2 (Letter), Listening Part 3 (Multiple matching)
Unit 11	Moving around	Transport, travel, holidays	Speaking Parts 3 and 4 (Decison-making task and discussion), Use of English Part 4 (Key word transformations), Writing Part 2 (Article)

Unit number	Title	Topics	Exam practice
Unit 12	Time off	Leisure time, hobbies and games, cinema and theatre	Writing Part 1 (Letter), Reading Part 3 (Multiple matching)
Unit 13	Around town	Cities and towns, facilities, traffic	Use of English Part 1 (Multiple choice lexical cloze), Speaking Part 4 (Discussion), Writing Part 2 (Report)
Unit 14	Shared tastes	Food and drink, meals, art	Use of English Part 3 (Word formation), Listening Part 2 (Sentence completion), Speaking Part 1 (General conversation)
Unit 15	Media mania	Television and radio, newspapers and magazines, books	Reading Part 1 (Multiple choice), Writing Part 2 (Review)
Unit 16	Stages of life	Different ages, university, school	Speaking Part 2 (Comparing photographs), Use of English Part 4 (Key word transformations)
Unit 17	Shopping in style	Clothes, shopping, money	Reading Part 2 (Gapped-text sentences), Use of English Part 4 (Key word transformations)
Unit 18	Home territory	Houses and homes, household problems	Speaking Parts 3 and 4 (Decision-making task and discussion), Use of English Part 2 (Open cloze), Use of English Part 3 (Word formation)
Unit 19	Green planet	Science, the environment	Use of English Part 3 (Word formation), Listening Part 4 (Multiple choice)
Unit 20	My judgment	Crime, opinions	Speaking Parts 3 and 4 (Decision-making task and discussion), Writing Part 2 (Essay), Listening Part 1 (Multiple choice)

Acknowledgements

The authors would like to thank their editors, Martine Walsh, Caroline Thiriau and Nicholas Murgatroyd, for their positive and professional support. They would also like to thank Rowland and Paul for their support and encouragement.

The book has also benefited enormously from the useful feedback we have received from teachers and students. In particular we would like to thank the following teachers who reviewed and piloted the material throughout its development:

Christine Barton, Greece; Gillian Davidson, UK; Stephanie Dimond-Bayir and her students at the Bell School, Cambridge, UK; Jayne Herzog, UK; Brendan Ó Sé, Eire; Jonathan Marks, Poland; Marek Doskocz, Poland; Peter Lucantoni, Cyprus; Helen Naylor, UK; Gabrielle Schiegg Cleary, Switzerland.

Development of this publication has made use of the Cambridge International Corpus (CIC). The CIC is a computerised database of contemporary spoken and written English, which currently stands at over one billion words. It includes British English, American English and other varieties of English. It also includes the Cambridge Learner Corpus, developed in collaboration with the University of Cambridge ESOL Examinations. Cambridge University Press has built up the CIC to provide evidence about language use that helps to produce better language teaching materials.

The publisher has used its best endeavours to ensure that the URLs for external websites referred to in this book are correct and active at the time of going to press. However, the publisher has no responsibility for the websites and can make no guarantee that a site will remain live or that the content is or will remain appropriate.

Produced by Kamae Design, Oxford

Illustrations by Robert Calow, Yane Christensen, Mark Duffin, Peter Kyprianou, Laura Martinez

The publishers are grateful to the following for permission to reproduce copyright photographs and material:

Key: l = left, c = centre, r = right, t = top, b = bottom

Alamy/©Alex Segre for p10 (r), /©Oxford Events Photography for p19, /©images-of-france for p22 (r), /©Colin Underhill for p43 (b), /©JTB Photo Communications Inc for p45 (l), /©Stock Image/Pixland for p54 (tl), /©Ros Drinkwater for p58 (l), /©foodfolio for p63; Art Archive/©Dagli Orti for p64; Art Directors & TRIP for p58 (r); Cassop Primary School for p85; Corbis/©Creasource for p43 (t);

Education Photos for p75 (t); Getty Images for pp 22 (l) and 54 (bl); Lonely Planet Images/©Sara-Jane Cleland for p10 (l); Punchstock/©Image Source for p33 (l), /©Stockbyte for p33 (r), /©Radius for p45 (r), /©Brand X for p54 (tr), /©Image 100 for p54 (br), /©Radius for p75 (b); Still Pictures/©Marcus Dlouhy for p28.

Photos researched by Hilary Luckcock

The authors and publishers acknowledge the following sources of copyright material and are grateful for the permissions granted. While every effort has been made, it has not always been possible to identify the sources of all the material used, or to trace all copyright holders. If any omissions are brought to our notice, we will be happy to include the appropriate acknowledgements on reprinting.

p. 17: Penguin Group (UK), Penguin Group (Canada) and Random House Inc for the extract from *The Minotaur* by Barbara Vine. Copyright © Kingsmarkham Enterprises 2006. Reprinted by permission of the Penguin Group (UK), Penguin Group (Canada) a Division of Pearson Canada Inc, and Random House Inc;

p. 39: Orion Publishing Group and A P Watt Ltd for the extract from *Maggie Smith, A Particularly Bright Star* by Michael Coveney. Reprinted by permission of Victor Gollancz, a division of the Orion Publishing Group and A P Watt Ltd on behalf of the author;

p. 63: Wagamama Limited for the adapted text 'Hungry? Thirsty?' Adapted from the Wagamama Website www.wagamama.com. Reproduced by kind permission of Wagamama Limited;

p. 69: Curtis Brown for the adapted extract from *The Angry Mountain* by Hammond Innes. Reproduced with permission of Curtis Brown Group Ltd, London on behalf of the Estate of Hammond Innes. Copyright Hammond Innes, 1964;

p. 79: Extract 'Shopping for a Living' from the Salary.com website, www.salary.com;

p. 81: Random House Group Ltd, and Random House, Inc for the adapted extract from *A Painted House* by John Grisham. Copyright © 2000, 2001 by Belfry Holdings, Inc. Published by Century. Reprinted by permission of the Random House Group Ltd and Random House, Inc;

p. 85: The Guardian for adapted article 'The Sustainable School' by John Vidal, from *The Guardian* 27 June 2006. Copyright Guardian News & Media Ltd 2006.

Introduction

本书的编撰目的是什么？

　　为使考生在FCE考试中取得好的成绩，本书提供了考生备考期间需要掌握的非常有用的词汇；并配有考试练习，可以让考生复习前面学到的词汇。

本书的目标读者是谁？

　　本书是为想要复习和扩展词汇的自学考生而设计的。本书也可以在课堂中作为FCE课程的一部分使用，或者由教师布置为课后作业。

应该按照什么顺序学习书中各个单元？

　　考生可以按照任何顺序学习这些单元。如果想为考试做好充分的准备，考生应该学习完所有的单元。考生可能会从某个特定的单元开始学习，因为它与教材中的某一话题或考生的某一特定写作任务相关。

如何使用本书？

　　最好的方法是将一个单元从头学到尾，因为每一个练习都可能复习到前面练习中出现的词汇，而考试练习部分（Exam practice）会涉及整个单元的词汇。

本书中的学习单元是如何组织的？

　　本书共有20个单元。每个单元有4页，内容是关于一个普通的话题，而这个话题通常又会被细分为几个较小的话题。每个单元包含3页的一般练习和1页的考试练习（Exam practice）。考试练习涉及了FCE考试的每一种题型（参见本书第4页的FCE考试概述）。即使不参加考试，这些练习对于英语学习者来说也是很有用的。

本书附赠的光盘中是什么内容？

　　考生需要听光盘来做书中的一些练习。听力考试练习也在光盘中。考试时，每段录音会听两遍；因此，考生在练习中需要将每段录音重放一次。光盘中还有一些口语考试练习的参考答案，考生可以作为范例使用。

如何使用单词列表？

　　本书的最后附有每个单元的单词列表，包括了考生应该学习的主要词汇。每个单词旁有国际音标（IPA）标注的读音。有些单词考生在口语或写作中可能永远都用不到，但是当看到或听到它们时，应该能够理解它们的意思。考生在结束每个单元的学习后，可以浏览单词列表，查看是否已经掌握每个单词或表达的意思。标出没记住的单词，返回到相应的单元中进行复习。考生还可以记录一些单词的翻译，或将单词记在思维发散图、表格或单词树中（参见本书第2页）。

如何进行写作考试练习？

　　在写作练习中，考生可以使用单元中学到的单词。附录5是写作一览表，列出了考生在做写作考试练习时的基本注意事项。考生可以在每次写作时查看一下这些注意事项，这样对写作过程会很有帮助，同时，也能知道在检查自己的答案时应该关注些什么。

如何进行口语考试练习？

　　在口语练习中，考生可以使用单元中学到的单词。附录4是口语一览表，列出了考生在口语考试练习中的基本注意事项。考生可以在每次做题时查看一下与问题相关的注意事项。

应该什么时候使用词典？

　　一些练习旁边有词典样式的图标📖。考生可以使用《剑桥高级英语学习词典》（*Cambridge Advanced Learner's Dictionary*）或其他任何合适的英英词典，查找不认识的单词。考生可以将这些单词记在笔记本中，包括它们的意思和其他重要的信息，如读音、语体风格（正式／非正式）、例句等等（参见第2、3页关于如何记录词汇的更多方法。）

How do I learn and revise vocabulary?

考生可以在词汇笔记本中记录下所有的新单词，这对学习会很有帮助。标注出每个单词的主要特性，日后就可以将笔记本作为工具书使用。

下面的例子记录了所给单词的主要特性。如果第一次记录单词时不能完成所有的方框，可以先把它们空着，以后再补充完整。

如果在考生自己的语言中没有与该单词意思相对应的词汇，可以将翻译一栏空着。

Orchard	pronunciation: /'ɔːtʃəd/	part of speech: countable noun
definition:	an area of land where fruit trees grow	
translation:		
example sentence:	We saw some people picking apples in the orchard.	

考生在真正学会一个单词之前，可能需要复习或使用该单词多达20次。因此，即使考生已经记录过单元中的一些单词，再记录一次对复习也是很有用的。考生可以在学习一个单元的同时记录单词，也可以在浏览单词列表进行复习时记录。

下面提供了一些记录单词的方法：
• 画思维发散图，例如，与食物相关的单词：

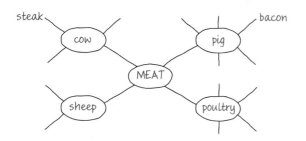

• 画单词树，如：

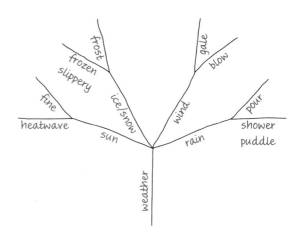

试着把所有的名词放在一起，所有的动词放在一起，以此类推。当考生认为自己已经认识思维发散图或单词树中的单词时，可以再画一次，并试着不看以前的图把单词重新填进去。
• 将单词分组，填写在圆圈或方框中。其中一些可能会重叠，例如：

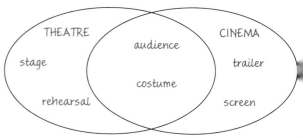

当考生认为自己已经学会了这些单词，可以将圆圈或方框再画一次，看记住了多少。
• 对于构建单词体系，表格很有用，例如：

Noun	fear	amazement
Verb	to frighten	to amaze
Adjective	frightening, frightened	amazing, amazed

•将几组短语动词写在一起，例如：

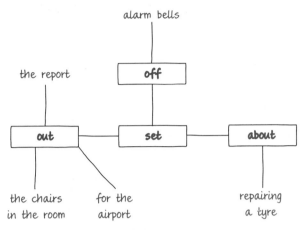

•将单词标注在图片上，例如：

或者使用图画来提示单词的意思，例如，表情符号适于表达积极的情感☺和消极的情感☹，或者表示喜欢、不喜欢，以及同意、不同意。

• 当练习中有"固定词组"的标题时，画出这些词组并且记录在笔记本中。考生需要把它们作为词组而不是单个的单词进行学习。例如第10单元中与*get*有关的词组。

• 一些单词后面总是跟着某个介词，因此需要将该单词和介词一起记下来。例如第4单元中的 *worried about*（对……担心）。

• 将意义相似的单词写在一起，如与*surprised*意思相似的形容词（=*amazed*, *astonished*）。
也可以将反义词写在一起，如*hard-working*（勤奋的）≠ *lazy*（懒惰的）。

• 选择一个单词，记录下经常与其一起使用的其他单词。

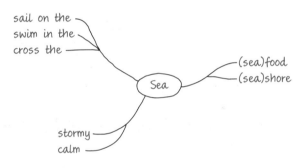

FCE Exam Summary

Paper 1 Reading (1 hour)

There are three parts and 30 questions.

Part	What are the tasks?	What do I have to do?	How many questions?	Where can I get practice?
1	Multiple choice	You read a text and, for each question, you choose from four possible answers (A, B, C or D).	8	Units 8, 15
2	Gapped text-sentences	You read a text from which seven sentences have been removed. You choose one of them to fit each space. There is one sentence which does not fit any of the spaces.	7	Units 2, 17
3	Multiple matching	You scan the text(s) and decide which paragraph/text each of the questions refers to. Some questions may have more than one answer.	15	Units 7, 12

Paper 2 Writing (1 hour 20 minutes)

There are two parts: a compulsory question in Part 1 and a choice of questions in Part 2.

Part	What are the tasks?	What do I have to do?	How many questions?	Where can I get practice?
1	Letter or email	You are given some information in a letter or email with some notes. You write a letter or email in 120–150 words using the information.	1	Units 3 (email), 12 (letter)
2	Questions 2–4 are from the following possible task types: article letter report essay review story Question 5 is about a set book. Two set books are offered and there is one question on each.	You choose one from five possible tasks and write your answer in an appropriate style in 120–180 words.	5 but you choose 1	Units 5, 11 (article) Units 1, 7, 9, 10, (letter) Units 13 (report) Units 6, 20 (essay) Unit 15 (review) Unit 4 (story)

Paper 3 Use of English (45 minutes)

There are four parts and 42 questions. They test your grammar and vocabulary.

Part	What are the tasks?	What do I have to do?	How many questions?	Where can I get practice?
1	Multiple choice lexical cloze	There are 12 numbered gaps in a text. For each one you choose from four possible answers (A, B, C or D).	12	Units 5, 13
2	Open cloze	You read a text with 12 numbered gaps and write the missing word in each gap.	12	Units 1, 3, 18
3	Word formation	You complete the gaps in a text with the correct form of the words at the end of the lines.	10	Units 4, 14, 18, 19
4	Key word transformations	You are given a sentence followed by a second sentence with gaps. You rewrite the second sentence in two to five words using a 'key word' which you are given.	8	Units 1, 8, 9, 11, 16, 17

Paper 4 Listening (40 minutes)

There are four parts and 30 questions. You hear each part twice.

Part	What are the tasks?	What do I have to do?	How many questions?	Where can I get practice?
1	Multiple choice	You hear eight recordings of people talking in different situations. You choose from three possible answers. A, B or C.	8	Units 4, 20
2	Sentence completion	You use the information you hear to complete sentences with gaps.	10	Unit 14
3	Multiple matching	You hear five speakers. You match a statement or opinion from a list of six options to each speaker.	5	Unit 10
4	Multiple choice	For each question, you choose A, B or C.	7	Unit 19

Paper 5 Speaking

There are four parts. They test your ability to communicate in conversational English. You do this with another student.

Part	What are the tasks?	What do I have to do?	Where can I get practice?
1	General conversation	You answer questions about topics such as family life, daily routines, likes and dislikes etc.	Units 10, 14
2	Comparing photographs	The examiner gives you two colour photographs and you talk about them for one minute.	Units 2, 9, 10, 16
3	Decision-making task	You work with the other student to carry out a task based on some pictures which the examiner gives you.	Units 11, 18, 20
4	Discussion	You and the other student have a discussion on topics related to Part 3.	Units 6, 11, 13, 18, 20

1 Good life plan

Health and fitness, illness and treatment

Health and fitness

1.1 Look at these two pictures. Why are these meals healthy or unhealthy? Use the words in the box to complete the sentences below.

salt	fat
vitamins	protein
fibre	carbohydrate
sugar	calories

A    B

Meal A is high in .... and low in ....
Meal B is high in .... and low in ....

1.2 Which of these things are generally good for you, and which are generally bad? Put a G in front of the good things, and a B in front of the bad things.

G fruit	B salt	vegetables	sugar	exercise	stress
salad	smoking	chocolate	alcohol	water	junk food
fish	cutting out fat	putting on weight	joining a gym	going on a diet	getting enough sleep

1.3 ⏺ 1a Now listen to a sportsman talking about his lifestyle. As you listen, underline the things above that he mentions.

1.4 What would the sportsman say to these statements? True or false?

1 I eat lots of fruit and vegetables.   .... True ....
2 I never drink alcohol.   ....
3 I drink a lot of water.   ....
4 I've cut down on chocolate.   ....
5 I go to the gym regularly.   ....
6 I never have to go on a diet.   ....
7 I make sure I get plenty of sleep.   ....
8 I eat a lot of junk food.   ....
9 I've never smoked.   ....
10 There's no stress in my life.   ....

> Ⓥ **Vocabulary note**
>
> **diet**可以表示某个人或一群人日常的饮食: *I'm an athlete so I eat a healthy diet.* （我是一名运动员，因此我的日常饮食很健康。） *Rice is the staple diet of people in India.* （大米是印度很多人的主食。） 但是，**diet**也可以用于某人由于医疗原因或减肥而设定的特殊饮食: *The doctor put me on a low-salt diet.* （医生限定我要吃低盐的食物。） *My jeans are tight, so I'm going on a diet.* （我的牛仔裤很紧，所以我要节食。）

1.5 Now decide whether the statements in 1.4 are true or false for you. Correct any false statements to make them true for you.

1.6 Complete the paragraph below using the correct form of one of these verbs.

go for   cut out   join   get   put on   ~~make~~   cut down on

If you want to stay healthy, (1) ....*make*......... sure you have a healthy diet. Eat plenty of fruit, vegetables and salad and (2) .... salt, fat and processed sugar. And if you want to avoid (3) .... weight, it's probably best to (4) .... junk food completely, because it contains all those things. And whatever your age, it's important to (5) .... enough exercise, so think about (6) .... a gym, or (7) .... a regular walk or run.

Illness and treatment

2.1 Even the fittest person suffers minor illnesses and injuries! Match the problem and the cause. Why would you

1	get a blister?	A	you've been working in a very noisy office
2	have a stomach upset?	B	you're just recovering from flu
3	be sunburnt?	C	you're about to go down with a cold
4	get a splinter in your finger?	D	you've eaten some undercooked meat
5	have a headache?	E	you've been making some bookshelves
6	feel run down?	F	you've just done a long flight
7	have a sore throat?	G	you've spent too long lying on the beach
8	be jet-lagged?	H	you've been wearing new shoes

2.2 Choose the correct word.

1 If you have burnt yourself badly, you go to the <u>casualty department</u> / *local surgery*.

2 If you cut your hand and need *scars* / *stitches* the doctor will give you a local anaesthetic.

3 If you suffer from hay fever, the doctor will give you *antihistamines* / *antibiotics*.

4 If you need medicine, the doctor will give you a *recipe* / *prescription* to take to the local pharmacy.

5 If you break your leg, the doctor will put a *plaster* / *bandage* on it.

6 When you are a child, you have lots of *injections* / *vaccinations* for common illnesses.

7 If you have a temperature, a nurse will take it with a *syringe* / *thermometer*.

8 If you need weighing, the nurse will ask you to step on the *stethoscope* / *scales*.

9 If someone is seriously injured, they are lifted into an ambulance on a *stretcher* / *wheelchair*.

Error warning

单词**prescription**（药方）和**recipe**（食谱）经常会被混淆。**prescription**是医生为病人所需的药品书写的一张单子。*The doctor gave me a prescription for antibiotics.*（医生给我开了一张抗生素的药方。）**recipe**是关于如何准备和烹饪食物的一系列介绍。*My mother gave me a really good recipe for bread.*（妈妈给了我一份很好的制作面包的食谱。）

2.3 ⓟ 1b Listen to three people talking about a medical problem they had recently. As you listen, fill in the box.

Person	Problem	Where they got help	Treatment
1			
2			
3			

3.1 IDIOMS ⓟ 1c Listen to five people talking about their health. Put a tick (✓) if they are feeling well and a cross (✗) if they are feeling unwell.

1 .....   2 .....   3 .....   4 .....   5 .....

3.2 Which words or expressions gave you the answer? Read the recording scripts for 1c and underline them.

4 COMMON EXPRESSIONS There are lots of expressions with *make*. Use one of the nouns below in each sentence.

arrangements   changes   decision   phone call   effort   mistake   speech   ~~appointment~~   suggestion

1 Before you go to the doctor's, you need to make a(n) ....*appointment*.......... at the surgery.

2 Carla made a very helpful .... about how the waiting room could be rearranged.

3 I've got to make a firm .... about which malaria tablets to take.

4 If you're stressed, it's easy to make a really stupid .... and have an accident.

5 They've made a lot of .... to my local surgery and it looks really good now.

6 The .... that the doctor made at his retirement party was hilarious.

7 The hospital has made a huge .... recently to improve the appointments system.

8 By the end of the afternoon, they had made all the .... for the operation.

9 It was noisy in the waiting room, so John went outside to make an important ....

5 PHRASAL VERBS Read sentences 1–5, then match them to the descriptions A–E.

1 I didn't want to play hockey, so I made up a story about twisting my ankle.

2 She didn't visit me when I was in hospital, but she made up for it by buying me some chocolates.

3 Sophie didn't know which ward her brother was on, so she made for the information desk.

4 The nurse spoke so softly that I couldn't make out what she was saying about my medicine.

5 The old operating theatres are no longer used, so the hospital has made them into accommodation for nursing staff.

A Someone is doing something good to compensate for something they didn't do before.

B Someone is heading in a particular direction.

C Someone has decided to use something in a different way.

D Someone has invented a reason for something which happened to them.

E Someone was unable to hear what another person was saying.

Exam practice

USE OF ENGLISH Part 2

For questions 1–12, read the text below and think of the word which best fits each space. Use only one word in each space. There is an example at the beginning.

Exam Tip
想想每条横线上应该填哪个单词。检查该单词是否与其前后的单词或表达相匹配。

The Benefits of Physical Activity

The pace **(0)** .....of..... modern life is fast, and most people have busy and demanding lives. So eating **(1)** .... balanced diet and doing physical activity can **(2)** .... a big difference to overall health. Regular physical activity is good **(3)** .... your whole body, from your brains to your bones. Yet many people do not get **(4)** .... exercise. The good news is that **(5)** .... is easier than you may think to fit physical activity **(6)** .... your day because you can do it at **(7)** .... time and almost anywhere. No matter **(8)** .... your age and stage of life, there are plenty of ways to take exercise.

Your feet were made for walking, so use them **(9)** .... you get the chance. Walk around town. Ignore lifts and escalators and build up your leg muscles by climbing stairs. Next, get out and play. Kicking a ball about is fun, and it is also a great way to spend time together **(10)** .... a family. Finally, try doing two things **(11)** .... once! While you talk on the phone or watch television, stretch, lift weights or **(12)** .... household chores.

USE OF ENGLISH Part 4

Complete the second sentence so that it has a similar meaning to the first sentence, using the word given. *Do not change the word given.* You must use between *two and five words*, including the word given.

Exam Tip
确保第二个句子包含第一个句子中的所有信息。

Example

0 The staff will have to work hard tomorrow to compensate for the time they've lost today.

MAKE

The staff will have to work hard tomorrow to ....make up for.................. the time they've lost today.

1 I've reduced the amount of chocolate I eat, but I'm not losing any weight.

CUTTING

I've tried .... chocolate, but I'm not losing any weight.

2 No one appreciated that what Anna suggested was helpful.

MADE

Anna .... but no one appreciated it.

3 If you want to lose weight, you'll have to think about starting a diet.

GOING

If you want to lose weight, you'll have to think .... diet.

WRITING Part 2: letter

This is part of a letter you have received from your English-speaking penfriend, Annie. Write a letter to your penfriend, giving her the information she asks for. Write 120–180 words.

> I'm collecting ideas for a project I'm doing called 'Staying Fit and Healthy'. Could you write and tell me what you do to stay fit and keep healthy? Perhaps you can tell me about what physical activities you do, and what kind of food you eat.
>
> Write soon, Annie

2 Earth, sea and sky
Geography, climate and weather

Geography

1.1 Look at the photographs below. Where do you think the places are?

1.2 Read the description below. It is about one of the places. Put one word from the box into each gap.

flowers	forests
orchards	paths
~~peaks~~	slopes
streams	valleys

Manali is surrounded by towering snow-capped mountain (1) ...._peaks_......... and thick pine (2) .... Shallow (3) .... of clear mountain water flow into the Beas River. Around the town the landscape is breath-taking. The gentle wooded (4) .... of the hillsides are covered with wild (5) .... and fertile apple (6) .... Above Manali, travellers can walk along the winding (7) .... through the narrow (8) .... and high mountain passes to the Himalayas.

Match the description to one of the photographs.

1.3 Match the adjectives from the box with their opposites.

low	~~deep~~
muddy	straight
wide	steep
cultivated	

shallow ...._deep_..........   narrow ....   winding ....
clear ....   wild ....
gentle ....   high ....

1.4 Write two or three sentences about the place in the other photograph. Use words from 1.2 or 1.3.

....

....

2.1 Choose the best word to fit each gap in these definitions.

1 A ....*river*........ is bigger than a .... Both of them are natural but a .... is manmade. A .... happens when there is too much water.

stream	canal
flood	~~river~~

2 A .... is bigger than a .... and in tropical areas is called a .... When trees are cut down, the wood or .... is used for furniture, houses etc.

wood	forest
rainforest	timber

3 A .... is higher than a .... A .... has one steep side and is often on the coast. A .... is a natural hole in the side of a mountain, cliff or hill.

mountain	cliff
hill	cave

4 The .... is the salty water which covers a large part of the earth's surface. The .... is very similar in meaning but is used for very large areas of water, e.g. the Pacific. A .... is completely surrounded by land. When water drops suddenly from a high point to a low point we call it a ....

sea	ocean
lake	waterfall

5 We use .... for the edges of a river and .... for the edges of a sea or lake. An area of sand or stones beside the sea or a lake is called a .... The .... is where the land meets the sea.

banks	shores
beach	coast

6 .... is on the ground and we grow plants in it. When it is very wet it becomes .... On the beach or in the desert there is often .... on the ground. In very dry places there is a lot of .... blowing in the air.

sand	soil
dust	mud

2.2 Read the email. Choose the correct word (A, B, C or D) for each gap.

Hi Jackie

I'm writing to tell you about my holiday. We hired bicycles and on the first day we cycled beside the Grand Union 1 ..ᴮ.. , which was built in 1793 to carry goods from the Midlands to London. It was very relaxing. The next day we cycled around a 2 ... . That took a few hours but there was a small sandy 3 ... and a little 4 ... where you could sit in the shade. We camped there and the next day we hired a boat. The only problem was there was a lot of thick 5 ... at the side of the lake which we got stuck in. We weren't in danger because the water was 6 ... , but there was a risk of not being able to get the boat out. On another day we went for a walk to the top of a 7 ... . It wasn't very high but we had a lovely view. We came down the other side and stopped in the village at the bottom for lunch in a really nice café. I'd recommend it. See you soon.

Love Maria

	A		B		C		D	
1	Stream		Canal		Flood		River
2	sea		ocean		lake		waterfall
3	banks		shores		beach		coast
4	wood		forest		rainforest		timber
5	sand		soil		dust		mud
6	little		shallow		narrow		gentle
7	mountain		cliff		hill		cave

> ### Vocabulary note
> 一些单词有不止一个意思，并且第二个意思常常是习语的用法：*I've got a **mountain** of work to do.* = a lot of work（我有很多工作要做。）*There was a **flood** of applications for the job.* = suddenly a large number of applications（突然有很多人申请这份工作。）

Climate and weather

3.1 Read these sentences about two different climates. Guess which are about picture A and which are about picture B in 1.1. Write A or B next to each one.

1   It is always hot and humid. B

2   Summers are mild and wet.

3   As it's near the Equator, there is little difference in temperature between the warmest and the coolest months.

4   Rain falls nearly every day and there is no dry season.

5   In winter the temperature drops to below 0°C.

6   In the rainforest, the morning of almost every day begins with a clear blue sky.

7   The area is often cut off because of snow.

8   By mid-afternoon every day there are sudden hard downpours and thunderstorms are common.

9   The heavy snowfall in winter attracts skiers and tourists.

10 It can rain heavily in July and August during the monsoon.

11 The temperature at night is 20°C–25°C but during the day it rises to above 30°C.

12 Skies are often cloudy in the mountains, whether it is summer or winter.

3.2 Check your answers and then put the sentences into two paragraphs to make two separate descriptions, keeping the sentences in the same order as in 3.1. Join some of them with *and* and *but*. Use your notebook.

Picture A: Summers are mild and wet. In winter ....

3.3 🎧 2 Listen to a description of the climate in another country. Which part of the world do you think it is?

3.4 Using 3.1–3.3 to help you, write a description of the climate in your country in your notebook.

4.1 COMMON EXPRESSIONS Each of these sentences is about different weather conditions. Write *rain*, *snow/ice*, *sun* or *wind* next to each one.

1   I nearly fell over because the path was slippery.
snow/ice

2   There was a strong breeze coming off the sea.
…………..

3   The heatwave went on for weeks. …………..

4   We got caught in a shower. …………..

5   They had fine weather for the match. …………..

6   The lake was frozen so we went skating. …………..

7   My feet were soaked because I trod in a puddle.
…………..

8   They couldn't get home because of the blizzard.
…………..

9   The gale blew the tree down. …………..

10 It poured all day. …………..

11 The ground was covered in frost. …………..

12 The hailstones were as big as golfballs. …………..

4.2 Underline the words which helped you to decide and write them on a word tree – see pages 2–3.

5 WORD BUILDING Make the weather nouns below into adjectives. Be careful with spelling.

breeze …….breezy…….   wind ………………….   sun ………………….
storm ………………….   rain ………………….   fog ………………….
cloud ………………….   dust ………………….   ice ………………….

Exam practice

READING Part 2

You are going to read a magazine article about a mountain in Africa. Five sentences have been removed from the article. Choose from the sentences A–F the one which fits each gap. There is one extra sentence which you do not need to use.

Exam Tip

在考试中，共有7个需要补充的句子，文章也会更长。考生可以凭借词汇和语法知识决定每句话应填在哪里。

On a clear day Mount Kilimanjaro is visible from Nairobi. However, when the sun is low and the clouds light, the enormous, snow-capped peak appears to be floating in space. [1 [ ]]

Kilimanjaro is 5895m above sea level and is on the equator. [2 [ ]] They'll start in tropical temperatures, go through milder weather to high alpine desert and then permanently snow-capped summits.

Despite its tremendous altitude, it is possible to get to the top without any technical climbing ability. With its accessible slopes, abundance of porters and relatively mild climate, the trek to the summit is considered a moderately easy climb in mountaineering circles. [3 [ ]]

The ascent is recognised as one of the great walks of the world by the climbers who complete it. [4 [ ]] They will take home memories of colourful scenery, stunning natural beauty, warm and friendly locals and a unique sense of isolation. This last impression is reinforced when they realise that until more than 100 years ago, nobody had ever climbed this vast volcano.

Ever since Hans Meyer's first ascent in 1889, more and more people have tackled the mountain. [5 [ ]] Be aware of the scenic variety, remoteness and popularity of each option, but most importantly, be aware of the degree of difficulty. The ascent is a gruelling but wonderful trek with magnificent views, unmatched in Africa. Whichever route you opt for, to make the most of it walk slowly with your eyes open. Then you'll come home with something far more valuable and important than a summit certificate.

A Those who do so will be rewarded by what they see.
B As a result of this, trekkers will go through several different climates in the course of only five or six days.
C Even so, surprisingly few people make it all the way there.
D This is the most difficult path to follow.
E If you'd like to join them, it's essential to select the route that is most appropriate for you.
F At such times, that kind of beauty appears almost supernatural.

SPEAKING Part 2

1 **Look at the photos in Exercise 1.1 again and think about your answers to these questions.**
   What can you see in each photograph?
   What is different about the two places?
   What season do you think it is? What is the weather like?
   What would you enjoy about each place? What would you find difficult?

Exam Tip (also see speaking checklist on p. 99)

考生需要比较两幅照片，同时要表达自己的观点。

2 **Practise speaking for a minute about one of the photographs. Record yourself and then listen. Try to improve what you said.**

3 Sound waves

Music, sounds

Music

1.1 How musical are you?
Read the questions
and answer them.

Quiz

1. Are you musical? *Yes / No*
2. Do you come from a musical family? *Yes / No*
3. Can you play a musical instrument? *Yes, I play the .... / No, I can't*
4. Have you ever sung in a choir? *Yes, in the past / Yes, and I still do / No, never*
5. Do you ever go to concerts? *Yes, frequently / Yes, occasionally / No, never*
6. How often do you listen to music? *As often as I can / Quite often / Hardly ever / Never*

1.2 3a Now listen to a woman talking about music. Mark the answers she would give in a different colour.

1.3 3a Listen to the woman again, and then practise speaking for one minute about yourself, using the questions and answers you gave in 1.1 to help you.

2.1 Read the music reviews below. Match the kind of music and the review.

rock ...... pop ...... classical ...... world music ......

1
Having produced an **album** of African rumba tunes the group have now turned to Cuba for inspiration. But instead of using the original Spanish **lyrics**, they've added their own. The rhythm and lead guitars and the variety of voices and crisp arrangements effectively maintain interest. A brilliant addition to their repertoire.

2
This album is built around the work of legendary **composer** Johnny Mercer, whose songs defined much of 20th century music and went to the top of the charts. Yet **fans** of his work may be surprised by these arrangements. **Old favourites** with **catchy tunes**, from the 50s to the 80s, are effortlessly transformed into the **band**'s own **distinctive style** with some very pleasing **harmonies**. Buy this one for your collection!

3
This is much better than their first album, and nothing here is a **cover version**. Some of the **tracks** feature heavy metal guitar solos, and the drums are alive with rhythm. A marvellous album that gets better with every listening.

4
This is an album of Argentinian chamber songs, written in the early 1900s. There's everything here from a beautiful **duet** to a passionate tango. It's all beautifully performed, superbly recorded and packaged with an imagination and care that does the designers credit. Fantastic.

2.2 Look at the words in bold. Find the correct word(s) or expressions for

1 a song sung by two people ....*duet*...............

2 a combination of voices singing together in tune ....

3 a collection of songs on a CD ....

4 a person who writes music ....

5 a musical group ....

6 individual songs on a CD ....

7 a recording of a song previously done by another singer or group ....

8 the special way someone does something ....

9 familiar songs that everyone likes ....

10 people who like a particular singer or group ....

11 the words written for a song ....

12 music that is easy to remember ....

2.3 Look at the reviews again and highlight all the words and expressions that give you a positive impression.

2.4 Use words from 2.1 and 2.2 to complete the following review.

The new (1) ....*album*............... from BlueLite is a real treat for all (2) .... of this lively young Irish rock (3) .... It features a few (4) .... that everyone will know, but it also has some great new tracks with meaningful and very moving (5) .... written by Lizzie Sullivan. The words reflect her own life and experiences. Some of these songs are performed as (6) .... by Lizzie and Tim O'Reilly. They have already developed their own very (7) .... and the (8) .... of the old Beatles hit 'Help' is real magic.

3 🎧 **3b** Listen to four people describing different kinds of music. Which type is each person describing?

jazz   folk   rock 'n' roll   country and western

1 ....   2 ....   3 ....   4 ....

4 Complete each definition of the puzzle with an appropriate musical word. If you complete it correctly, the letters circled make another musical word. These pictures may help you

1 a wind instrument often used to play jazz   s a x (o) p h o n e

2 another word for a band   _ (_) _ _ _

3 this musical performance is usually held in a hall   _ _ _ (_) _ _ _

4 you find the top 20 hits here   _ (_) _ _ _ _

5 a large classical string instrument   _ (_) _ _ _

6 a person who writes music   _ _ _ _ _ (_) _ _

7 a string instrument popular in rock bands   _ _ _ (_) _ _

8 a musical play in which words are sung   _ _ _ (_) _

9 a large instrument with black and white keys   _ _ (_) _ _

Sounds

5.1 📖 (◎ 3c) Look at the words in the box. They each describe a sound. Many of them sound like the noise they are describing. Now listen to the recording and match each word to a sound.

roar	crash	hiss	howl	bark	grunt	splash	bang	creak	hum	whistle	croak

1 .... 7 ....

2 .... 8 ....

3 .... 9 ....

4 .... 10 ....

5 .... 11 ....

6 .... 12 ....

> **Vocabulary note**
>
> 以上很多单词都可以在一系列不同的语境中使用：*In the dark forest, a wolf **howled** at the moon.*（在黑暗的森林中，一只狼对着月亮嗥叫。）*The child **howled** when she realized she had lost her favourite toy.*（当孩子意识到丢了自己最喜爱的玩具时，号啕大哭起来。）*As the storm struck, the wind **howled** through the trees.*（风暴来袭时，狂风在树隙间咆哮。）

5.2 Complete the sentences by matching the beginnings (1–10) with the endings (A–J).

1 I tried to speak to Tim

2 As we entered the factory

3 As Peter fell head first into the lily pond

4 I had almost lost my voice

5 I knocked over the enormous vase

6 When we walked through the harbour

7 My legs were stiff when I stood up

8 I opened the bottle

9 The PE instructor was very strict

10 When the villain walked on to the stage

A the wind was whistling through the sails.

B and my knees made a strange creaking sound.

C and the cork flew out with a loud bang.

D and he barked out his orders to his pupils.

E we could hear the hum of machinery.

F the audience hissed its disapproval.

G there was an impressive splash.

H but he just grunted and wouldn't reply.

I and when I tried to speak I just croaked.

J and there was a deafening crash as it shattered.

5.3 Use these words to create the sound effects in the paragraph below.

whistling	creaking	~~barking~~	howl	crash	hum	bang	grunted	hissed

Something had woken me. I could hear a dog (1) ....._barking_..... in the distance and the continuous (2) .... of the traffic on the motorway. I heard it again. It was the sound of someone (3) .... softly outside the window, trying to catch my attention. There was a sudden (4) .... as a ladder hit the wall. I heard the (5) .... of footsteps on the rungs as someone came up. 'Pst ... Melanie are you awake?' the voice (6) .... , urgently. 'I am now,' I (7) .... , grumpily. I knew exactly who it was. Suddenly there was a loud (8) .... and a (9) .... of pain as my big brother hit the bushes below.

> **Vocabulary note**
>
> 写作时，使用形容声音的词汇可以为故事或描写增加趣味。

Exam practice

USE OF ENGLISH Part 2

For questions 1–12, read the text below and think of the word which best fits each space. Use only one word in each space. There is an example at the beginning.

I was awakened (0) ....by.... birds singing. It was half-past four (1) .... the morning and the first time my sleep (2) .... ever been disturbed by birdsong. I lay there listening (3) .... these sounds which both are and are not music. Light came quickly and my room filled with (4) .... much song that at six I couldn't stay there (5) .... longer but had to get (6) .... and go out.

Dew was on the big lawn and in the middle of it two green birds (7) .... long beaks and red stripes on their heads (8) .... searching for food in the grass. They looked up, but otherwise took (9) .... notice of me as I passed along the sandy path. Walking softly so (10) .... not to disturb the birds, I made (11) .... way towards the shrubberies I had only glanced (12) .... the day before.

WRITING Part 1: email

You have received an email from your English-speaking friend, Sam, who is helping to organise a music festival. Read Sam's email and the notes you have made. Then write an email to Sam, using *all* your notes.
Write your reply in 120–150 words.

From: Sam Martinson
Sent: 4th April
Subject: Music Festival

I'm really glad you want to take part in the music festival in July. Could you just give me some more info?

Yes!

The festival lasts for five nights and I'm trying to arrange the programme, so could you tell me something about the kind of music your band plays?

Explain

The other thing I'd like to know is whether you'd prefer to play on the first night of the festival or the last.

Say which and why

And where do you and the band want to stay? We're going to camp at the festival, so do you want to do that too?

No, because …

Reply soon

Sam

4 Highs and lows
Feelings, adverbs and adjectives

Feelings

1.1 ⏺ 4a Listen to a boy called Nick talking about something that happened recently. Answer these questions.

1 Who came to watch Nick's team play? Why? ....

2 What happened after the match? ....

3 Who was chosen? ....

1.2 Do you know the meaning of the adjectives below? Which are positive ☺ and which are negative ☹ ? Check in a dictionary if you need to. Draw ☺ above the positive ones and ☹ above the negative ones.

☹

ashamed   confident   disappointed   embarrassed   excited   guilty   jealous   proud   relaxed   upset

1.3 ⏺ 4a Listen again. How do you think Nick felt …

1 after he scored the goal? ....   2 at the end of the day? ....

1.4 ⏺ 4b Now listen to Nick continue his story. Choose three adjectives from the list to describe how he felt at the end of Saturday. ....

2.1 Read the email below. The underlined adjectives have similar meanings to those in the table below. Write them in the correct column.

amazed	annoyed	depressed	frightened	pleased	worried
				glad	

Hi Helga

I want to tell you about last Saturday when I went to the seaside with my friends. I was really <u>glad</u> that they phoned me because I was feeling <u>fed up</u> so I was relieved to have something to do. But when we got to the seaside I realised they wanted to spend their time at a theme park and I'm <u>scared</u> of going on the big rides. I got <u>cross</u> with them because they hadn't told me. In the end they persuaded me to try. As I sat there waiting for the first ride to begin, I could feel my heart beating fast and I felt like screaming, but as soon as it started I forgot to feel <u>anxious</u> about it because it was fun. When I got off I was <u>surprised</u> to realise how much I'd enjoyed it and I went on all the other rides! Next time you must come too.

Love Tina

2.2 These words also have similar meanings to the underlined words. Put them in the correct column in 2.1. If you think there is a word in a column which is stronger than the others, underline it.

| afraid astonished concerned delighted |
| miserable furious terrified |

 Vocabulary note

使用**afraid**一词可以使消极的表达显得委婉一些：*I'm afraid the train's already left.*（**恐怕**火车已经开走了。）

3.1 Look at the people in the picture. Do they feel the same as Tina in Exercise 2? Write down as many adjectives as you can about how they feel.

They look ....

They seem ....

How would you feel? Tick the adjectives in the table in 2.1 which would describe your feelings on a funfair ride.

3.2 Complete these phrases from Tina's email.

1 I was really glad .... me
2 I was relieved .... something to do
3 I'm scared .... the high rides
4 I got cross .... them
5 I forgot to feel anxious .... it
6 I was surprised .... how much I'd enjoyed it

 Vocabulary note

考生如果无法确定一个形容词后跟**with**，**about**还是**of**，可以查一下词典，然后记下整个短语。很多表示感觉的形容词后面也可以接（**that**）+主语+动词，或者接动词不定式（**to**...）：*Maria was sorry that she had missed the party.*（玛丽亚很遗憾错过了晚会。）*Maria was pleased to get the invitation.*（玛丽亚很高兴获得了邀请。）

3.3 Think about something you did recently, e.g. a sports match you played in, a place you visited, a party you went to. Choose two of the adjective phrases below and write a sentence with each one.

worried about   surprised that   afraid of   upset that   pleased to   annoyed with

Adverbs and adjectives

4.1 Tina said she was feeling miserable. We can change the meaning of *miserable* with an adverb, e.g. *I'm very miserable* or *I'm quite miserable*. Some adverbs are stronger than others.

STRONG:	very	LESS STRONG:	quite

Add these adverbs to the table.

> **Error warning**
>
> 检查*quite*的拼写。不要把它同*quiet*混淆。

extremely   fairly   really   terribly

4.2 In spoken English, we often use *a bit* or *so*: *I was so tired, I was a bit impatient*. Add *a bit* and *so* to the table.

5 IDIOMS There are lots of different ways of saying we are happy or sad and many of them are idioms. Are these people happy or sad? Draw ☺ for happy or ☹ for sad.

1 I'm **feeling on top of the world** after my holiday. ☺

2 She waved goodbye and then she **burst into tears**.

3 I've got the job so I'm **thrilled to bits!**

4 My sister's **feeling sorry for herself** because she lost her phone and can't afford a new one.

5 She's been **walking on air** ever since she met Mark.

6 You're **full of the joys of spring** today. Has your team won the championship?

6.1 WORD BUILDING Choose the correct adjective in each of these sentences and then finish the rules in 6.2.

1 I was really *boring / bored* on holiday. There was nothing to do.

2 Last night's show was really *disappointing / disappointed* – we wasted our money.

3 We were very *surprising / surprised* when we got to the hotel and it was closed.

4 Tom was so *exciting / excited* when he received your letter with the good news.

5 He hated talking in public so he felt very *worrying / worried* about giving a speech.

6 Sourav gave me a ride on his motorbike. It was absolutely *terrifying / terrified*.

7 I didn't find the holiday *relaxing / relaxed* because my friend wanted us to go out all the time.

6.2 Put *–ed* or *–ing* in the sentences below.

Adjectives ending in .... describe a feeling.   Adjectives ending in ...... describe what caused the feeling.

6.3 Complete this table.

Noun	fear	amazement	....	....	annoyance	....
Verb	....	amaze	embarrass	please	....	excite
Adjective	frightening frightened	....	embarrassing embarrassed	pleased pleasing	....	exciting excited

Noun	depression	....	pride	anxiety	misery	....
Adjective	....	angry	....	....	....	jealous

Exam practice

LISTENING Part 1

 4c **Listen to the recordings and choose the best answer A, B or C.**

1   You overhear a woman telling a friend about a conversation she had with her parents.
    How did her parents feel about her news?
    A   furious
    B   astonished
    C   pleased

> **Exam Tip**
> 仔细听与问题相关的单词。例如，如果问题中有 *frightened*（害怕的）这个单词，考生可能会在录音中听到 *scared, afraid* 或 *terrified*。

2   You hear a man talking about an activity holiday he went on.
    How did he feel at the end of it?
    A   annoyed
    B   relieved
    C   upset

 Listen again.

USE OF ENGLISH Part 3

For questions 1–10, read the text below. Use the word given in capitals at the end of each line to form a word that fits in the space in the same line.

> **Exam Tip**
> 有时候，考生需要将单词变成否定形式。

Jealousy is a **(0)** ......*confusing*........ emotion and it can make people behave   CONFUSE
in totally **(1)** .... ways. It can of course have a   EXPECT
wide **(2)** .... of causes and some people feel jealous more   VARY
easily than others.
It could be that you are **(3)** .... that your team didn't win the   DISAPPOINT
(4) .... and you can't bear to watch the other team receive the   CHAMPION
cup. The acceptable response is to offer them your **(5)** .... and   CONGRATULATE
not to show your jealous feelings.
Jealousy may also have its origins in other more **(6)** ....   PERSON
circumstances such as a friend getting a job you wanted yourself.
You should not show your **(7)** .... as this can make you look   ANNOY
(8) .... small-minded. If you do express your views, it will   REAL
be **(9)** .... for the other person, who can't do anything about   EMBARRASS
their success, and you may even lose a friend unless you **(10)** ....   APOLOGY
immediately.

WRITING Part 2: story

Your teacher has asked you to write a story for an international magazine. The story must begin with the following words:
Jakob was absolutely furious when he saw what was going on outside his window.

Write 120–180 words.

> **Exam Tip** (also see writing checklist on p. 100)
> 考生需要想想在将要写的故事中会发生什么。人物的感觉是什么？故事要怎样结尾？

5 Looking back
The past, time

The past

1 When did these events happen? Match each event (1–8) with an appropriate time expression (A–H).

1	The Beatles pop group played together	A	millions of years ago.
2	Vaccinations were not invented	B	in the 1940s.
3	Humans started painting pictures in caves	C	from 1960 to 1970.
4	Dinosaurs lived on earth	D	in 1961.
5	The first helicopter was flown	E	about 30,000 years ago.
6	The Great Wall of China was built	F	until the eighteenth century.
7	Nelson Mandela became president of South Africa	G	more than 2000 years ago.
8	The first man went into space	H	towards the end of the 20th century.

2.1 Look at the two photos below. Where do you think they are?

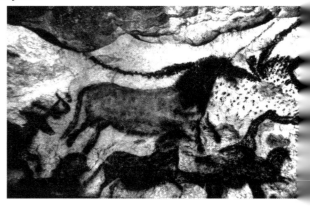

2.2 🔊 5a Now listen to a student talking about the two photographs. Complete the gaps with his answers.

1 In the first picture there's a very ....*old wall*.......... and in the second there are some ....*cave paintings*.......... .

2 The .... are older than the ....

3 The wall was built about ....

4 The paintings were done ....

5 The wall is in .... and the paintings are in ....

2.3 🔊 5b Now listen to the student talking about these questions and note his answers.

What is the oldest thing you can see in your country? ....

When was it made? ....

Check your answers, then answer the two questions about your own country.

3.1 Read this text and choose the correct words to complete it.

Prehistoric Britain

We have archaeological (1) _evidence_ / _facts_ of people living in Britain dating back to about 10,500 years ago. This period is known as prehistory, and there are no written (2) _catalogues_ / _records_ which go back this far. The (3) _population_ / _community_ of Britain must have been very small in prehistoric times. Historians have no precise (4) _scores_ / _figures_, but they think that there were no more than a million (5) _residents_ / _inhabitants_. These prehistoric Britons belonged to different (6) _tribes_ / _dynasties_ and spoke a number of different languages. All of them are the (7) _ancestors_ / _descendants_ of modern British people.

They survived by (8) _hunting_ / _chasing_ animals and gathering berries and fruit in the wild. About 2,750 years ago people in Britain began to lead a more (9) _settled_ / _seated_ life and farming techniques improved. People began to grow crops and keep animals to provide them with the (10) _goods_ / _produce_ they required such as meat, wool and milk. They also made (11) _tools_ / _machines_ out of iron, and this period is known as the Iron Age. The people of this time built huts to live in and had quite sophisticated (12) _beliefs_ / _opinions_. We know that they had a strong tradition of telling (13) _histories_ / _stories_ orally, but they left no trace of a written language behind. It was only when the Romans (14) _invaded_ / _attacked_ Britain just over two thousand years ago that the written word arrived.

> **Error warning**
>
> **history**（历史）是指过去发生的所有事件：_She's studying for a degree in ancient history because she's fascinated by it._ （她正在攻读古代史的学位，因为她对这门学科很着迷。）**story**（故事）是对真实的或想象的事件的描述，常常用于娱乐他人：_The story is about three boys who explore an old castle._ （这个故事是关于三个男孩探索一座古老的城堡。）

3.2 WORD BUILDING Complete the different parts of speech. (Sometimes there are two nouns.)

Noun	history	prehistory	archaeology	evidence
Noun (person)	historian	————		————
Adjective	historical			

Verb	populate	civilise	invade	reside
Noun	population			
Noun (person)	————			

Verb	inhabit	descend	believe	survive
Noun				
Noun (person)				

Noun	discovery	abolition	cause
Verb	discover		

Noun	invention	colonisation	introduction
Verb			

> **Error warning**
>
> **historic**是指在历史上有（或可能有）重要意义的：_a historic building_（一座有历史意义的建筑），_a historic event / day_（一个历史性事件/日子）。**historical**是指与研究或表述过去事件有关的：_a historical novel_（一部历史小说），_historical documents_（历史文件）。

3.3 Now do a mind map with the headings History, Prehistory and Archaeology to help you remember the vocabulary. See pages 2–3 for an example.

Time

4.1 **Choose the correct answer.**

1 Several years have *spent / passed* since I saw Jenna.

2 School music lessons usually *last / pass* an hour.

3 If I travel during the rush hour, it *lasts / takes* me an hour to get to work.

4 The talks *went on for / spent* three days, but no decisions were reached.

5 I *spent / lasted* three hours writing the report for today's meeting.

> **ⓥ** *Vocabulary note*
>
> 用**last**表示某事进行多长时间：*The film lasts an hour.* （电影持续了一个小时。）如果一个人**spend**（花）时间做某事，那么从这段时间的开始到结束都在做这件事：*He spent all day planning the trip.* （他花了一整天来计划这次旅行。）动词**pass**表示时间已经过去了：*Several weeks have passed since I saw my sister.* （自从上次见过我姐姐后，几个星期过去了。）某事**take**（花费）时间，即需要一些时间来做这件事：*It may take us several weeks to get back.* （我们也许要花几个星期才能回去。）

4.2 **Answer these questions by writing a sentence about yourself in your notebook.**

1 How long does it take you to fly from your country to London?

2 How long does summer last in your country?

3 How many years have passed since you left primary school?

4 How long have you spent studying English today?

5 How long does it take you to get from home to work / college every day?

6 What's the longest film you've ever seen? How long did it go on for?

5 COMMON EXPRESSIONS **What is the difference between the expressions in A and B?**

1 A The party started at eight, and we arrived **on time**.

   B We arrived at the party **in time** to see Diana cut her birthday cake.

2 A I **have a lot of time for** Anna because she's always so pleasant and helpful.

   B I **have no time for** Lisa – she's always rude and negative about everything.

3 A I spent three hours walking around the gallery and the **time flew**!

   B I spent several hours at the airport just **killing time**.

6.1 **Choose the correct answer to each question.**

1 Do you usually arrive on time for lessons?

2 Do you get home in time to eat with your family?

3 Who do you have a lot of time for?

4 Who do you have no time for?

5 Does time fly when you read a book?

6 When did you last have to kill time?

A After I missed my train home.

B People who are always grumpy.

C Of course I do!

D My sister – she's important to me.

E Yes, we always have a meal together.

F Always, I don't know where it goes.

6.2 **Now answer each question for yourself.**

Exam practice

USE OF ENGLISH Part 1

For questions 1–12 read the text below and decide which answer (A, B, C or D) best fits each space.

THE FIRST PEOPLE

From the arrival of the first modern humans to the beginning of recorded history is a (0)..C.. of about 100 centuries, or 400 generations. We know very little about what (1)..... at this time because these (2)..... people left no written records of themselves. What we know about them comes from the (3)..... archaeologists have found at different (4)..... .

We know that throughout prehistoric times there were many small-scale societies, and a lot of different (5)..... living in the British islands. These groups were often in (6)..... with their neighbours and frequently attacked each other. They also had contact with peoples in other parts of Europe and (7)..... trade with them. The many objects found in tombs and burial chambers (8)..... this.

The first written accounts of Britain (9)..... from the time when Julius Caesar invaded Britain just over two thousand years (10)..... . The Romans did not colonise the islands of Britain to any significant extent. To a population of about three million, Caesar's army and administration (11)..... only a few percent. The towns and villas of the new Roman province were nearly all built by wealthy people from the British islands who later became Roman (12)..... .

0	A	spell	B	term	C	period	D	stretch
1	A	went on	B	passed out	C	went through	D	passed by
2	A	elderly	B	ancient	C	antique	D	old
3	A	marks	B	proof	C	evidence	D	signs
4	A	sites	B	positions	C	settings	D	grounds
5	A	families	B	dynasties	C	tribes	D	classes
6	A	contest	B	fight	C	battle	D	conflict
7	A	did	B	had	C	made	D	kept
8	A	try	B	prove	C	test	D	check
9	A	belong	B	exist	C	begin	D	date
10	A	ago	B	previously	C	since	D	earlier
11	A	grew	B	increased	C	added	D	raised
12	A	residents	B	citizens	C	inhabitants	D	tenants

> **Exam Tip**
>
> 如果感觉一个答案是正确的，就要相信自己的直觉！如果不确定，就尝试排除那些错误的选项。然后看剩下哪些选项，如果仍不确定，就猜吧！

WRITING Part 2: article

You have seen this announcement in an international student magazine.
Write 120–180 words.

Articles wanted!

FAMOUS BUILDINGS

We're doing a series on famous historical buildings. Could you write about a famous ancient building in your country? If so, write and tell us where it is, what it's called, and something about it. The best articles will be published.

> **Exam Tip** (also see writing checklist on p. 100)
>
> 给文章定个题目，尽量使其生动有趣。

Test One (Units 1–5)

Choose the correct letter: A, B, C or D.

1. She burst into .... when she opened the letter.
   A crying   **B** sadness   **C** misery   **D** tears

2. Don't stand too near the edge of the .... because you might fall.
   A peak   **B** valley   **C** cliff   **D** hill

3. I felt extremely .... when I couldn't remember my neighbour's name.
   A embarrassed   **B** embarrassment   **C** embarrass   **D** embarrassing

4. I prefer string instruments so the .... is my favourite.
   A flute   **B** saxophone   **C** cello   **D** drum

5. My dad was .... with me when I told him I'd lost the camera he bought me.
   A scared   **B** guilty   **C** worried   **D** furious

6. Rio de Janeiro was the capital of Brazil .... 1822 to 1960.
   A until   **B** in   **C** on   **D** from

7. We were too far away to make .... what the sign said.
   A for   **B** into   **C** out   **D** up

8. We got off our bikes because the hill was too .... to cycle up.
   A high   **B** steep   **C** straight   **D** tall

9. Mickey couldn't stand up so two men carried him off the football pitch on a ....
   A trolley   **B** surgery   **C** ambulance   **D** stretcher

10. We were a .... surprised when we realised the hotel didn't serve food.
    A quite   **B** bit   **C** so   **D** fairly

11. I've .... down on salt and fat in my diet because they're not good for me.
    A cut   **B** put   **C** got   **D** gone

12. We had a perfect view from the aeroplane because the skies were ....
    A empty   **B** cloudy   **C** open   **D** clear

13. The ball we were playing with landed in the water with a huge ....
    A crash   **B** splash   **C** bang   **D** howl

14. The path was very .... because of the wet weather.
    A stony   **B** muddy   **C** sandy   **D** dusty

15 I haven't done any sport this week because I'm feeling a bit off ....
    A shape   **B** colour   **C** fitness   **D** sorts

16 The crowd .... as the team came onto the pitch.
    A roared   **B** grunted   **C** hummed   **D** barked

17 There is .... that people lived in eastern North America at least 50,000 years ago.
    A belief   **B** evidence   **C** opinion   **D** fact

18 I'm really .... of my son who won first prize in the art competition.
    A pleased   **B** proud   **C** delighted   **D** happy

19 I put on lots of extra .... when I stopped walking to work.
    A weight   **B** strength   **C** energy   **D** exercise

20 The last track on this .... is the best one.
    A solo   **B** duet   **C** album   **D** single

21 I was trying to be very quiet but the door .... as I opened it.
    A hissed   **B** creaked   **C** whistled   **D** croaked

22 People can .... by eating berries and fruit.
    A survive   **B** descend   **C** inhabit   **D** civilise

23 There has been a decrease in the .... of Italy during the last five years.
    A residents   **B** people   **C** population   **D** community

24 I took the .... which the doctor gave me to the pharmacy and got some medicine.
    A thermometer   **B** recipe   **C** vaccination   **D** prescription

25 I .... two hours on the internet last night looking for a cheap holiday before I eventually found something.
    A passed   **B** spent   **C** took   **D** lasted

26 Paula couldn't help feeling .... before her driving test, as she really wanted to pass.
    A anxious   **B** disappointed   **C** ashamed   **D** relieved

27 The .... of the singer's latest song are about her childhood.
    A lyrics   **B** instruments   **C** tunes   **D** harmonies

28 The rain was so .... we were soaked after a few minutes.
    A long   **B** strong   **C** deep   **D** heavy

29 There are lots of mountain .... which flow into the River Colorado.
    A streams   **B** floods   **C** lakes   **D** canal

30 I've always enjoyed reading .... novels because they bring the past to life.
    A ancient   **B** antique   **C** historical   **D** historic

6 Getting the message across

Advertising, computers, telephoning

Advertising

1 Match these different ways of advertising (1–5) with their dictionary definitions (A–E). Which one can be either written or spoken?

1 catalogue .....   2 commercial break .....   3 mailshot .....   4 poster .....   5 slogan .....

A

noun a short, easily remembered phrase used to advertise an idea or product.

C

noun a large printed picture, photograph or notice which you stick or pin to a wall or board.

E

noun a short period of advertisements between TV or radio programmes.

B

noun a list, usually in the form of a book, of things you can buy, often by mail order.

D

noun the posting of material to a lot of people at one time.

2.1 Read advertisement A and decide which of these slogans best matches the content.

An island with something for everyone

An island looking to the future

A

Come to Sicily and experience its amazing colours, stunning landscapes and delicious, healthy food.

Visit the city of Catania, which is a perfect combination of spectacular 17th century architecture, lively nightlife and musical traditions.

Relax on fine, golden, sandy beaches watched over by Europe's biggest active volcano, Mount Etna.

Last but not least, enjoy the wonderful flavours of top-quality products such as olives, pistachio nuts, honey, vegetables and dried fruit.

B

Come to Sicily and experience the bright colours, beautiful landscapes and tasty food.

Visit the city of Catania, which is a combination of 17th century architecture, busy nightlife and traditions.

Relax on the nice beaches watched over by the volcano, Mount Etna.

Last but not least, enjoy the good flavours of products such as olives, pistachio nuts, honey, vegetables and dried fruit.

2.2 Now read advertisement B and compare it with A. Underline the differences.

2.3 Complete the table with the words used in the adverts to describe the nouns.
Which advert most makes you want to visit Sicily? Why?

	Advert A	Advert B		Advert A	Advert B
Colours:	amazing		Traditions:		
Landscapes:			Volcano:		
Food:			Beach:		
Architecture:			Flavours:		
Nightlife:			Products:		

3.1 Advert A uses the phrase *perfect combination*. Tick five adjectives in the box you could use instead of *perfect*. Why did you not choose the others?

> agreeable extraordinary fantastic magical
> nice pleasant remarkable unique

3.2 Some of these sentences should contain *only* instead of *unique*. Correct them.

1 I'm the unique person in my class who has been to Alaska.

2 This sculpture is unique and that's why it's so valuable.

3 This is the unique opportunity I have to see this film.

4 The band produces a unique combination of sounds on this track.

Error warning

unique和only都有"唯一"的意思，但是unique用于表示某样东西很特别或者不寻常：*The recipe is unique because I invented it myself.*（这张食谱很独特，因为它是我自己发明的。）

3.3 Complete this advert with information about your country. Try to use the adjectives from 2.3 and 3.1.

> Come to .... and experience its .... , ... and ....
>
> Visit the city of .... which is a perfect combination of .... and ....
>
> Relax ....
>
> Enjoy ....

4.1 Read these phrases from a radio advert. Decide which word best fits each gap.

1 Direct Books has a special ..A.. just for you.

  A offer   **B** advertising   **C** publicity

2 We're giving you a unique ..... to save money.

  A possibility   **B** occasion   **C** opportunity

3 We're offering up to 40% ..... selected books.

  A off   **B** lower   **C** down

4 ..... you pay is the price of your books.

  A Only   **B** All   **C** Just

5 Postage and packing is ..... free.

  A extremely   **B** very   **C** absolutely

6 You'll receive a free mystery gift worth at ..... £5.

  A least   **B** less   **C** most

7 To ..... advantage of this offer, put your order in now.

  A make   **B** take   **C** have

8 It's only for a ..... period.

  A limited   **B** little   **C** reduced

9 We also offer a ..... allowing you to return any book within seven days.

  A compromise   **B** protection   **C** guarantee

10 We will give you a ..... refund.

  A sufficient   **B** full   **C** whole

11 If you're looking for a ..... book, please contact us.

  A particular   **B** personal   **C** peculiar

4.2 🔊 6a Now listen and check your answers.

Computers

5 Read the text from Direct Books' internet website and put the correct word in each gap.

Nouns:	bestsellers basket home page keyword password support	**Adjectives:** online secure **Verbs:** ~~browse~~ click enter sign

Search

You can (1) ......browse...... for books under the main subject categories. Look for a specific book using the search boxes on the (2) .... or type in a (3) .... (e.g. rugby). To check out the latest (4) .... and to see what's coming up just go to the webpage for that sport.

Order

Ordering from directbooks.co.uk is (5) .... .You should (6) .... in using your email address and you will be asked for a (7) .... Add your books to your shopping (8) .... and then (9) .... on 'checkout'. We will give you a unique personal account number after you have placed your first order to allow you to enter your account number (10) .... so that you don't have to (11) .... your personal and credit card details every time.

Help

Click help on our website or call 0845 678944 for customer (12) ....

Telephoning

6.1 *Call* sometimes means 'to phone' and sometimes means 'to visit' (usually a short, spontaneous visit). What does *call* mean in these sentences? Write *phone* or *visit* next to each sentence.

1 I'll **call on** Paolo next time I pass his flat. .....visit.....

2 Don't forget to **call** when you get there. ....

3 I'll **call in** when I have time. ....

4 She **called** Alan **back** but he'd already sold the ticket. ....

5 We **called by** but you were out. ....

6.2 PHRASAL VERBS Put the correct word in each space to make a phrasal verb.

away   ~~for~~   off   out   over

1 Shall I call ....for.... you and then we can go together?

2 I didn't notice Suzi until she called .... my name.

3 The match was called .... because of bad weather.

4 He was called .... on business.

5 I called Jon .... because I wanted to introduce him to my friends.

7.1 🔊 6b Listen to Tanya's messages. For each person choose the best answer A–F.

			Which person
1	Lara	A	tried to speak to Tanya yesterday?
2	Mum	B	has hardly any credit?
3	Joe	C	got a wrong number?
4	Sarah	D	couldn't get a signal?
5	Dad	E	will ring again?
6	Peter	F	will send a text message?

7.2 PHRASAL VERBS Put a verb in each gap to make phrasal verbs from the recording in 7.1.

1 ...hang.. up = put the phone down

2 .... through = be connected

3 .... up = call or phone

4 get .... off = lose the connection

5 .... up = answer

6 .... back = return a call

Error warning

打电话是*make a phone call*，不是*do a phone call*。

Exam practice

WRITING Part 2: essay

1 Read a model answer to an exam question. Underline the advantages and disadvantages the student mentions.

What are the advantages and disadvantages of computers?

The main advantage of computers is that it's easy to find out information like how to travel somewhere. This means that people don't need to look in books or newspapers. However, there is sometimes too much information available. Also, when we read facts on the internet, we don't always know what is true.

A further disadvantage is that people throw their computers away after a few years. This results in a lot of waste. There are a number of advantages for children such as being able to play games. In addition, they make learning more fun. But this leads to children spending too much time on the computer.

It is easier to stay in touch with friends by email and another advantage is that you can send photos. But people send emails rather than talk to each other. I sometimes think people rely on computers too much and if a computer goes wrong, for instance in a hospital, it might be dangerous.

In conclusion, I think computers improve our lives in lots of ways and the advantages are more important than the disadvantages.

2 Look at the groups of words and expressions below. They are all from the model answer. Find them and highlight them. Which group of words and expressions is used ...

to explain something? ..... to give an opposite opinion? ..... to introduce the next argument? .....
to give examples? .....

A ... such as ... , ... like ... , for instance ...
B However, ... , But ...
C This means that ...   This leads to ...   This results in ...

D The main advantage of ... is that ...
In addition, ...
A further / Another advantage is that ...
There are a number of disadvantages of ...
Also, ...

3 Write an answer like the one above to the following exam question. Use the words and expressions you have learnt.

You've had a discussion in your English class about the use of mobile phones. Now your teacher has asked you to write an essay answering the following question.
What are the advantages and disadvantages of mobile phones?

Write between 120 and 180 words.

Exam Tip (also see writing checklist on p. 100)

不要忘记在文章的结尾得出结论。

SPEAKING Part 4

Think about these questions.
Do you take your mobile phone everywhere with you?
Do people use mobile phones too much?
Practise saying your answers aloud.

How important are computers to you in your daily life?
What are the best and worst things about computers?

7 The world of work

Jobs, personal qualities, employment and unemployment

Jobs

1 If you are looking for a job, some websites may help you. Here is a list of job categories on one website. Which category would you click on if you were looking for the following jobs? Write them in the spaces.

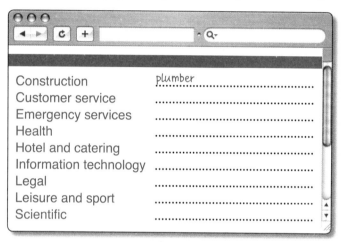

Construction	plumber ....
Customer service	....
Emergency services	....
Health	....
Hotel and catering	....
Information technology	....
Legal	....
Leisure and sport	....
Scientific	....

call centre manager	chef
electrician	firefighter
kitchen assistant	plumber
lab assistant	lifeguard
optician	police officer
psychologist	software engineer
solicitor	

2.1 Below are some adverts for job vacancies. Which job is each one advertising? Choose from the list below.

accountant   architect   builder   cleaner   mechanic   nursery assistant   receptionist   sales manager

A

....

You need to be efficient, well-organised and self-motivated and be able to work without supervision. You should also have good communication skills to deal with our customers. Salary is dependent on qualifications and experience. Some training is available.

If you would like a permanent job in a local hotel, then call 0987 864829 for an application form.

B

....

Temporary job available in a local store for a reliable and flexible person. Previous experience preferred but not essential as training can be given. You will be required to do shift work when the shop is closed (early mornings and evenings) and some overtime. Excellent wages for an honest hard-working person. Please contact James Havard to obtain an application form and a job description.

C

....

Enthusiastic person required to join our team. We are looking for a dynamic, creative person. A full training programme will be given to the successful candidate so no previous experience with young children is necessary. Good rate of pay and possible promotion in the future. Further details and an application form are available from office@mpr.co.uk.

2.2 Answer these questions by choosing Job A, B or C and write the words from the adverts which give you the answers.

1 Which job is not forever? ..B..
Word(s) in advert: .... temporary ....

2 Which job is for a long time or forever? .....
Word(s) in advert: ....

3 Which job suggests you may get a higher position? .....
Word(s) in advert: ....

4 Which job has hours which change? .....
Word(s) in advert: ....

5 Which jobs needs you to get on well with others? .....
Word(s) in advert: ....

6 Which job may involve extra hours? .....
Word(s) in advert: ....

2.3 Each advert mentions how the person will be paid. Put *salary*, *rate of pay* and *wages* into the definitions below.

1 .... – an amount of money agreed for a year and paid every month.

2 .... – usually paid every week, often for work which does not require a lot of qualifications.

3 .... – how much someone will be paid per hour.

2.4 Use the words in brackets to form a word that fits in the gap.

Dear Sir
I saw your advertisement in the local newspaper last Friday. I am interested in the **(1)** ...vacancy.. (vacant) for assistant manager in your hotel. Please find enclosed an **(2)** .... (apply) form.
I have worked in the **(3)** .... (cater) industry for several years and before that in an office. I have several secretarial **(4)** .... (qualify) and am familiar with different computer programs. I enjoy working with people and I am **(5)** .... (rely), efficient and hard-working. I have recently finished a **(6)** .... (train) course at the local college in administration. I am very **(7)** .... (enthusiasm) about a career in the hotel business. I am **(8)** .... (ambition) and I would like to run my own hotel one day.
Yours faithfully
Adam Piekarski

Personal qualities

3.1 Look back at 2.1 and underline the personal qualities needed for each job.

3.2 7a Listen to the two people in the photographs talking about themselves. Which speaker does which job?

Speaker .... is a hairdresser.
Speaker .... is a carpenter.

3.3 Look at the recording script and underline all the words which helped you to answer. Can you think of any more personal qualities useful for each job in the photographs?

Employment and unemployment

4 Several things usually happen between seeing an advert and getting a job. Put these into the right order on the flowchart below.

Phone or email for an application form   Accept the job offer   ~~See an advert~~

Have an interview   Email or post the application form   Fill in the application form   Receive a job offer

See an advert.	▶		▶		▶		▶		▶		▶	

5.1 COMMON EXPRESSIONS ⊙ 7b Listen to some people talking about work. Write ✓ for people who have a job and ✗ for people who don't have a job.

1 ….   2 ….   3 ….   4 ….   5 …..   6 ….   7 …..   8 ….

5.2 Look at the recording script at the back of the book and underline all the words which told you whether the person was working or not.

Two people decided to leave their jobs. What do they say? …………………………………………………………

One person had to leave their job. What do they say? …………………………………………………………

5.3 Here are some sentences from the recording. Put *work*, *job* or *career* in each gap. Use the recording script to help you if you need to.

I'm trying to change (1) …*career*… and I'm looking for (2) …………… as a teacher.

I've just applied for a (3) …………… at the theatre.

I had a long (4) …………… in the police force.

The journey takes an hour each way so I don't have time to do much after (5) …………… .

I do four long days which is very hard (6) …………… .

I gave up my (7)…………… as a chef a year ago and I'm still out of (8) …………… .

I'm going to do some unpaid (9) …………… experience soon in an agency.

I was promoted last week so that's very good for my (10) …………… .

5.4 Now complete these summaries with *work*, *job* and *career*.

1 …………… is a countable noun and is used to talk about something specific.

2 …………… is a countable noun which is used to talk about what someone chooses to do over a lifetime.

3 …………… is a verb or an uncountable noun which is used to talk generally about what someone does to earn money.

Ⓥ Vocabulary note

it's a good job 表示幸运的意思：*It's a good job we didn't go to the concert because it was cancelled.* （很幸运我们没有去那场音乐会，因为它被取消了。） **to do a great job** 表示某事做得好的意思：*You've done a great job tidying the flat.* （你整理公寓的工作做得很好。） **to work** 也可以表示运转或起作用的意思：*The computer isn't working. I can't send an email.* （电脑不工作，我没法发邮件了。）

Error warning

occupation 很正式，通常只用于正式的语境中："我喜欢我的工作" 应为 *I enjoy my job*，而不是 *I enjoy my occupation*。

Exam practice

Exam Tip

考试中会有更多要阅读的信息，并有15个问题。
问题中的单词总是与文章中的单词不同。

READING Part 3

You are going to read a newspaper article in which three
people talk about their jobs. For questions 1–10, choose from
the people A–C. The people may be chosen more than once.
Which woman

started a company with others?

feels her private life might suffer from her commitment to her job?

is likely to do very well in the future?

feels that others don't always recognise her qualities?

says she values the input of others?

has had varied experiences in one organisation?

has not yet achieved her main ambition?

is not self-confident about her own abilities?

had the opportunity to carry out some research?

is hoping to improve the lives of others through her present job?

1	
2	
3	
4	
5	
6	
7	
8	
9	
10	

A   Carol Jackman, chef
Jackman joined the restaurant, Cranberry, eight years ago as a waitress. She soon became restaurant manager before
making the big leap into the kitchen. After working under head chef and owner Peter Godden's guidance, she rose to
become under-chef. She may be shy and modest (she says she still has a lot to learn), but with her fabulous technique,
great organisational ability and impressive creative instincts, her boss says she should go far. During her time at
Cranberry, she has also had two children and she feels they have benefited from seeing a mother getting pleasure from
her work.

B   Sarah Brookes, architect
Brookes set up a business with two friends to design and build a community centre. They then won a competition run by
the government to find out more about the effects of architecture on schooling. The firm is currently renovating a school
in London. The design will allow flexible, adaptable classrooms and outdoor teaching. Brookes says they hope they will
make a difference to the children's lives. Although there is no doubt about that, she worries that she doesn't always do
so well fitting her work and her children into her day and that she often puts work first.

C   Monika Myles, TV Director
Myles worked as a TV director for four years, then went on to make some award-winning documentaries. She starts
filming this week on a big-budget drama for TV but her eventual dream is to make a full-length feature film. She wants to
make films that have a message at the end of them. Because she is small and young-looking, she says people initially
are unsure about what she is capable of. But when she sees a script, she has a vision and is able to translate it into a
moving image. She acknowledges the fact, however, that film-making is also about a team putting their heads together
to create a piece of art.

Writing Part 2: letter

You have seen this advertisement for a job in your
local English language newspaper.
Write your letter of application in 120 – 180 words.

WEEKEND WORK IN OUR COMPUTER SHOP

We want an enthusiastic English-speaking person to
work in our computer shop at weekends.

– Are you interested in all types of computer games?

– Do you have good computer skills?

– Do you enjoy dealing with people?

Write to Mr Pitt, Manager of Computer Games,
explaining why you would be suitable for the job.

Exam Tip (also see writing checklist on p. 100)

求职信要以*Dear Mr...*或*Mrs...*或*Ms...*开头，以*Yours
sincerely*结尾。

8 Everyone's different

Physical appearance, personality

Physical appearance

1.1 🎧 8 Listen to a conversation between two people. Which boy is Sam and which boy is Toby? Write the names below the pictures.

A: ....

B: ....

1.2 Look again at the picture of Sam and read this description of Sam's dad. Does Sam take after his dad? Underline the things which are similar.

Sam's dad has a thin pointed face and freckles. He's got straight brown hair but he's going bald. He's got pale blue eyes and a long straight nose. He doesn't wear glasses.

Now read this comparison.

Sam looks like his dad. They've both got freckles and the same shaped face. Their hair is similar although Sam's is fairer and thicker. Sam's nose is just like his dad's and they have the same eyes. They're very alike but Sam wears glasses.

1.3 Look at the picture of Toby and read this description of his mother. Underline the things which are similar about them and write a comparison like the one above in your notebook.

Toby's mum has got a round face. She's got long wavy hair which was dark but it's going grey now. She's got a small turned-up nose, large green eyes and quite full lips.

1.4 Write below the words used in 1.1 and 1.2 to describe someone's face, hair and eyes.

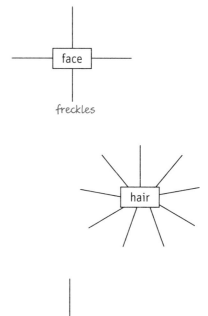

1.5 📖 Think about yourself and your friends and add any other words you can think of.

1.6 Write sentences in your notebook like those in 1.2 and 1.3 comparing yourself with someone in your family or a friend.

Ⓥ *Vocabulary note*

take after只能用于同一家庭的人：*Jessica takes after her mum.*（杰西卡和她妈妈长得很像。）**look like**可用于表示任何人：*Mark looks like John Lennon.*（马克与约翰·伦农长得很像。）

Personality

2.1 📖 Here is a letters page from a magazine. Read the letters and choose the best word for each gap.

Dear Geri

I used to love playing with Sam when we were small because he's so (1) .C.. – he was really good at making up exciting games to play. But he didn't enjoy being in large groups because he was very (2) ..... and he didn't like other children playing with us. He's a bit more (3) ..... now so he's got more friends. But we had an argument the other day. I made a joke about his clothes and now he won't speak to me. He's much too (4) ..... – it's really easy to upset him. I don't know what to do.

Patrick

Dear Geri

I've only known Trina a few months. The best thing about her is that she's great fun to be with as she's always (5) ..... . She never seems to be in a bad mood. She's always got something to say – in fact, she's the most (6) ..... person I've ever met. She never gets anxious but in some ways she's far too (7) ..... about everything – she nearly always arrives late when we've arranged to meet. I don't really mind though. The only thing I don't like about her is that she can be (8) ..... to other people – she sometimes makes fun of them. I want to tell her but I don't want to lose her as my friend. What shall I do?

Carla

1	**A** easy-going	**B** thoughtful	**C** imaginative
2	**A** shy	**B** selfish	**C** thoughtless
3	**A** nosey	**B** sociable	**C** bossy
4	**A** sensitive	**B** sensible	**C** sympathetic
5	**A** big-headed	**B** cheerful	**C** moody
6	**A** talkative	**B** generous	**C** considerate
7	**A** outgoing	**B** lively	**C** relaxed
8	**A** impatient	**B** unreliable	**C** unkind

> **Error warning**
>
> **sensitive**（敏感的）描述某人情绪很容易受干扰：*Tim cries if he hears a sad story. He's very sensitive.*（如果提姆听到一个悲伤的故事，他就会哭泣。他很敏感。）**sensible**（明智的）表示某人有很实际的生活方式：*Sam always has a bottle of water with him in case he gets thirsty - he's very sensible.*（山姆总是随身带着一瓶水以防自己口渴——他很明智。）**sympathetic**（有同情心的）表示某人理解其他人的问题：*My teacher was sympathetic when I explained why I was late.*（当我解释为什么迟到时，老师对我表示理解。）

2.2 Using these expressions from the letters, write two positive and two negative sentences about someone you know.

He's very/really .... He's so .... He's a bit .... He's much/far too .... She's never/always .... The only thing I don't like about her is that she .... The best thing about her is that she .... She can be ......

3.1 Match the adjectives in column A with their opposites in column B.

Column A	Column B
funny	aggressive
generous	shy
gentle	big-headed
hard-working	rude
modest	lazy
polite	mean
self-confident	serious

3.2 Choose the correct adjective for each sentence.

1 After Steve won the prize, he became rather ...big-headed... and expected everyone to praise him.

2 The people I met were very .... We were offered meals everywhere we went.

3 It's .... to walk into someone's office without knocking.

4 She could be a really good musician but she's too .... to practise.

5 I saw a really .... film on TV. I couldn't stop laughing.

6 Animals are only .... towards people if they are frightened or hungry.

4.1 Some adjectives are missing from this personality quiz. Choose the correct word below.

bad-tempered ~~bossy~~ dishonest moody nosey

1 Are you ....bossy............? Do you like to tell other people what to do?

2 Are you ....? Are you interested in other people's business?

3 Are you ....? Are you happy one day and miserable the next?

4 Are you ....? Do you feel angry a lot of the time?

5 Are you ....? Do you sometimes tell lies?

4.2 How many questions would you answer *yes* to? Are these good or bad things about your personality?

Look back at all the vocabulary about personality. Choose some adjectives which describe yourself and write them in the table.

POSITIVE	NEGATIVE

5.1 WORD BUILDING 📖 We can add a prefix to some adjectives to make an opposite. The most common prefix is *un-*. Others are *dis-, in-, ir-* and *im-*.

Put the correct prefix above these groups of adjectives.

polite patient possible	popular kind imaginative sociable	considerate convenient expensive	honest satisfied	relevant responsible regular

Complete this rule.
.... is added to some adjectives beginning with *p-*.
.... is added to some adjectives beginning with *r-*.

> **V** *Vocabulary note*
>
> 可以将前缀**un-** 和**dis-** 添加到一些动词前面（*unpack*打开行李，*unlock*开锁，*dislike*不喜欢，*disagree*不同意）和一些名词前面（*unhappiness*不开心，*disapproval*不赞同）。

5.2 We can add *-ful* to some nouns to make positive adjectives meaning 'having': *thoughtful, cheerful*.

We can add *–less* to some nouns to make negative adjectives meaning 'lacking': *thoughtless, friendless*.

Add *–ful* or *–less* to the nouns below to make adjectives which fit in the sentences below.

care   colour   harm   pain   power   ~~thank~~   grace

1 We were really ....thankful......... that we'd reserved seats as the hall was full.

2 That's the second wallet you've lost. Why are you so .... ?

3 Water is a .... liquid.

4 The president is the most .... person in the country.

5 My foot is still .... from when I hurt it last week.

6 You can stroke the pony. He's quite ....

7 I love watching Mary dance because she's so ....

Exam practice

READING Part 1

You are going to read an extract from a biography about an actor called Maggie Smith. For questions 1–3, choose the answer (A, B, C or D) which you think fits best according to the text.

Maggie Smith is an extremely talented actor whose obsessive attention to detail in her performances carries over into photography sessions. She will not sit for photographs if she does not feel that everything is absolutely right. And if she can choose her photographer, it will usually be Zoe Dominic, who remembers Maggie cancelling a photo-call because she was dissatisfied with her earrings. 'With any other actor,' says Dominic, 'I would have forced the issue. But with Maggie I would never argue.'

Zoe Dominic finds Maggie a great subject and a great actress, who is above all physically funny: 'I've always found her hysterically funny. She has **immense physical grace**, which is why I like to catch her in action. On a bad day – and I try not to photograph her if she's unhappy, or not ready – she shrinks, in face and body. But when she feels good, and that's the ideal time to photograph anyone, she positively blossoms and she looks like a wonderful peach. Whether she's conscious of **that** or not I don't know. I wouldn't dream of discussing it with her.'

1   What do we find out about Maggie in the first paragraph?
  A   She likes to argue with her photographers.
  B   She prefers to wear a lot of jewellery.
  C   She is very careful about her appearance.
  D   She does not enjoy having her photograph taken.

2   What does Maggie's 'immense physical grace' mean
    in the second paragraph?
  A   her way of moving
  B   her inner strength
  C   her height
  D   her sense of humour

3   What does 'that' refer to at the end of the second paragraph?
  A   Maggie's reactions are difficult to predict.
  B   Maggie often has bad days.
  C   Maggie is not easy to talk to.
  D   Maggie's mood affects the way she looks.

> **Exam Tip**
>
> 考试中的阅读文章更长，并有8个问题。通常会有一个问题是关于某个单词、短语或句子意思（mean）是什么或指（refer）什么。

USE OF ENGLISH Part 4

Complete the second sentence so that it has a similar meaning to the first sentence, including the word given. Do not change the word given. You must use between two and five words, including the word given.

1   Marta has the same personality as her father, who is very outgoing and optimistic.
  AFTER
  Marta .... father, who is very outgoing and optimistic.

2   Tanya has such a good imagination that she can make up amazing stories.
  IS
  Tanya .... that she can make up amazing stories.

3   My sister and I are completely different because she has dark hair and eyes.
  LOOK
  I .... my sister who has dark hair and eyes.

> **Exam Tip**
>
> 检查第二个句子是否与第一个句子的意思相同。

9 Get active
Movement, sport

Movement

1.1 Look at these verbs of movement. Which are fast and which are slow?

~~run~~ ~~walk~~ dash rush stroll
stride creep sprint crawl wander

FAST run ....
SLOW walk ....

1.2 Who or what moves in this way? Complete the table with the verbs above. Some subjects match more than one verb.

an athlete	sprint, run	traffic	
a tourist		a burglar	
a baby		someone late for work	

1.3 Use one of the verbs above in the correct form to complete these sentences. There may be more than one correct answer.

1 Andrew ....crept.......... into the house, trying not to wake the rest of the family.

2 She saw the bus in the distance and .... to the bus stop.

3 .... is a good form of exercise for anyone of any age.

4 The athlete .... to the finishing line and broke all records.

5 Paul was a fast walker, and he was soon .... ahead of me.

6 We .... through the park, admiring the flowers.

7 He only had ten minutes to catch the bus, so he .... into the house, grabbed his coat and .... out again.

2.1 IDIOMS Look at these sentences which contain idioms with *run*. Try to answer these questions without using your dictionary.

1 Do you ever eat breakfast **on the run**? Or do you prefer to sit down and eat at a table?

2 Did you ever **run wild** as a child? Did your parents try to stop you?

3 Do feelings **run high** in your family when your national team is playing in a big international sports match? Do you shout and jump up and down?

4 Do you **run yourself into the ground** when you're studying for an exam? Do you get very tired?

5 Have you spent a morning **running round in circles** recently? Did you have a lot to do? Did you achieve anything?

6 Is there a particular talent which **runs in your family**? For example, are several people in your family artistic or musical?

2.2 Now match each of the idioms (1–6) to one of the explanations (A–F).

1	do something on the run	A	go from one generation to the next
2	run wild	B	make yourself tired by working too much
3	people's feelings run high	C	do something without stopping what you're already doing
4	run yourself into the ground	D	behave in an uncontrolled way
5	run round in circles	E	be very active without succeeding in doing much
6	run in the family	F	people are very excited

2.3 PHRASAL VERBS 📖 Choose the correct phrasal verb in these sentences.

1 If you criticise people, you _run them down_ / run over them.

2 If you encounter a problem, you run *up against* / *through* it.

3 When you meet someone unexpectedly in the street, you run *across* / *over* them.

4 If you want someone to explain something to you, you ask them to run *out of* / *through* the details with you.

5 When children are very naughty, their parents run *up against* / *out of* patience.

6 If you're very busy, you're always running *around* / *down*.

2.4 Complete these sentences so they are true for you.

1 I don't like running people down because ....

2 If I run up against a problem, I ....

3 If I run across a friend when I'm out shopping, I ....

4 I ask someone to run through something again if I ....

5 I run out of patience very quickly when I ....

6 I find I'm always running around when ....

Sport

3.1 Write the activities from the box in the correct column.

running	volleyball	skating
cycling	judo	squash
jogging	yoga	rugby
aerobics	walking	swimming
badminton	athletics	climbing
skateboarding	skiing	diving
hockey	snorkelling	football
table tennis	baseball	gymnastics
sailing	snowboarding	hiking
martial arts	surfing	ice hockey

GO	PLAY	DO
running	volleyball	judo

3.2 TRUE or FALSE? Correct the sentences if they are wrong.

1   Golf is played with clubs on a court.

2   You play squash on a court with a bat.

3   You play hockey on a track using a stick.

4   You go skating at a pitch, and take your skates with you.

5   Tennis is played on a clay court or a grass court, but you always need a racket.

6   Good skateboarders use a ramp.

7   Baseball is played with a stick.

8   Footballers wear boots on their feet.

3.3 What do you call the people who play sports?

Someone who goes running is a *runner*. Which of the other sports in 3.1 add *–er*?

Someone who plays volleyball is a *volleyball-player*. Which of the other sports add *–player*?

What is the name of the person who does these sports?

cycling – ....*cyclist*.........
gymnastics – ....
athletics – ....

4.1 🎧 9a Listen to three people talking about different sports/activities. Which sports do they describe?

Speaker 1 ....   Speaker 2 ....   Speaker 3 ....

4.2 Now write four sentences in your notebook about a sport you play. Say how you feel about it, what you do and what equipment you use.

5.1 COMMON EXPRESSIONS Complete these sentences with the correct form of *win* or *beat*.

1   They ....*beat*........ the favourites in the second round, and went on to .... the semi-final.

2   After years of training, Alison finally .... her great rival in the final and .... the trophy.

3   Peter .... a gold medal in the 10,000 metres, ... the world record by two seconds.

4   Fitzpatrick went on to .... the race, ... his rival by a tenth of a second.

5   There is no one to .... them now – they're bound to .... the cup.

> **Ⓥ Vocabulary note**
>
> 赢得比赛或奖品时用***win***：*win a race, a semi-final, a cup, a medal, a trophy*。打败对手或打破纪录时用***beat***：*beat another team, an opponent, a rival, a record, a time*。在游戏或体育运动中击败某人用***beat***：*My brother always beats me at chess.*

5.2 IDIOMS Match the beginnings of these sentences (1–5) with the endings (A–E).

1   We left very early in the morning,

2   I was going to buy Mum a watch for her birthday,

3   Constanza doesn't want to take a long haul flight

4   At first I didn't want to go clubbing with the others

5   Everyone laughed at his idea of selling kites

A   but it turned out **to be a winner**.

B   but I think **we can win her round**.

C   but **if you can't beat them, join them**.

D   but my sister **Helena beat me to it**.

E   but **we still didn't manage to beat the rush**.

5.3 Put the idioms in bold into this table and write their meaning.

WIN	to be a winner = to be extremely successful to win someone round
BEAT	

Exam practice

USE OF ENGLISH Part 4

For these questions, complete the second sentence so that it has a similar meaning to the first sentence, using the word given. Do not change the word given. You must use between two and five words, including the word given.

0 The burglar quietly entered the house through the back window.
CREPT
The burglar .....*crept into the house*..... through the back window.
1 It took John's boss a long time, but he explained all the details of the contract to him.
RUN
It took John's boss a long time .... all the details of the contract with him.
2 I tried to be the first in the bathroom this morning, but my sister got there first.
BEAT
I tried to be the first in the bathroom this morning, but my sister .... it.
3 The builders faced many problems when they started laying the foundations of the house.
RAN
The builders .... of problems when they started laying the foundations of the house.
4 I think Susie inherited her musical ability from her mother and grandmother.
RUNS
I think being musical .... family.

SPEAKING Part 2

Look at the two photographs. Think about vocabulary to describe them. When you are ready, take a minute to describe the two photographs.
What is the sport?
What's happening in the picture?
What are the people wearing?
What equipment are they using?
How are they feeling?
What are the differences between the two sports?

9b **Listen to the model answer.**

WRITING Part 2: letter

This is part of a letter you have received from your Canadian penfriend Michael.
Write a letter to Michael, giving him the information he asks for. Write 120–180 words

... so I need some information for the project I'm doing on sport. Could you write and tell me which sport is most popular in your country and why? And what about you – do you like playing sport or watching it?
Write soon,
Michael

10 My world
Family and relationships, celebrations, friends

Family and relationships

1.1 Complete the sentences with the relationship words below.

classmates	colleagues	~~cousins~~	nephew	flatmates	a married couple
neighbours	penfriends	step-sisters	sisters-in-law		

1 Our mothers are sisters. We're ......*cousins*...... .

2 We share an office. We're ....

3 My parents are divorced. My dad has just married Claire's mum. Claire and I are ....

4 We had our wedding anniversary last week. We're ....

5 I'm married to Mary's brother. Mary and I are ....

6 We share a flat. We're ....

7 We sit next to each other at school. We're ....

8 We live next door to each other. We're ....

9 My sister has a son and a daughter. They're my .... and niece.

10 We write to each other but we've never met. We're ....

1.2 People who belong to the same family are relatives. Look at 1–10 above. Which of the people are related to each other?

Error warning

谈论对其他人的感觉时，可以说与其有好的或坏的关系，例如："我和我的姐姐关系很好／坏"应为 *I have a good / bad relationship* **with** *my sister*，而不是 *I have a good / bad relationship* **to** *my sister*。

Celebrations

2.1 Read the letters on the opposite page about two different weddings and put the missing words into the crossword.

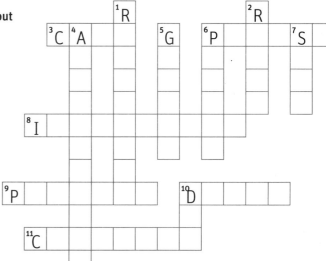

Vocabulary note

同某人结婚／订婚：We get / are married / engaged **to** someone。

同某人离婚：We get / are divorced **from** someone。

Dear Bill

I'm glad you got the **[8 across]** to my brother's wedding and that you're able to come. It will be a traditional wedding and will take place in the garden of the bride's family. The wedding **[10 down]** will begin with the groom arriving there on a horse. The **[11 across]** starts with the couple bowing to each other and to the **[6 across]**. You will have to be patient as there are no chairs! The bride and groom will both wear colourful, traditional clothes and all my relatives will probably wear traditional clothes too but the other **[5 down]** just dress smartly. However, don't dress too informally or wear black. After the wedding we'll go to a restaurant to have a traditional lunch. You can give the couple any kind of **[9 across]** but we usually give money. If you want to take **[6 down]** of the couple, you can but you shouldn't go too close.

Dear Satya

I'm so pleased you're coming to my sister's wedding in our village. She's getting married on the same day as my parents' silver wedding **[4 down]** – they've been married for 25 years. So first of all everybody will go to the Town Hall for a civil **[11 across]** and then we'll go to the village church where the bride and groom will exchange gold **[2 down]**. In the church the bride's family sit on one side and the groom's on the other. My sister is going to wear a long white **[10 across]** and the groom will wear a **[7 down]**. Most people dress formally and some women wear hats. On the way out of the church everyone throws rice or flower petals over the couple for good luck. Then we'll go to the **[1 down]** which will be in a hotel nearby. There'll be lots to eat and drink and a **[3 across]** which is cut by the bride and groom. If you want to bring a **[9 across]**, most people buy something for the couple's new home.

2.2 Here are some photos of the weddings. Can you guess which country they are in?

2.3 Read both letters again and find the answers to these questions. Underline where you find the answers.

1 Where will it take place?

2 How will the day begin?

3 What will happen next?

4 What will people wear?

5 Where do people eat?

6 Do people give presents? What?

Friends

3.1 (🔊 10a) Listen to four people talking about a friendship. How well do they know the person they are talking about? Write A, B or C in the gaps.

Speaker 1 .....   Speaker 2 .....   Speaker 3 .....   Speaker 4 .....

A very well   **B** quite well   **C** not well at all

3.2 Here are some phrases from the recordings. Put one verb in each gap. Then listen again to check.

enjoy	fell	fell	get	get	got	had	keep	lost	make
make	spoken	told							

Speaker 1   I (1) ....*fell*....out with Mike over money.
we haven't (2) .... to each other for three months.
I should (3) .... in touch with him to (4) ....up
we (5) .... each other everything.

Speaker 2   I (6) .... in love with her.
we (7) .... on well together
I'd really like to (8) .... to know her.

Speaker 3   we (9) .... touch for a while
we (10) .... each other's company
we (11) .... in touch now.

Speaker 4   I don't (12) .... friends easily
we (13) .... things in common

3.3 Read again what Speaker 1 and Speaker 3 said. Which adjectives do they use with *friend(s)*?

We were very .... friends.
He was my .... friend.

Our fathers were .... friends.
Jasmine and I became .... friends.

4.1 COMMON EXPRESSIONS There are lots of fixed phrases with *get*. Three of them are in 3.2. Write them here.

get .... touch   get .... together   get .... someone

4.2 *Get* sometimes has a similar meaning to *become*. Can you replace *become* with *get* in any of these sentences? Write the correct form of *get* in the sentences where it fits.

1   Jasmine and I *became* good friends.

2   That singer *is becoming* more and more popular.

3   The speaker *became* nervous when he realized he'd forgotten his notes.

4   I never expected to *become* a millionaire.

5 Choose the correct word for each gap in this essay called 'New friends'.

My family recently moved to a new town and it was the beginning of the summer holidays. My **(1)** *parents/relatives* were both busy at work and I didn't know anyone. So I decided to join some dancing classes as I thought it might be a way to **(2)** *know/meet* people. But when I got there I nearly went home again as there seemed to be lots of married **(3)** *couples/pairs*. Then I realised that was the class for **(4)** *traditional/typical* dances and I wanted to learn modern dance. When I found the correct room, some people came to talk to me and I soon **(5)** *got/made* friends. After a few days I realised that I wasn't very good at dancing. But then I never expected to **(6)** *get/become* a brilliant dancer. All I wanted was to **(7)** *get/learn* to know some people. I found out one girl was a **(8)** *neighbour/colleague* who lived in the next flat to ours and we had lots of things **(9)** *in/on* common. She is now my **(10)** *top/best* friend. We see **(11)** *the/each* other every day. We get **(12)** *on/with* well together and we never fall **(13)** *down/out*. And one of my friends is now married **(14)** *with/to* someone she met at that class.

Exam practice

SPEAKING Part 1

1 **Think about your answers to these questions.**

Who are the most important people in your life? Why?
Do you and your friends share the same ideas?
Who is your best friend? What is he/she like?

Exam Tip (also see speaking checklist on p. 99)

考官会问考生一些关于生活方面的问题。考生需要谈谈自己、个人兴趣和家庭。

2 **10b** **Listen to what a student says, then look at the recording script at the back of the book and underline some useful words and expressions.**

3 **Record yourself answering the questions above. Listen to the recording and try to improve what you said.**

SPEAKING Part 2

Look at the two photographs in 2.2 and compare and contrast them. How are the two weddings different? Think about the answers to the questions below.
Who can you see?
Where are the people?
What is happening?
How are they feeling?
Which kind of wedding would you prefer?

WRITING Part 2: letter

This is part of a letter you have received from your English penfriend, Kim. Write a reply giving her the information she asks for. Write 120–180 words.

...and now I'm doing a project on family celebrations in different countries. Could you write and tell me about a family celebration you've been to recently? It could be about a wedding or a party. Tell me what happened and why.
Thanks,
Kim

LISTENING Part 3

10c **You will hear five different people talking about a family party. For questions 1–5, choose from the list A–F what each speaker says about the party. Use the letters only once. There is one extra letter which you do not need to use.**

A The arrangements were unclear.

B It was less formal than expected.

C The quality of the food was poor.

D There wasn't enough for the children to do.

E The location was unsuitable for some people.

F There wasn't enough space.

Speaker 1	**1**	☐
Speaker 2	**2**	☐
Speaker 3	**3**	☐
Speaker 4	**4**	☐
Speaker 5	**5**	☐

Listen again.

Exam Tip

录音中的说话者都提到了与聚会有关的事，如孩子或食物，指出了对聚会不满的地方。

Test Two (Units 6–10)

Choose the correct letter: A, B, C or D.

1 I know I should be more .... but I don't want promotion because I enjoy what I'm doing.
   A honest   **B** ambitious   **C** reliable   **D** flexible

2 When I was shopping, I ran .... Stephanie. I hadn't seen her for ages so we had a chat.
   A across   **B** through   **C** over   **D** down

3 We didn't know what was wrong with the car but the .... was able to tell us as soon as he saw it.
   A architect   **B** electrician   **C** lifeguard   **D** mechanic

4 Cheap flights .... in increased air traffic.
   A mean   **B** result   **C** make   **D** lead

5 I'm sure Jake didn't leave the door unlocked. He's much too ....
   A sensitive   **B** sensible   **C** selfish   **D** sympathetic

6 We left the hotel and .... slowly through the town admiring everything.
   A wandered   **B** sprinted   **C** crept   **D** dashed

7 The football .... was really muddy after all the rain.
   A track   **B** court   **C** course   **D** pitch

8 My .... vary because the amount I get depends on how many hours I work in the restaurant.
   A wages   **B** money   **C** salaries   **D** pay

9 I didn't see much of my grandmother when I was small but I've got a really good relationship ....
   her now.
   A to   **B** from   **C** by   **D** with

10 Stefan is hoping to get a temporary .... in a shop during the summer.
   A work   **B** job   **C** occupation   **D** career

11 I'll sing a song as long as you don't .... fun of me.
   A make   **B** be   **C** do   **D** have

12 Go to our website and .... on the map to get information about buses in your area.
   A click   **B** sign   **C** enter   **D** browse

13 Training is given so no previous .... of catering is required for this job.
   A application   **B** vacancy   **C** qualification   **D** experience

14 The wedding .... took place in a church and lasted for 45 minutes.
   A reception   **B** ceremony   **C** anniversary   **D** celebration

15 Marina is so .... – sometimes she's really happy and then a few hours later she refuses to speak to me.
    A dishonest   **B** bossy   **C** impatient   **D** moody

16 They had to call the party .... when Yan became ill.
    A over   **B** away   **C** off   **D** out

17 My sister has had a baby boy. I'm really pleased to have a new ....
    A cousin   **B** nephew   **C** aunt   **D** niece

18 I've got two tennis .... in case I break one during a match.
    A rackets   **B** clubs   **C** sticks   **D** bats

19 Too much stress can be .... to your health.
    A painful   **B** harmful   **C** graceful   **D** careful

20 When I went to live in China, I .... touch with some of my old friends because I didn't write or phone them.
    A got   **B** kept   **C** lost   **D** stayed

21 Everyone has a(n) .... number that allows them and nobody else to look at their account online.
    A only   **B** single   **C** unique   **D** extraordinary

22 I've got a .... face like my father.
    A round   **B** straight   **C** curly   **D** turned-up

23 The shop also has a(n)...................... so you can buy clothes by mail-order if you can't get to town.
    A advertisement   **B** mailshot   **C** catalogue   **D** poster

24 None of the guests were dressed .... in jeans and T-shirts. They were all wearing their best clothes.
    A traditionally   **B** typically   **C** smartly   **D** informally

25 Alan and I used to be very good friends but we fell .... last summer and I haven't spoken to him since.
    A apart   **B** down   **C** out   **D** away

26 My mother's side of the family are all tall so I take .... them.
    A after   **B** to   **C** from   **D** on

27 I've tried Luca's number lots of times but I can't .... through.
    A phone   **B** ring   **C** dial   **D** get

28 I used to play .... but I hurt my knee and had to stop.
    A gymnastics   **B** rugby   **C** jogging   **D** athletics

29 Although I've applied for lots of jobs, I've been .... since I left school.
    A unemployed   **B** unqualified   **C** retired   **D** redundant

30 I finished first in the race so I won the ....
    A record   **B** opponent   **C** cup   **D** time

11 Moving around
Transport, travel, holidays

Transport

1.1 The vocabulary in the box is from the text below. Is the text about a journey by train, car, plane, bus or underground?

seat	headset	pass	crew	departure	control	~~passport~~	board
check-in	conveyor	gate	belt	refreshments	security		

Read the text below and complete it with the correct words from the box.

First of all, don't forget to pack your ticket and your (1) ....passport........ in your hand luggage. When you arrive at the (2) .... desk, your bags will be weighed and put on a (3) .... belt. You will be given a boarding (4) ...., allocated a seat and told to go to the (5) .... lounge. To get there, you will pass through passport (6) .... and a (7) .... check. Look at the departure (8) .... in the lounge so you know which (9) .... number you must go to when it's time to board.

The cabin (10) .... will direct you to your (11) .... when you board, and you have to fasten your seat (12) .... before take-off. You will be served (13) .... and most companies provide an entertainment system with a (14) ....

Choose the best word to complete the title for the text.

Making your first *journey/ crossing/ flight/ trip*

1.2 🎧 11a Listen and check you have filled in the gaps correctly.

1.3 🎧 11b Listen to a short description of four other journeys. What type of travel is each person describing?

1 ....   2 ....   3 ....   4 ....

1.4 Read the recording script for 11b and underline all the words related to each kind of travel. Then put them in the correct circle below. Highlight any words which appear in more than one circle.

BUS   UNDERGROUND   TRAIN   TAXI

Travel

2.1 Use the words below to complete the sentences.

travel   hotel   equipment   storm   camera   weather   car   transport
~~luggage~~   suitcase   money   guidebook   accommodation   information   journey   coin

1 There's no need to take a lot of ....*luggage*.......... when you travel – you should be able to pack all your clothes into one ....

2 We searched for .... on the internet and eventually found a really nice .... in the centre.

3 The .... was very changeable while we were on holiday, and at the end of the week we had a big ....

4 You don't have to take much .... on a walking holiday apart from waterproof boots and clothing, but it's a good idea to take a digital .... if you want to take pictures.

5 You don't need to have a lot of .... with you when you travel, but make sure you've got a .... for the trolley at the airport.

6 I'd always enjoyed all kinds of .... , but by the time I'd finished a long motorway .... to Scotland in thick snow and icy winds, I'd changed my mind!

7 I wanted some .... about the city, so I went into a bookshop and bought a ....

8 I found that public .... in Barcelona was excellent, so I never used my .... to get around.

2.2 Check your answers and then decide whether the words in the box are countable or uncountable. Put a C or U next to them in the box. Write them in a word tree. See page 000 for advice on recording vocabulary.

Holidays

3.1 Answer the questions in the questionnaire below.

Reader survey
It's holiday time ...

❶ How do you usually travel when you go on holiday?
  A by car
  B by train
  C by plane

❷ Where do you usually go for a holiday?
  A to visit friends and family
  B to a city or resort in your own country
  C to a city or resort abroad

❸ What kind of holiday do you usually take?
  A an activity holiday
  B a beach holiday
  C a sightseeing holiday

❹ What do you like doing on holiday?
  A visiting galleries, museums and archaeological sites
  B getting fit and doing some exercise
  C just relaxing and taking it easy

❺ Where do you stay on holiday?
  A in a hotel or guesthouse
  B at a relative or friend's home
  C on a campsite

❻ What is the best thing about having a holiday?
  A getting away from routine
  B getting to know new places
  C getting together with friends

3.2 🎧 11c Listen to a man and a woman talking about the kind of holidays they like. Write the answers they would give to the questionnaire on p 51 below.

Man	1	2	3	4 .....
	5	6		
Woman	1	2	3	4 .....
	5	6		

3.3 What do you think? Complete the answers to the questions.

1 Is it better to book a holiday at the last minute or well in advance?
I think it's better to ....
because ....

2 Would you prefer to go on a package tour or travel independently?
I'd always prefer to ....
because ....

3 Would you rather stay in a small guesthouse or a luxurious five-star hotel?
I'd rather .... *because*
....

4 Complete the sentences using *travel*, *journey* or *trip*.

1 In August, I'm going on a ....*trip*......... to Mexico City with my wife.

2 They set off on the difficult .... before dawn, and they didn't arrive until after dark.

3 Drive carefully and have a safe .... home!

4 He's away on a business .... all next week, but I'll give him the message when he returns.

5 I know rail .... takes longer than going by plane, but I really enjoy it.

6 I'm really looking forward to my .... to New Zealand. I'll have lots to talk about when I get back.

7 My parents have always said that .... makes you more independent.

8 How long is your .... to college each morning?

Vocabulary note

travel可以用作动词或名词。当它作名词时，是不可数的，描述旅行的活动：*Air travel is becoming increasingly popular.*（乘飞机旅行变得越来越受欢迎了。）**journey**用来描述从一个地方去另一个地方。它是可数名词。*The journey from home to work takes two hours.*（从家去工作地点要花两个小时。）**trip**用来描述一段短期的旅行：去某地一段时间，然后回家。它是可数名词。*My friend and I went on a weekend trip to Amsterdam.*（我和朋友周末去阿姆斯特丹旅行了。）

5.1 PHRASAL VERBS Some phrasal verbs have more than one meaning. Look at how *set out* is used in these sentences. Match each sentence 1–4 with one of the meanings A–D below.

1 He **set out** to find the cave he'd seen marked on an old map. B

2 He **set** the main points of his report **out** clearly, so we could all understand it.

3 Alison **set** the chairs **out** so that everyone could see the speaker.

4 We **set out** for the airport before it got light.

A arrange something neatly

B do something with a clear aim or intention

C give well organised written information

D begin a journey

5.2 Look at these other phrasal verbs with *set*. Match each sentence 1–4 with one of the meanings A–D below.

1 The stormy weather **set in** on Monday, and it was still raining four days later.

2 When we opened the boot, it **set off** the car alarm.

3 He **set up** a helpgroup called NightWatch for people who had problems sleeping.

4 I took my bike to the shop because I've got no idea how to **set about** repairing a puncture.

A an action caused something to happen

B something unpleasant started which continued for a long time

C something was established

D to start to do something

Exam practice

SPEAKING Parts 3 and 4

Look at the drawings below.

Answer the questions. Write some notes and then use them to help you speak about the pictures.

What are the advantages and disadvantages of each holiday?
Try to think of something to say about each picture.
Which holiday would you prefer to go on and why?
Where did you spend your last holiday? What did you do?

🎧 **11d** **Listen to a model answer.**

Exam Tip (also see speaking checklist on p. 99)
在考试中，考生会和一名搭档进行讨论，并且要试着一起决定一件事。

USE OF ENGLISH Part 4

Complete the second sentence so that it has a similar meaning to the first sentence, using the word given. Do not change the word given. You must use between two and five words, including the word given.

0 There are a few details in the report that need explaining.
INFORMATION
There ....*is some information*.................... in the report that needs explaining.
1 We travelled from Edinburgh to London by car.
JOURNEY
We .... from Edinburgh to London by car.
2 My friend and I took a short break in Copenhagen last week.
TRIP
My friend and I went .... Copenhagen last week.
3 I'd like to fix the washing machine, but I don't know where to begin.
SET
I've got no idea how .... the washing machine.
4 Have you succeeded in booking a room in London yet?
ACCOMMODATION
Have you managed .... in London yet?

WRITING Part 2: article

You see the following announcement in an international magazine.

> **THE LONGEST JOURNEY**
>
> What is the longest journey you have ever done?
> Write an article describing your journey, explaining how you felt about it and why you were doing it.
> The best articles will be published next month.

Exam Tip (also see writing checklist on p. 100)
考生需要使自己的文章尽可能生动有趣。使用适当的习语或表达，说些有趣的事或提出问题。

Write 120–180 words.

12 Time off
Leisure time, hobbies and games, cinema and theatre

Leisure time

1.1 🎧 12a Listen to two people talking about what they do in their free time.

What do they prefer doing? Going out or staying in?

1 .... 2 ....

1.2 Read the recording script for 12a and underline the phrases the people use to describe what they do in their free time. Which phrases could you use to describe your leisure time?

1.3 COMMON EXPRESSIONS Put the expressions into the correct place in the chart below.

TV	a party	swimming	the cinema	a quiet night in	cards	a drink	friends round
a concert	surfing	a restaurant	a drive	the theatre	a barbecue	the beach	a walk
games	a film	shopping	a club	a play	a DVD	clubbing	a match

STAYING IN	GOING OUT
to have a party	*to go*
to watch	*to go to*
to play	*to go for*

1.4 Do you prefer going out or staying in? Use the expressions above and the words below to talk about yourself.

When I have some free time, I prefer to ...... , and I also enjoy ...... and ....
But I don't really like ...... or...... .

Hobbies and Games

2.1 Match pictures A–H with the games and pastimes 1–8.

A   B  C   D  E

F  G   H

1	jigsaw puzzle		2	crossword ......
3	cards		4	dominoes ......
5	snakes and ladders		6	backgammon ......
7	chess		8	su doku ......

2.2 Put a tick next to the ones that are popular in your country.

> 🔽 **Vocabulary note**
>
> 玩游戏时用动词**play**，如*play chess*（下国际象棋）。进行其他的娱乐消遣／活动时用**do**，如*do a crossword*（猜字谜）。收集物品时用**collect**，如*collect stamps*（收集邮票）。

2.3 Complete this paragraph about hobbies using the correct form of *play*, *do* and *collect*.

Everyone in my family has a hobby. My brother (1) ....plays....... chess; he only took it up recently and he plays really well. My sister (2) .... unusual shells and my parents (3) .... the crossword in the newspaper every day. As for me, someone showed me how su doku puzzles work and I've really taken to them, so I (4) .... them all the time now. When we're all together at the beach or at home in the winter, we (5) .... cards and we sometimes (6) .... board games like snakes and ladders or backgammon too.

3.1 PHRASAL VERBS Match these phrasal verbs with *take* with an object and a meaning.

TAKE
after	your hat	hear and remember
in	a business	accept
off	a new friend	resemble someone
on	information	fill up
over	space	develop a liking for
to	someone in your family	gain control of
up	work	remove

> 🔽 **Vocabulary note**
>
> **take**和**up**连用表示开始把某事作为兴趣爱好：*I took up chess last year.*（我从去年开始玩国际象棋。）**take**和**to**连用表示真的很喜欢做某事：*I've really taken to su doku puzzles.*（我真的很喜欢数独游戏。）

3.2 Use one of the phrasal verbs with *take* to complete these sentences.

1 I ...took to... Gemma's flatmate, Kate, as soon as I met her.

2 There was so much to .... at the lecture that I found it hard to make notes about everything.

3 The piano .... a lot of space downstairs, but we all enjoy playing it.

4 Now you're here, why don't you .... your coat and sit down and have a cup of coffee?

5 Peter .... his father – he looks and sounds just like him at times.

6 Amanda's decided to .... some more teaching now the children are older.

7 GDC Electronics has finally .... its rival, Telectrical.

Cinema and theatre

4.1 Look at the words below. Write *C* in the space if they are for the cinema, *T* if they are for the theatre or *B* if they are for both.

actor	B	critic	.....	performance	.....	special effects	.....
audience	.....	director	.....	plot	.....	stage	.....
box office	.....	documentary	.....	rehearsal	.....	studio	.....
cartoon	.....	drama	.....	reviews	.....	subtitles	.....
cast	.....	dressing room	.....	science fiction	.....	thriller	.....
costumes	.....	location	.....	screen	.....	trailer	.....
comedy	.....	musical	.....	soundtrack	.....		

4.2 (12b) Listen to two people talking about whether they prefer going to the cinema or theatre. Which does each one prefer, and why?

The woman prefers going to the .... because ....

....

The man prefers going to the .... because ....

....

Which do you prefer, and why?

I prefer going to the .... because ....

....

5 (12c) Listen to these reviews of popular films. Which kind of film is being described in each one? Choose the correct word from the box. There is one word you will not use.

western   thriller   romantic comedy   horror   cartoon   documentary   drama

1 ....   2 ....   3 ....

4 ....   5 ....   6 ....

6.1 Look at the recording script for 12c. All the words in *italics* are *adjectives*. They are all *positive* in meaning. They can all be used with the word *film*, *play* or *story*. But not all reviews are good, and some will contain negative adjectives.

Look at the adjectives below. Mark them P for positive, or N for negative.

gripping P	unimpressive	stunning	uninteresting	tedious	entertaining
brilliant	imaginative	uninspired	fascinating	wooden	

6.2 Choose the appropriate adjective to complete the paragraph.

Friends had recommended a new thriller called 'Green Line'. They said that the plot was absolutely *fascinating/unimpressive* and that lead actor Gene Bruno gave a really *wooden/brilliant* performance. But I was bitterly disappointed when I went to see it. I found the plot totally *imaginative/uninteresting* and halfway through the film, I guessed the ending. The directing was totally *uninspired/gripping* as well; probably because the story, which was based on a case of mistaken identity, was horribly *tedious/stunning*.

Exam practice

WRITING Part 1: letter

You are staying in an English-speaking country and have received this letter from the manager of the film club you belong to. Read the letter and the notes you have made. Then write a reply to Mr Johnstone using all your notes.

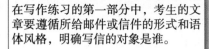

Exam Tip
(also see writing checklist on p. 100)

在写作练习的第一部分中，考生的文章要遵循所给邮件或信件的形式和语体风格，明确写信的对象是谁。

Write a **letter** of between **120–150** words.

Dear Student

We are planning to make a few changes to the film club next year, so I am writing to all our members, asking them for their answers to a few questions. — Yes...!

First of all, I would like to know if you enjoy the film club and the films we offer? — Suggest....

Second, we are particularly interested in what students would like, so do you have any suggestions about new films we could show? — Tell Mr Johnstone

Next, do you think it would be a good idea to have a café in the cinema where people could get drinks and snacks?

Finally, do you think it would be a good idea to run the film club on a Thursday afternoon as well as a Friday evening? — No, because ...

Thanks for taking the time to write back.

Yours sincerely

Robin Johnstone

READING Part 3

You are going to read some film reviews. For questions 1–6, choose from the films A–C. The films may be chosen more than once.

Which review mentions

some amusing moments?	1
the story being based on a true event?	2
a well-designed plot?	3
the impressive performances of the main actors?	4
a storyline which is rather unimaginative?	5
making excellent use of technology?	6

A

Sally Strikes Again!

Other recent films about sea creatures have managed to appeal to both adults and kids, but I don't feel this one necessarily has all the ingredients to do that. One fish looks much like another to me, but there are some good lines which make you laugh out loud and the computer animation is amazing.

B

The heat of summer

Harry Elfondo and Heather Mackenzie play the leading roles in this film aimed at teenagers. Elfondo adds class and assurance and Mackenzie is affecting and affectionate. Despite the fact that there are few original thoughts in the plot and parts are quite tedious, you can't help wanting to find out what happens to their characters in the end.

C

The Triangle

This murder mystery is director Jimmy Syke's most accessible, entertaining work since *Live Again*. In his usual style, a dozen or so key characters cross paths in unexpected ways until everything becomes clear in the last ten minutes. The film is set in a fictional mining town but it is about a struggle for survival which actually took place in a town in western Canada.

13 Around town

Cities and towns, facilities, traffic

Cities and towns

1.1 Which of the following describe the place where you live?

a port   a market town   a new town/city   a seaside town
a capital city   an industrial town/city   a rural area   a historic town/city

1.2 Match each sentence below to one of the cities in the photographs.

1   In addition, its wide open spaces and the latest leisure facilities make it an ideal location for a family day out.

2   But now that cars have been banned from the narrow cobbled streets, a walk through the picturesque centre is even more pleasant.

3   The city is in the heart of one of the country's fastest growing regions and is only 40 years old.

4   You'll certainly want to stop for a while in the beautiful old market square.

5   During that time it has grown into a modern city with up-to-date shopping centres and lively nightlife.

6   The city has always been famous for its ancient churches and impressive medieval buildings.

City A

City B

1.3 The sentences are from tourist information brochures but they are mixed up. Put them in the correct order.

City A   Sentences ..6.. , ... , ...   City B   Sentences ...... , ... , ...

1.4 Underline any words or expressions in 1.2 which you could use to describe your home town or city or the town nearest to where you live. Which words below could you use about your town or city?

many attractions	delightful parks	huge temple	cosmopolitan atmosphere	ancient mosque
famous art gallery	interesting museum	ruined castle	quiet and peaceful	full of life

2.1 〔 13a 〕 Listen to someone talking about living in a city. Which of the cities in the photographs does she live in now, A or B?

2.2 〔 13a 〕 Listen again and decide if these statements are true (T) or false (F).

1 She lives on the edge of the city. ..T..

2 The part of the city where she lives is very crowded. ......

3 Her office is close to the shopping centre. ......

4 She takes the bus to the centre because it's hard to park there. ......

5 She moved because she wanted to live somewhere more peaceful. ......

6 The area where she used to live was well looked after. ......

2.3 Find words in the recording script for 13a to complete these definitions.

1 A .....housing....... estate is a large group of houses or flats and an .... estate is where people work, often in a .... district.

2 A .... area is a part of a city or town where people live. People often live on the edge of a city which is sometimes called the .... or ....

3 A building with many offices is sometimes called an .... block and a .... block is a tall building made up of flats.

4 Towns sometimes have a pedestrian .... where people do their shopping.

5 A car park on several levels is called a .... car park.

6 Areas or buildings that are in bad condition are ....

7 Bicycles and buses are sometimes separated from other traffic in a bus/cycle ....

Facilities

3.1 Where do people do the things below (1–10)? Each answer is two words (choose the second word from the box below the puzzle). Write the words in the puzzle.

1 go swimming and do other fitness activities

2 visit the doctor

3 leave their vehicle

4 look at paintings

5 listen to music

6 hire a cab

7 watch matches

8 go skating

9 roll heavy balls along a narrow track

10 buy things

alley	centre	centre	centre	gallery
ground	hall	park	rank	rink	stadium

3.2 Find one word going down the puzzle and match it to the remaining word from the list above. What do people do there?

3.3 Think about the eleven places in the puzzle. How often do you visit them?

Traffic

4.1 (🎧 13b) Two cars were in a traffic accident. Listen to the drivers explaining what happened. Mark each driver's route on the map and where the accident took place.

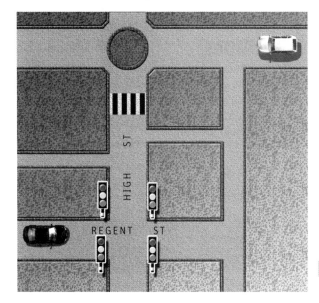

4.2 Complete this newspaper report about the accident.

Two cars crashed on the High Street yesterday afternoon at 5.30 pm during the (1) ......rush..... hour. A black Renault was approaching a pedestrian (2) .... having just turned left at the traffic (3) ....where the High Street meets Regent Street. The driver (4) .... a van which had stopped. She says she was doing about 20 km (5) .... hour but was (6) .... down. A white Fiat came out of a (7) .... road onto the High Street and drove into the side of the Renault. The police were called and the driver of the Fiat admitted he was at fault because he was driving down a (8) .... street the wrong (9) .... He said he was taking a short (10) .... to avoid a traffic (11) .... on the (12) .... near the river. It was blocked yesterday for an hour because a lorry (13) .... down on the roundabout.

5.1 PHRASAL VERBS Underline the phrasal verb in these sentences (1–6), then match them to their meanings (A–F).

1 The car slowed down as it came to the roundabout.

2 We're late because the car broke down.

3 Can you write your phone number down in my address book?

4 I'll definitely be there when you sing in the concert. I won't let you down.

5 I was offered a place on the law course but I turned it down.

6 The building was pulled down because it was unsafe.

A	disappoint	......let somebody down......
B	reduce speed	....
C	demolish	....
D	refuse	....
E	stop working	....
F	record on paper	....

5.2 These phrasal verbs have the same meaning as two of those in 1–6. Match them to their meanings.

put down .....   knock down .....

6 WORD BUILDING We can put *under-* or *over-* before a noun, verb or adjective to add to the meaning, e.g. *overtake, underground*. Put *under-* or *over-* before the word in bold in each of these sentences.

1 It's safer to go through the ......under.....**pass** than to try to cross the road.

2 She is very thin and ....**weight**.

3 More people have come to work in my office and it's really ....**crowded**.

4 I love to swim ....**water** and look at the fish.

5 Your library books are ....**due** – you'll have to pay a fine.

6 I can't eat this – it's so ....**cooked** it's almost burnt.

7 The shop assistant must have ....**charged** me. He hasn't given me enough change.

8 I know what my sister's bought me for my birthday because I ....**heard** her telling my mum.

Exam practice

USE OF ENGLISH Part 1

For questions 1–12, read the text below and decide which answer (A, B, C or D) best fits each space.

NEW YORK CITY

New York city has **(0)** ..B.. into the second largest city in North America. It is now a major business, cultural and shopping centre **(1)** ..... millions of visitors each year. Most tourists stay in the **(2)** ..... of the city, in Manhattan. It is easy to see the sights of Manhattan on foot or you can take a tourbus. There are cycle **(3)** ..... in the city if you want to hire a bicycle but you need to be brave! The subway is the quickest means of public transport but you will want to avoid the **(4)** ..... hour. And, of course, there are the famous yellow taxis. There are few taxi **(5)** ..... – just wave your arm at a taxi with its light on. You will certainly want to visit Central Park, a huge open **(6)** ..... which is ideal for relaxing on a hot summer day. The city is rich in restaurants but remember that smoking is **(7)** ..... . One of the many boat trips goes to Ellis Island where you may want to stop for a **(8)** ..... to read about the history of immigration. The main residential areas are in the **(9)** ..... of the city where, as in all large cities, some districts are quite **(10)** ..... down. Many tourists visit Queens which is the **(11)** ..... of some interesting art galleries and Brooklyn for cafés, shops and **(12)** ..... nightlife.

0	**A** become	**B** grown	**C** increased	**D** extended
1	**A** appealing	**B** advancing	**C** arriving	**D** attracting
2	**A** heart	**B** interior	**C** focus	**D** eye
3	**A** roads	**B** streets	**C** lanes	**D** ways
4	**A** busy	**B** rush	**C** crowded	**D** hurry
5	**A** ranks	**B** stalls	**C** kiosks	**D** stations
6	**A** surface	**B** region	**C** space	**D** estate
7	**A** banned	**B** excluded	**C** refused	**D** dismissed
8	**A** period	**B** while	**C** length	**D** piece
9	**A** outdoors	**B** outskirts	**C** outsides	**D** outlines
10	**A** broke	**B** let	**C** run	**D** turned
11	**A** location	**B** place	**C** position	**D** area
12	**A** alive	**B** lifelike	**C** live	**D** lively

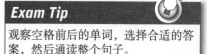

Exam Tip

观察空格前后的单词，选择合适的答案，然后通读整个句子。

SPEAKING Part 4

1 **🎧 13c** Think about your answers to these questions, then listen to somebody answer two of them. Are their answers the same as yours?
   - What is special about your capital city?
   - What are the disadvantages of living in a big city?
   - Would you prefer to live in a modern city or a historic one?
   - Why do people choose to live in the centre of cities?
   - Is there a city you'd like to visit in the future?

2 Practise answering each of the questions above. Record yourself, then listen and try to improve what you said.

WRITING Part 2: report

A group of English-speaking students is going to visit your college. Your teacher has asked you to write a report telling the students about the places of interest in your town, both old and new. Write 120–180 words.

14 Shared tastes
Food and drink, meals, art

Food and drink

1 Use the words in the box to complete the mind map below.

~~beef~~   ~~trout~~   lamb   chicken   chop   ham   wing   cod   plaice   bacon   steak
squid   burgers   tuna   breast   salmon   pork   mussels   duck   prawns   sausages   lobster

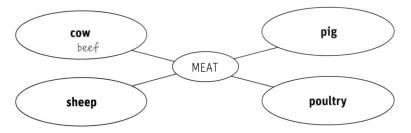
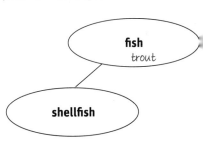

cow
beef

pig

MEAT

sheep

poultry

fish
trout

shellfish

2.1 Put the verbs in the box into the chart below.

roast   fry   boil   stir fry   bake   grill   stew

Where you cook	How you cook	What you cook	What you use
Under the grill		steak	a grillpan
On the hob		an egg fruit fish vegetables	a saucepan a saucepan a frying pan a wok
In the oven		beef a cake	a roasting tin a cake tin

2.2 🎧 14a Listen to three people. What kind of food is each person describing: English, Italian or Chinese?

1 ....   2 ....   3 ....

2.3 📖 Read the recording script for 14a and underline the words that gave you the correct answer.

2.4 📖 The verbs in bold describe ways to prepare food. Choose the correct word to complete each sentence below.

1 I **poured** myself a glass of *orange juice/coffee*.

2 To make an omelette, **beat** the *potatoes/eggs* together.

3 **Chop** the *vegetables/salad* very small.

4 You can't eat a(n) *banana/apple* without **peeling** it first!

5 **Grate** the *cheese/meat* before putting it on the pizza.

6 You'll need to **melt** the *butter/cream*.

7 **Mix** all the ingredients for the *milk/cake* together.

8 **Slice** the *lemon/flour* very thinly.

9 **Stir** the *bread/sauce* regularly while it cooks.

Meals

3.1 ⓟ **14b** Listen to an English person describing what she eats on a typical day and complete the chart.

Everyday meals	Breakfast: Lunch: Dinner:	Special meal	Day: Food:
What she doesn't eat:			

3.2 Practise speaking for one minute about what you usually eat.

3.3 Read the text. Then decide whether the sentences below are true (*T*), false (*F*) or not given (*NG*).

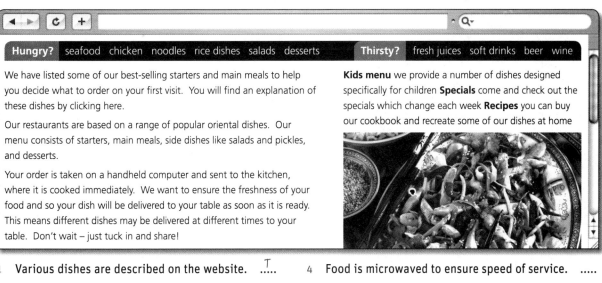

Hungry? seafood chicken noodles rice dishes salads desserts   **Thirsty?** fresh juices soft drinks beer wine

We have listed some of our best-selling starters and main meals to help you decide what to order on your first visit. You will find an explanation of these dishes by clicking here.

Our restaurants are based on a range of popular oriental dishes. Our menu consists of starters, main meals, side dishes like salads and pickles, and desserts.

Your order is taken on a handheld computer and sent to the kitchen, where it is cooked immediately. We want to ensure the freshness of your food and so your dish will be delivered to your table as soon as it is ready. This means different dishes may be delivered at different times to your table. Don't wait – just tuck in and share!

Kids menu we provide a number of dishes designed specifically for children **Specials** come and check out the specials which change each week **Recipes** you can buy our cookbook and recreate some of our dishes at home

1 Various dishes are described on the website. ..T...
2 The restaurant serves only Japanese food. .....
3 This is a self-service restaurant. .....
4 Food is microwaved to ensure speed of service. .....
5 This restaurant caters for family dining. .....
6 The meals served are easy to make at home. .....

3.4 COMMON EXPRESSIONS We use the word *taste* literally when we talk about food. But we also use it figuratively to talk about more abstract things like art, fashion or films. Look at these examples and match the two halves of the sentences.

The sauce smells lovely   A I thought it was really tasteless.

I've always loved   B landscapes are more to my taste.

I enjoyed the dinner last night   C so I told her she had good taste in clothes!

I loved Emma's new dress   D but I'll taste it to see if it needs salt.

I didn't enjoy the film;   E because it's really tasteful.

I don't like abstract paintings;   F because everything I ate was really tasty.

I like the way the gallery is decorated   G the taste of garlic.

3.5 Match these adjectives to the definitions below: *tasty, tasteful, tasteless.*

1 in bad taste ....   2 delicious ....   3 in good taste ....

Art

4.1 Choose the best word to fit each gap in these definitions.

1 prints   oil paintings   ~~drawings~~   water colours
If you want to do ....*drawings*.......... , you'll need a pencil, but to do .... , you'll need a brush and some water. Many of the famous pictures which are on display to the public, like the Mona Lisa, are .... Even if you can never buy these pictures, you can often get .... of them so you can have a copy of your favourite picture on the wall.

2 sculptures   textiles   jewellery   pottery
We use the word .... to describe objects made out of clay, like vases. Materials woven by hand or machine are known as .... Since ancient times, people have worn .... such as necklaces and bracelets and made .... of their gods and animals.

3 still life   abstract   portrait   landscape
A(n) .... is a picture of a person, but a(n) .... is a picture of objects that do not move, like fruit, flowers or bowls. A(n) .... is a picture of the countryside, but a(n) .... shows line, shape and colour and does not attempt to be realistic.

4 gallery   studio   collection   exhibition
A(n) .... of paintings is on display to the public, and it usually takes place in an art .... An artist usually paints in a .... Millionaires often own a number of very valuable pictures in their own private ....

4.2 Read the questionnaire below about art.

HOW ARTY ARE YOU?

1 How artistic are you?
Very / a little / not very / not at all

2 What type of art do you do?
Painting / drawing / sculpture / pottery / other ....

3 Do you go to art exhibitions and galleries?
Yes, occasionally / frequently
No, hardly ever / never

4 What type of art do you like? ....

5 What is your favourite picture? ....

6 Who is your favourite artist? ....

(🔊 14c) Listen to a man talking about art and answer the questions in the questionnaire for him.

4.3 Practise speaking for a minute about your taste in art. Use the questionnaire to help you.

Exam practice

USE OF ENGLISH Part 3

Use the word given in capitals at the end of each line to form a word that fits in the space. There is an example at the beginning (0).

THE RED FLOWER RESTAURANT

With its mixture of charm, character and excellent **(0)** ....hospitality.., The Red Flower   **HOSPITABLE**
is one of those **(1)** .... treasures you don't often find. The owners, Fritz   **HIDE**
and Gemma will make sure you and your guests will **(2)** .... enjoy your   **THOROUGH**
meal.

   A really **(3)** .... welcome is guaranteed to everyone who dines at The   **FRIEND**
Red Flower. The restaurant is open all day every day for hot and cold food, and
whether you're looking for a **(4)** .... midday snack, an evening meal with   **TASTE**
the family or a venue for a special **(5)** ...., The Red Flower can provide   **CELEBRATE**
exactly what you're looking for.

   The restaurant is well-known for its **(6)** .... menus, which offer a range   **SEASON**
of English and international dishes at **(7)** .... prices. This explains the   **REASON**
restaurant's **(8)** .... with both locals and tourists. The bar offers soft   **POPULAR**
drinks as well as a wide **(9)** .... of wines. It's an ideal place to meet up   **SELECT**
with friends and family or to enjoy a **(10)** .... evening out with someone   **ROMANCE**
special.

LISTENING Part 2

(𝕇 14d) **You will hear an interview with an Australian artist called
Anna Roberts. For questions 1–10, complete the sentences.**

Anna is well known for pictures of very | 1 ⬚ | places.

Anna often gets to these places on foot, but occasionally she gets there
by | 2 ⬚ | .

In her paintings Anna always tries to show that | 3 ⬚ | is very beautiful.

Some of Anna's paintings are so | 4 ⬚ | that they look like photographs.

Anna has recently done some paintings of the | 5 ⬚ | using yellow and orange.

Anna thinks her paintings are special because of the way she shows the | 6 ⬚ | .

Anna has a strong preference for doing her paintings on | 7 ⬚ | .

Although she has used other types of paint, Anna prefers to do her paintings in | 8 ⬚ | .

Anna's paintings are sold to | 9 ⬚ | as well as private collectors.

In addition to being a painter, Anna has written | 10 ⬚ | about painting.

(𝕇 14d) **Listen again.**

SPEAKING Part 1

Think about how you would answer these questions.

Do you like cooking?   What sort of things do you cook?
What's your favourite food?   Why do you like it?

15 Media mania

Television and radio, newspapers and magazines, books

Television and radio

1.1 Read this information from a TV awards website. Match the names of the programmes with their explanations. Write A–F in the gaps.

A Comedy   B Current affairs programme   C Drama series

D Reality TV   E Soap opera   F Documentary

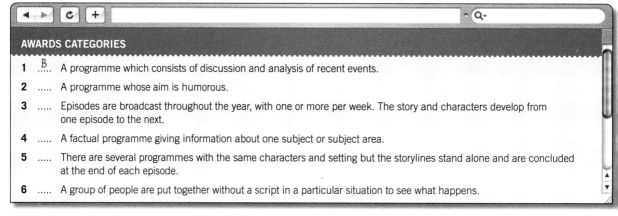

AWARDS CATEGORIES

1   .B....   A programme which consists of discussion and analysis of recent events.

2   .....   A programme whose aim is humorous.

3   .....   Episodes are broadcast throughout the year, with one or more per week. The story and characters develop from one episode to the next.

4   .....   A factual programme giving information about one subject or subject area.

5   .....   There are several programmes with the same characters and setting but the storylines stand alone and are concluded at the end of each episode.

6   .....   A group of people are put together without a script in a particular situation to see what happens.

1.2 🔊 15 Listen to three people talking about their favourite TV programmes. What kind of programmes are they?

Speaker 1 ....   Speaker 2 ....   Speaker 3 ....

1.3 Does your favourite TV programme fit into one of the categories in 1.1? Tick the expressions below you could use to talk about it.

It makes me laugh.   It's so entertaining.   The acting is brilliant.   The storylines are gripping.
It's really good drama.   I love the characters.   The plots are good.   It's quite compelling.

1.4 Decide if these nouns go with TV, radio or both. Write them in the correct place in the circles.

~~aerial~~   channel   disc jockey   highlights   remote control
repeats   screen   set   station   studio

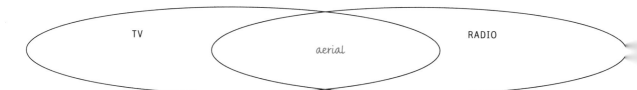

TV   aerial   RADIO

2.1 Complete the gaps with a word from the box.

heard	listened to	looked at	read about
saw	~~saw~~	watched	

1 I turned round and suddenly ....saw.......... Abby standing in the doorway.

2 Sadie always .... music while she was working.

3 Tim .... the map to see where they were.

4 I .... an advert in the newspaper yesterday for a course in jewellery-making.

5 I .... the sound of a motorbike coming down the road. It was Mark.

6 Kate stood by the window and .... her children playing in the snow.

7 I .... Johnny Depp's new film in a magazine.

Vocabulary note

人们不用努力就可 **see**（看到）：*I saw Rob when I was in the supermarket.* （我在超市看到罗布了）。当人们 **look at**，**watch** 或 **read about** 的时候，要做出努力：*She looked at the clock to see what the time was.* （她看看表，想知道几点了。）**watch** 是人们盯着事物看一段时间，并且所看的事物常常是移动或变化的：*I spent Saturday afternoon watching Jake play football.* （我整个星期六下午都在看杰克踢足球。）人们不用努力就可以 **hear**（听见），但是当要 **listen to**（听）的时候，就要做出努力：*We stopped playing when we heard the whistle.* （我们听到口哨声后就停止了玩耍。）*I like to listen to the radio on Sunday morning.* （我喜欢在周日上午听广播。）

2.2 What does *see* mean in these sentences? Match sentences 1–3 with A–C.

1 I want to see how they'll react.   A to meet

2 I'm seeing her at ten.   B to understand

3 I don't see what you mean.   C to find out

Newspapers and magazines

3 COMMON EXPRESSIONS There are lots of words which make expressions with *newspaper* or *magazine*. Some go before the noun and some go after. Which words can be used only with *newspaper* (mark them *N*) or only with *magazine* (mark them *M*)? Some can be used with both (mark them *NM*).

daily N	fashion ...	glossy ...	gossip ...	... advertisement	... article	... cover
local ...	monthly ...	morning ...	tabloid ...	... editor	... editorial	... headline
today's ...	travel ...	women's ...		... report		

4 Some verbs are often found in newspaper reports. Decide which verb fits best in each gap.

FESTIVAL LOSES MONEY

The company Musicfest (1) ..C.. that the two-day concert they organised at the weekend attracted far fewer fans than they had (2) ..... They had (3) ..... to raise £20,000 for charity but Chris Powell, the finance director, (4) ..... that they had actually lost money. He (5) ..... the bad weather but also (6) ..... that the local newspaper had not promoted the festival as they had (7) ..... He (8) ..... the fact that one act was cancelled at the last minute but he (9) ..... that another well-known performer had only played for ten minutes because of a dispute over pay. He (10) ..... to fans to attend the next one-day concert which will take place in September.

	A	B	C
1	proposed	described	announced
2	expected	warned	prepared
3	cared	hoped	believed
4	expressed	offered	admitted
5	suggested	blamed	accused
6	claimed	advised	predicted
7	declared	emphasised	promised
8	apologised	disapproved	regretted
9	refused	denied	opposed
10	appealed	demanded	threatened

Books

5 Write these books in the correct category.

atlas	biography	cookery book	detective story	diary	encyclopedia
ghost story	guidebook	poetry book	science fiction novel	textbook	thriller

Reference *atlas* ....

Fiction ....

Non-fiction ....

6.1 Quickly read this extract from a book. Do not worry about words you do not understand. What kind of book do you think it is from? Choose from the list in 5.

The bathroom door was open and I stepped back into the shadows as footsteps came running out of my room. A torch flashed in the corridor. 'Roberto! Agostino!' Somebody went hurtling past and flung himself down the stairs. I had a brief glimpse of a short, angry figure. Then a door opened along the corridor, near the red glow of the window. I peered out and caught sight of the silhouette of a man hurrying down the corridor towards me. As he passed me he switched on a torch and in the reflected light from the walls I made out the features of Roberto.

6.2 You may not understand every word when you are reading. There are four words/expressions in the extract which mean *see* or *look*. Underline them. Now read the extract again. Is it easier to understand?

6.3 Here are some more words often used in fiction. There is an odd one out in each group. Which one is it? Why?

1	notice	glimpse	breathe
2	smell	gaze	wink
3	spot	sniff	view
4	stroke	witness	stare
5	observe	overhear	glance

7.1 Choose the correct word in these definitions.

1 .A.. writes any kind of book. ..... writes fiction.
 ..... writes in newspapers and magazines.
 ..... writes poetry, sometimes in verses which rhyme.
 A An author   **B** A journalist
 C A novelist   **D** A poet

2 You keep books from ..... for only a short while but you buy them from ..... .
 A a bookshop   **B** a library

3 You ..... books from libraries. Libraries ..... them to you.
 A borrow   **B** lend

4 Real people have ..... . People in books, plays or films are called ..... .
 A personalities   **B** characters

7.2 Read this review and choose the correct words.

My (1) *favourite/best* thriller from the (2) *novelist/journalist* Hammond Innes is (3) *called/named* 'The Angry Mountain'. This is the book that really got me interested in reading when I was young and I will always (4) *remember/remind* it for that. It's a great example of adventure (5) *non-fiction/fiction*. The story is so well-written you feel as though you are in the same room as the (6) *characters/personalities* and the (7) *relationships/relatives* between them are brilliantly developed. It is now out of print but you may be able to (8) *borrow/lend* it from a (9) *library/bookshop* if you (10) *request/ask* it. Hammond Innes puts together a tightly-written story which is a thoroughly (11) *entertaining/entertained* read. It's a book you will not be able to put down until you have finished the last (12) *chapter/verse*.

7.3 Note any expressions you could use in a review about a book you like.

Exam practice

READING Part 1

You are going to read part of a novel. For questions 1-4, choose the answer (A, B, C or D) which you think fits best according to the text.

The whole night sky seemed on fire. The headlights of a car stabbed the countryside on the road to Avin. It slowed and stopped. Then the headlights went out. A door closed in the stillness of the villa below me. My muscles tensed. I thought I heard the creak of a stair board, and suddenly I knew someone was coming up the stairs, coming to my room. I swung the shutters shut and moved towards the door. The palms of my hands were sweating and the metal of the torch I held felt slippery. But the weight of it was comforting.

I stood with my head pressed close to the panelling of the door, listening. There was somebody outside now. I couldn't hear him, but I sensed him there. Very quietly the key was turned in the lock. I stiffened and then stepped back, so that I should be behind the door when it opened. I couldn't see it, but I felt the handle turning. Then my hand, which was touching the woodwork of the door, was pressed back as the door was opened. I grasped the heavy torch, raising it ready to strike out. But before I could hit him, the man was past me and in the room.

I slipped out into the passage, the sound of my movement lost in the deep pile of the carpet. A faint red glow showed through a window at the far end of the corridor. I reached the dark shaft of the stairs and hesitated because the villa was all silent and still, knowing that the sound of my own footsteps on the stairs would draw attention to myself.

And as I stood there, hesitating, there was a sudden shout from my room. 'Roberto! Agostino!' The bathroom was right opposite the head of the stairs. The door was open and I stepped back into the shadows as footsteps came running out of my room. A torch flashed in the corridor. 'Roberto! Agostino!' Somebody went hurtling past and flung himself down the stairs. I had a brief glimpse of a short, angry figure. Then a door opened along the corridor, near the red glow of the window. I peered out and caught sight of the silhouette of a man hurrying down the corridor towards me. As he passed me he switched on a torch and, in the reflected light from the walls, I made out the features of Roberto.

1 How did the writer feel after the car arrived?
  A relieved
  B anxious
  C confident
  D disappointed

2 The writer stood behind the door so that he could
  A see what was happening in the room.
  B prevent the man from opening the door.
  C escape quickly if he needed to.
  D attack the man if he entered.

3 Why didn't the writer go down the stairs immediately?
  A He knew the man was following him.
  B He thought someone might hear him.
  C He wasn't sure if that was the way out.
  D He was afraid of falling in the dark.

4 How did the writer recognise Roberto?
  A He shone a torch at Roberto's face.
  B The light from the window lit up Roberto's face.
  C Roberto's torch gave enough light to see clearly.
  D Roberto's face was reflected in a mirror on the wall.

WRITING Part 2: review

You recently saw this advertisement in an English language magazine called *Best Books*.

Write your review in 120–180 words.

Reviews Wanted!

Have you read any really interesting or unusual books recently? If so, could you write a review of the book you read? Include information on the content or the story and say whether you would recommend the book to other people.

The best reviews will be published next month.

Test Three (Units 11–15)

Choose the correct letter: A, B, C or D.

1 When I was twelve, my grandfather taught me how to .... chess.
   A do   **B** play   **C** make   **D** collect

2 The government .... major changes to the education system today.
   A warned   **B** declared   **C** announced   **D** expressed

3 I've never liked .... steak because it can be rather dry – the flavour is much better if you fry it.
   A roasted   **B** baked   **C** grilled   **D** boiled

4 One of the first successful .... films was *Fantasmagorie*, which was made up of 700 drawings and lasted two minutes.
   A comedy   **B** drama   **C** play   **D** cartoon

5 The road the children walk along on their way to school is very busy, but fortunately there's a pedestrian .... they always use.
   A path   **B** crossing   **C** precinct   **D** street

6 I'm trying to get more .... on the internet about how to reach the island from the mainland.
   A fact   **B** information   **C** detail   **D** knowledge

7 I .... on the news that the price of gas is going up again.
   A looked   **B** listened   **C** heard   **D** watched

8 I've never been much good at painting, but I've been going to .... classes for a year and have made several nice vases.
   A pottery   **B** drawing   **C** cookery   **D** sculpture

9 We stayed in comfortable .... not far from the city centre.
   A hotel   **B** resort   **C** accommodation **D** guesthouse

10 It'll take you over an hour to get to the city centre in the .... hour.
    A rush   **B** busy   **C** run   **D** crowded

11 It was very hot in Egypt, so we set .... at dawn to visit the Pyramids.
    A off   **B** about   **C** back   **D** in

12 I've just taken .... sailing, and I'm going to do a special course next month.
    A to   **B** over   **C** up   **D** after

13 I found it very stressful living in the centre of town, so I was pleased when we moved to a quiet residential area in the ....
    A edge   **B** suburbs   **C** estate   **D** outskirts

14 You'll find a pharmacy in the market .... , facing the clock tower.
    A way   **B** centre   **C** lane   **D** square

15 Peter was on his way to a meeting, so he only had time to .... at the report quickly.
    A glance   **B** stare   **C** glimpse   **D** gaze

16 At the airport, you have to go through passport .... before you get on a flight.
    A security   **B** check   **C** desk   **D** control

17 The leading actor gave the .... of his life and the audience cheered him at the end of the play.
    A performance   **B** rehearsal   **C** review   **D** show

18 In the UK, people often finish their meal with a .... like apple pie.
    A side dish   **B** starter   **C** main course   **D** dessert

19 My brother Richard is an artist, and he's well known for his .... of local people.
    A abstracts   **B** landscapes   **C** portraits   **D** still lifes

20 I was tired last night so I spent the evening .... television.
    A looking   **B** watching   **C** seeing   **D** viewing

21 When they heard their train was due to come in on a different .... all the commuters dashed over to it.
    A board   **B** escalator   **C** rank   **D** platform

22 Sally always reads gossip .... when she's bored.
    A magazines   **B** newspapers   **C** journals   **D** comics

23 As soon as we've finished decorating the kitchen, we'll buy a new electric .... and have it installed.
    A cooker   **B** wok   **C** saucepan   **D** dish

24 I love going to the cinema and watching the film on the big ....
    A stage   **B** studio   **C** location   **D** screen

25 I like the way my sister has designed her flat – it's really ....
    A delicious   **B** tasteful   **C** fresh   **D** tasty

26 There's a major junction controlled by traffic .... and that's where you turn left.
    A bypasses   **B** crossroads   **C** lights   **D** roundabouts

27 There was a good .... on the television last night about polar bears.
    A drama   **B** series   **C** forecast   **D** documentary

28 The .... from Dover to Calais only takes about an hour when the sea is calm.
    A trip   **B** crossing   **C** voyage   **D** travel

29 The .... of the thriller I saw last night was so complicated I want to see the whole film again.
    A plot   **B** subtitle   **C** soundtrack   **D** trailer

30 Most cities have at least one art .... worth visiting.
    A museum   **B** gallery   **C** centre   **D** hall

16 Stages of life
Different ages, university, school

Different ages

1.1 When we don't know exactly how old someone is or we want to talk generally, we can use these expressions:

He/She is: in his/her (early/late) teens   in his/her (early/late) twenties, thirties etc.   middle-aged   elderly

Finish these sentences about your country.

1   Most people go to university when they're ....*in their late teens.*............

2   People usually get married when they're ....

3   The majority of people have their first child when they're ....

4   People generally retire when they're ....

1.2 🎧 16a **Listen to five people talking. Complete each sentence with one of the age groups above.**

Martha is ....
Rob is ....
Jessie is ....
Callum is ....
Jim is ....

1.3 COMMON EXPRESSIONS **Write expressions from the recording which mean the same as the expressions below, then look at the recording script at the back of the book to check your answers.**

1   *My husband died twenty years ago:* I've been a ....*widow*............ for twenty years.

2   *When I was a child:* .... a child

3   *I have a three-year-old great-granddaughter:* I have a great-granddaughter who is ....

4   *I didn't have a year off between school and university:* I didn't have a ....

5   *I'm expecting a baby:* I'm ....

6   *My child has just started to walk:* I've got a ....

7   *My cousin is about the same age as me:* My cousin is ....

8   *He behaves like a child:* He's ....

9   *My children are adults:* My children are ....

10 *I still feel/look young:* I don't feel/look ....

> **Error warning**
>
> "我有一个三岁的女儿"应该表述为 *I have a three-year-old daughter*，而不是 *a three years old daughter*。"我怀孕了"应为 *I'm expecting a baby*，而不是 *I'm waiting for a baby*。**kid**（孩子）只在非正式的情况下使用，表示 **child** 的意思。

2   WORD BUILDING **We can add *-ish* ('quite, about or with certain qualities') to nouns or adjectives. Add *-ish* to one word in each of these sentences and make any other changes necessary.**

1   I'm not sure how old my teacher is – ~~around~~ thirty*ish* perhaps.

2   She's tall with glasses and she always wears jeans.

3   I look nothing like my brother because he's got red hair.

4   I'll see you about eight outside the cinema.

5   My boyfriend's got quite long hair and a beard.

6   It's a new building with a statue outside – you can't miss it.

3 COMMON EXPRESSIONS There are lots of expressions with the word *life*. Choose one expression to follow each sentence below.

She's always enthusiastic and loves being busy.　　　　　　　　　A That's life.

There's no point worrying about things that might not happen.　　　B Life's too short.

You should go out more instead of polishing your car every weekend.　C She's full of life.

I haven't seen you for ages.　　　　　　　　　　　　　　　　　D Get a life!

I don't want my daughter to give up her job but it's her decision.　　E How's life?

Every year we think we can win and every year we come second.　　　F It's her life.

University

.1 Read this text from a university website. Who is it aimed at?

> The university is on one campus which covers an area of 200 acres. There are five faculties – Humanities, Science and technology, Social sciences, Law, and Medicine and these are divided into departments like geography, art history etc. When you arrive, you can pick up a prospectus and book which tour you want to go on, according to your subject of interest. Your tour will begin with a talk by one of the lecturers, who will tell you more about the courses. All our courses consist of a mixture of formal lectures, seminars in groups of up to twenty students and at least two tutorials per term where groups of two or three students have the opportunity to discuss things in more detail with their own tutors. Most courses require students to write a dissertation in their last year.
>
> The tours will show you the halls of residence where students live, the students' union where lots of social events take place and other useful facilities like the supermarket and launderette.
>
> Our undergraduate courses all begin in October and most of our students are school-leavers – just four per cent are mature students of 21 and over. At present the university year consists of three terms but we are changing to a two-semester year in three years' time. We will have a slightly longer spring vacation and shorter summer vacation.
>
> We have separate open days for graduates who want to go on to do a postgraduate course.

.2 Complete these sentences with words from the text.

The university year is divided into ......*terms*...... or .... The breaks are called ....

Students attend .... , ... and .... where they are taught about their subject.

Students are taught by .... and ....

A long piece of written work is called a ....

Students who are studying for a first degree are called .... When they finish they are called .... A student who continues to study after a first degree is called a ....

The buildings of a university and the land that surrounds them are called a ....

Students live in .... and attend social events arranged by the ....

Information about the university can be found in a booklet called a ....

The university is organised by subject into different .... and a group of these form a ....

Students who are at least 21 are .... students.

School

5.1 Look at the words you've written in 4.2. Which of them can you also use to talk about a school?

5.2 Choose the correct words in this email to a penfriend.

Dear Tomo
You asked me about education in my country. I'm still at (1) school/ the school because it's (2) essential/ compulsory here up to the (3) age/year of 16. We go to a kindergarten or nursery school first and then we (4) start/join primary school, where we spend seven years, when we're four or five years of (5) old/age. Now I (6) go/attend a state secondary school which has about 1000 (7) pupils/undergraduates. We have six lessons a day and each subject is (8) taught/learnt by a different teacher. We have a lot of homework and projects and, if we (9) lose/miss an important deadline, we have to stay (10) following/ after school to finish the work and hand it (11) in/on. We have to wear a uniform until we're 15 but after that we're (12) let/allowed to wear our own clothes. When we're 16 we (13) take/pass some exams. Then we can either (14) leave/depart school or stay on for two more years. During those two years we (15) learn/study just three or four subjects. There are also (16) opportunities/occasions to do vocational courses like hairdressing or mechanics at a college of further education. I haven't decided what to do yet. Write back soon.
Ian

5.3 Rewrite the email in your notebook so it is true for your country.

6.1 PHRASAL VERBS Which of these sentences can you complete with the verb *give* or *hand*? In which sentences does only the verb *hand* fit? In which sentences does only the verb *give* fit? Put the correct forms of the verbs in each gap.

> **Vocabulary note**
>
> 参加考试用**take**, **sit** 或**do** an exam 表示。如果用**pass** an exam则指已经知道了结果并且考试合格了。相反的情况用**fail**。

1　This ring was my grandmother's. It was ....**handed**......... down to my mother and now it's mine.

2　The application forms should be .... in by Friday morning.

3　We .... over our passports when we got to the border.

4　Monica .... back the book she'd borrowed from me.

5　I .... away all the toys I didn't play with any more.

6　They were .... out free T-shirts in that new shop yesterday.

7　I had to .... up jogging because my knees started to hurt.

6.2 Complete the table below.

meaning	hand	give	particle
give to someone who will be alive after you have died	✓	✗	+ down
give to someone in authority			+ in
give to someone else			+ over
return something to someone			+ back
give to someone without asking for payment			+ away
give something to a large number of people			+ out
stop doing a regular activity			+up

Exam practice

Speaking Part 2

1 Look at the photos and think about your answers
to these questions.

   1 Where are the people?

   2 What are they doing?

   3 What else can you see?

   4 Compare the two classrooms. What things are
the same and what things are different?

   5 Which method of learning is best? Why?

> ### Exam Tip (also see speaking checklist on p. 99)
> 考试中，照片上方会有一个问题来提示考生作答，如：
> *Which method of learning is best?* 哪种学习方式是最
> 好的？

2 🔊 **16b** Listen to someone talking about the
photos. Then look at the recording script and
underline some useful expressions. Now record
yourself talking about the photos for one minute.

USE OF ENGLISH Part 4

Complete the second sentence so that it has a similar meaning to the first sentence, using the word given.
Do not change the word given. You must use between two and five words, including the word given.
Example:

0 When we lived in Germany, I attended the local school and learnt to speak German.

   WENT

   When we lived in Germany, I ....*went to the*........ local school and learnt to speak German.

1 My sister's pregnant so I'm going to be an uncle.

   BABY

   My sister's .... so I'm going to be an uncle.

2 I must stop eating so much chocolate because it isn't good for me.

   GIVE

   I must .... so much chocolate because it isn't
good for me.

3 My parents always allowed me to decide when to go to bed.

   LET

   My parents always .... when to go to bed.

> ### Exam Tip
>
> 所填单词不要多于 5 个。缩略词如*don't*
> 和*hasn't*算两个单词。

17 Shopping in style

Clothes, shopping, money

Clothes

1.1 Look at these lists of clothes and accessories. Which is the odd one out in each list? Why?

1	blouse	dress	skirt	(tie)	tights	*The others are clothes only women wear.*
2	cuff	buckle	collar	buttons	sleeves	
3	gloves	cagoule	coat	pyjamas	scarf	
4	jumper	pullover	socks	sweatshirt	T-shirt	
5	jacket	jeans	shorts	skirt	trousers	
6	hood	hat	laces	cap	scarf	
7	necklace	belt	bracelet	earrings	ring	
8	boots	nightdress	sandals	slippers	trainers	

1.2 Circle the words above which are plural. Which of these can never be singular?

2.1 [A–Z] Read Jasmine and Kariem's messages. Which picture did they each put on the website – A, B, C or D?

A  B  C  D

◄ ► | ↻ | + | | Q▾

☐ **Jasmine:** My favourite outfit is a knee-length sleeveless silk dress. It's got a V neck and two pockets. It's light blue and I have a necklace and some earrings to match. I wear it with some silver sandals with really high heels. I'm not very tall so I don't wear flat shoes. I can only really wear this dress to a party or somewhere special but I love the colour and the material and it makes me feel good.

☐ **Kariem:** My favourite trousers are dark brown and they've got straight legs. I don't like clothes which are too baggy and I hardly ever wear jeans. I like wearing my short-sleeved cotton shirt which has got a collar with buttons. It's very bright and cheerful. I prefer wearing a shirt to a T-shirt but I never wear a tie. When I go out I usually wear my leather jacket – it's old now but it's very comfortable.

2.2 Here is what the other two people in the pictures wrote. Match what each of them says to one of the pictures and fill in the gaps with a word from the box.

belt	boots	bracelet	buckle	collar	hood	~~jeans~~	laces	neck
pockets	sweatshirt	T-shirt	trainers	baggy	flat	long	short	

Andrew: I always wear denim (1) ......*jeans*...... everywhere I go. My favourite pair are quite (2) .... – I don't like things that fit. They've got big (3) .... which are usually full of stuff. Because they're a bit big I wear a large leather (4) .... to hold them up. It's got a big (5) .... I always wear a (6) .... – I like plain ones and I usually wear a (7) .... over the top. My favourite one has a big (8) .... And on my feet I always wear (9) .... with striped (10) .... So that's my favourite outfit and I wear it all the time!

Sangeeta: I have a dress I love to wear. It has (11) .... sleeves and is quite (12) .... – it comes below the knee but it's very cool because it's made of cotton. It's got a round (13) .... and a white (14) .... I've got a (15) .... made of beads which looks good with it but I don't usually wear a necklace. I have some black (16) .... that I wear with it. They're (17) ...., which I prefer because I'm quite tall.

.3 The adjectives below describe a material or pattern. Write them in the correct category below.

checked	cotton	flowery	leather
lycra	nylon	plain	polyester
silk	spotted	striped	wool

Material ....

Pattern ....

> ⒱ *Vocabulary note*
>
> 对于描述大多数材料来说，同一个单词可以被用作名词和形容词：*I bought a silk shirt*. （我买了一件丝绸衬衫。）*It's made of silk*. （它是由丝绸做的。）

.4 Write a short paragraph for the website about your favourite outfit.

Shopping

3 Choose the correct word to complete each sentence.

Gift *vouchers*/*cheques* are available in multiples of £5.

We're offering 25% *sale*/*discount* on all cameras.

Our *sale*/*discount* starts on Thursday at 9 am. Everything will be reduced.

We accept all major *cash*/*credit* cards.

If you need help pushing your *basket*/*trolley* to your car, please ask a member of staff.

Refunds/*Cashback* can only be given if you keep your *recipe*/*receipt*.

4.1 🎧 17a Listen to four customers in a clothes shop. Why don't they buy what they try on?

Match each customer to a reason.

Customer 1	A	It's a waste of money.
Customer 2	B	It doesn't fit.
Customer 3	C	It doesn't match another piece of clothing.
Customer 4	D	It doesn't suit him/her.

4.2 PHRASAL VERBS ⏺17b Read this conversation which one of the customers had later. Put the correct word into each space to make a phrasal verb. Then listen to the recording to check your answers.

back   into   into   off   on   on   out of   up

Simon   Mum. I got trousers, a jacket and a shirt to wear to Jason's wedding. I've put them (1) ...on... so you can see.
Mum   Good. You need to dress smartly. I'm sorry I couldn't come shopping with you.
Simon   So, what do you think?
Mum   Well, the jacket's a bit big but you might grow (2) .... it I suppose.
Simon   I've stopped growing, Mum. I couldn't find a smaller one. Anyway I like it and I've grown (3) .... my other one. I've had it since I was twelve. The trousers are good though, aren't they?
Mum   Mmm, well I'm not sure.
Simon   I went to loads of shops and tried lots of things (4) ....
Mum   Can you take the trousers (5) .... ?
Simon   I can but I think they're OK.
Mum   Well, OK but take them (6) .... now. Go and change (7) .... your jeans again before you get them dirty.
Simon   I'll hang them (8) .... and I'll decide tomorrow.

4.3 The pairs of sentences below have the same meaning. At the end of each pair are two verbs. Choose the correct one for each sentence.

1 a) I ..got.. dressed in a hurry.
   b) I ..put.. my clothes on quickly.
   [*put / got*]

2 a) I have to .... smartly for work.
   b) I have to .... smart clothes for work.
   [*wear / dress*]

3 a) The dancers were all .... in blue.
   b) The dancers were all .... blue.
   [*dressed / wearing*]

4 a) He .... undressed in the bathroom.
   b) He .... off his clothes in the bathroom.
   [*got / took*]

5 a) She fell asleep fully ....
   b) She fell asleep .... all her clothes.
   [*dressed / wearing*

Money

5 Choose the correct verb in each sentence. Then put them in the correct order to complete the biography of David Davies.

Error warning

付钱给某人用**pay**，为某物付钱用**pay for**：
I paid the builder the money I owed him.（我把欠建筑工人的钱付清了。）*I paid for the work the builder had done.*（我为建筑工人所做的工作付钱。）此外，付罚款、车票、账单或缴费，可以说*pay a fine, a fare, a bill*或*a fee*。

David Davies (1818–1890)

Correct order: D. ... ...

A   When he died, his family *earned/inherited* his fortune.

B   It *spends/costs* nothing to visit the exhibition there.

C   However, he *donated/saved* as much as he could from his wages and when he was in his twenties he had enough for a farm.

D   David Davies left school at the age of 11 and *put/earned* very little working on the land.

E   His granddaughters, Gwendoline and Margaret, *cost/spent* some of the money on paintings which are now among the most famous in the world.

F   After 15 months, they found some and Davies *put/saved* his money into developing coal mines.

G   But he didn't forget his local community and *paid/paid for* his village to have a new school and chapel.

H   He soon *inherited/made* a lot of money from the industry.

I   He later bought another farm and some land in a valley and *paid/paid for* some men to help him look for coal there.

J   When they died, they *donated/made* 260 of them to the National Museum of Wales.

Exam practice

READING Part 2

You are going to read an article about a woman who shops for clothes for film stars. Five sentences have been removed from the article. Choose from sentences A–F the one which fits each gap (1–5). There is one extra sentence which you do not need to use.

Shopping for a living
Helping Hollywood stars look their best

Wouldn't it be cool if you could shop for a living? | 1 |____| I'm talking about the latest fashions in the best shops. For Hollywood wardrobe stylists, this kind of shopping largely defines the job.

"Obviously it's fun to get paid to spend money," says Jami, "and to get to feel like one of the rich and famous. But I also like to help make people look good. | 2 |____| That's because every job is different, from game shows to commercials to movies."

Jami had no idea this job even existed until some actresses she knew kept telling her she'd be good at it. | 3 |____| "I basically carried around her shopping bags for free and learned the business, including stuff like who has the best evening wear and which tailor can do overnight alterations."

| 4 |____| "It's hard not to let your own tastes interfere, but ultimately you're not the final decision maker," says Jami, who thinks for a minute and then says, "My all-time favorite actor was a monkey, because he didn't talk back and he didn't drop his clothes on the floor."

It's no wonder these stylists are often credited with setting fashion trends around the globe. A stylist might give an actress a beautiful bag or amazing scarf to wear to a premiere. | 5 |____| The next thing she knows, she's got her own line of accessories and a boutique at Sunset Plaza.

So the next time someone compliments your sense of style, you could think of becoming a wardrobe stylist – it could be your introduction to the stars!

A Once it's splashed across the pages of every magazine across the country it becomes a trend.
B And I don't mean for groceries or socks.
C A stylist, of course, often has to deal with strong personalities as well as big budgets.
D But that's one of the few disadvantages of the job.
E She already had a distinctive personal style, so she apprenticed with a well-known stylist.
F And one of the best things is that it's never monotonous.

> ### *Exam Tip*
> 选完答案后将文章段落再读一遍，确保意思和语法都是正确的。

USE OF ENGLISH Part 4

For questions 1–4, complete the second sentence so that it has a similar meaning to the first sentence, using the word given. Do not change the word given. You must use between two and five words, including the word given.

Example:
0 The outfit I like best is my red skirt and white top.
FAVOURITE
My ....*favourite outfit*.... is my red skirt and white top.

1 Those shoes don't match your dress.
GO
Those shoes .... your dress.

2 Those jeans are too small for me now.
GROWN
I .... those jeans now.

3 I can return the jacket if I decide I don't want it.
TAKE
I can .... if I decide I don't want it.

4 Mary doesn't look at all good in that colour.
SUIT
That colour .... at all.

18 Home territory
Houses and homes, household problems

Houses and homes

1.1 Look at the pictures of houses below and read part of a letter from an American girl to her penfriend. Which house is she describing?

> You asked me to describe my home. Well, our house in the suburbs is modern and detached, like most houses in the US. It's made of wood and we have shutters at the windows. The house is quite spacious. Downstairs there's a large living room, a dining room, a study and a fitted kitchen. There's also a utility room which has the washing machine, drier and freezer in it. Upstairs there are four bedrooms. One of these has an ensuite bathroom and there is also a separate shower room. We have central heating and air-conditioning. It's hot and steamy in summer and cold in winter, so we need both! And there's a double garage – we keep a lot of junk in there as well the cars!

Underline the words which gave you the answer.

1.2 Match each of the types of houses below to a picture in 1.1.

1 villa ...D...
2 cottage ......
3 terraced houses ......
4 apartment block ......
5 detached house ......
6 bungalow ......

1.3 Look at the pictures again. Which of the houses above:

1 have more than one floor or storey? ....
2 have a double garage? ....
3 have a fence? ....
4 have a view of water? ....
5 have shutters? ....
6 have a hedge? ....
7 have a gate? ....

Vocabulary note
表示公寓时，英国英语用 **flat**，美国英语则用 **apartment**。

Add these words to the pictures to help you remember them.

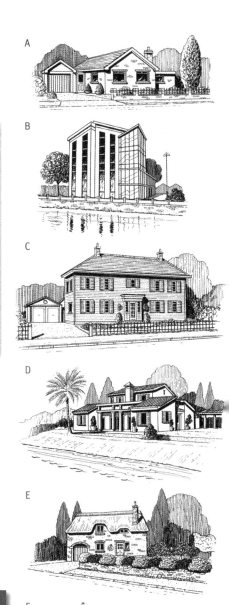

A

B

C

D

E

F

1.4 Read the email again. In your notebook, list the ways in which the house described is similar to yours, and the ways in which it is different.

1.5 Use your notes to write a paragraph about your house/flat. Use the email above as a guide.

2.1 Read this extract from a novel. Do not worry about any words you do not understand.

As we neared Black Oak, we passed the Clench farm, home of Foy and Leverl Clench and their eight children, all of whom, I was certain, were still in the fields. No one worked harder than the Clenches. Even the children seemed to enjoy picking cotton and doing the most **routine chores** around the farm. The hedges around the front yard were **perfectly manicured** into shape. The fences were straight and needed no repair. The garden was huge and its **legendary yield** fed the family all year.

And their house was painted.

Our house had been built before the First War, back when indoor bathrooms and electricity were unheard of. Its exterior was built from clapboards made of **oak**, probably cut from trees on the land which we now farmed. With time and weather the boards had faded to a pale brown colour, pretty much the same color as the other farmhouses around Black Oak. According to my father and grandparents, paint was unnecessary. The boards were kept clean and in good repair, and besides, paint cost money.

My mother **vowed** to herself that she would not raise her children on a farm. She would one day have a house in a town or in a city, a house with indoor plumbing and flowers around the porch, and with paint on the boards, maybe even bricks.

'Paint' was a **sensitive word** around our farm.

2.2 When you don't understand a word you should try to guess its meaning. Look at these words in the extract above and try to answer the questions without a dictionary.

Routine chores are
A everyday tasks
B repetitive games
C time-consuming jobs

The words **perfectly manicured** here refer to the hedges and mean
A well watered
B heavily fertilised
C carefully cut

The **legendary yield** of the garden refers to
A the flowers grown there
B the vegetables it produced
C the insects that lived there

4 **Oak** is a kind of
A brick   B cement   C wood

5 **Vowed** means
A encouraged   B promised   C dared

6 **Paint** was a **sensitive word** around the farm because the writer's mother
A had a row with the rest of the family about it.
B desperately wanted to live in a painted house.
C was jealous of the neighbours' farm.

3 COMMON EXPRESSIONS There are lots of common expressions related to the house and home. Match the two halves of the sentence below.

We just have to finish this section	A	that we shouldn't walk home late at night.
When I was younger I used to feel homesick	B	when he said everyone should work hard.
He hit the nail on the head	C	whenever I was away from my family.
You should put your own house in order	D	so please make yourself at home until then.
I shan't be there until 6.00pm	E	and then we're home and dry.
She really hammered home the message	F	before you start telling me what to do.

Household problems

4 Lots of people do household jobs and repairs themselves, and this is called DIY (Do It Yourself). However, sometimes you have to call in an expert. Who would you call for the following problems? Match each person (A–F) with a problem (1–6).

A electrician   B builder   C service agent   D decorator   E dry cleaner   F plumber

1 The tap in the kitchen is dripping and the pipe under the kitchen sink is leaking.   ..F...

2 The cushions on your sofa are stained with coffee.   .....

3 You'd like some new lighting put up.   .....

4 Your dishwasher has broken down while it's still under guarantee.   .....

5 You'd like a new patio made outside your house.   .....

6 You'd like your living room painted and you don't have time to do it yourself.   .....

5.1 PHRASAL VERBS Look at the sentences below and choose the correct answer.

1 Decorating that room was really tiring – it's done *me in* / *away with me* .

2 I was in the middle of doing *without* / *out* the room when the money ran out.

3 I need an electric saw for this job, but I'll have to do *away with* / *without* one.

4 I'd like to buy a really old house and do it *up* / *in* .

> **Vocabulary note**
>
> **do**通常指从事一项活动或工作。**make**通常指创造或生产某物。例如在居家生活方面，人们会谈论*make a cake or bookshelves*（制作蛋糕或书架）。注意：*make a bed*（铺床）是个例外，它的意思是将床单和毯子铺在床上。

5.2 Put these meanings under the correct phrase in the table.

renovate   ~~exhaust~~   manage without   decorate

do	someone in	out a room	up a building	without something
meaning	exhaust			

5.3 Answer these questions.

1 Have you ever done out your room? What colours did you use?

2 Does learning English do you in? Do you enjoy learning languages?

3 Can you do without a car? Do you use a bike?

4 Have you ever done up a flat? Did it take a long time?

> **Error warning**
>
> 使用表示移动的动词如**go**（去）或**come**（来）与**home**（家）搭配时，不需要使用介词：如"你什么时候回的家？"，正确的说法是*What time did you go home?* 而不是*What time did you go to home?*

Exam practice

SPEAKING Part 3

Look at the pictures of houses on page 80. First think about the advantages and disadvantages of living in each type of house. Then decide which house you would live in if you had the choice, and think about your reasons. Record yourself speaking for one minute and then listen to your recording.

SPEAKING Part 4

Read the questions, think about your answers, then record them.

Would you prefer to live in a house or flat?
Which room is most important for you? Why?
Would you rather live in an old or new house?

Is it important to live near to where you work or study?
How could the area where you live be improved?
Are you friendly with people in your area?

USE OF ENGLISH Part 2

Read the text below and think of the best word which fits each space. Use only one word in each space. There is an example at the beginning (0).

THE BEST CITY TO LIVE IN?

Vancouver has just **(0)** ...*been*.... rated top in a survey of cities across the world. According **(1)** .... the survey, its natural beauty **(2)** .... temperate climate are the main reasons **(3)** .... it being chosen as **(4)** .... of the best cities in the world to live. But Vancouver also scored highly in the survey **(5)** .... Canada is politically stable and a country **(6)** .... levels of personal safety and security are high. **(7)** .... addition, it offers a high standard **(8)** .... medical care and education, a good public transport system, good quality housing and excellent recreational activities.

Other Canadian cities **(9)** .... also placed high in the survey, with Toronto, Ottawa, Montreal and Calgary all being ranked in the top thirty. **(10)** .... is thought to be **(11)** .... to the fact that Canada also has strict law enforcement and low crime rates, **(12)** .... makes all its cities amongst the safest in North America.

USE OF ENGLISH Part 3

Read the text below. Use the word given in capitals to form a word that fits in each space. There is an example at the beginning.

> **Exam Tip**
> 想想从语法上讲需要哪一类的词，例如形容词、副词、名词或者动词。

SUNNY COTTAGE

This bright, **(0)** ....*spacious*......... cottage is **(1)** .... located in open and
very **(2)** .... countryside. It is within walking distance of a village with a
shop and a school and it takes just 20 minutes to drive to the **(3)** .... city
of Bath. It is light and **(4)** .... in summer, yet cosy in winter. The cottage
offers a pleasant **(5)** .... of traditional and modern amenities, and provides
an excellent base for exploring the **(6)** .... area.
On the ground floor you will find a living room with a **(7)** .... floor, and a
modern **(8)** .... kitchen, which is well-equipped with all necessary
(9) .... Upstairs there are three bedrooms and two shower rooms. In
the drive there is parking for four cars, with **(10)** .... roadside parking.

SPACE/PERFECT
PICTURE
HISTORY
AIR
COMBINE
SURROUND
WOOD
FIT
APPLY
ADDITION

19 Green planet
Science, the environment

Science

1.1 Tick the things that you think a scientist might do during a typical day at work.

work as part of a team
enter data into a computer
make an exciting discovery
make observations
test a theory
analyse statistics
attend a conference
carry out an experiment
work outside

1.2 What will these scientists study? Match 1–7 with A–G.

1	physicist	A	rocks
2	biologist	B	substances
3	ecologist	C	stars
4	chemist	D	the environment
5	mathematician	E	living things
6	geologist	F	matter and energy
7	astronomer	G	numbers and shapes

1.3 Complete the table.

person (noun)	astronomer			ecologist			
subject (noun)	astronomy		chemistry			mathematics	
adjective		biological			geological		physical

1.4 Read texts A and B and answer the questions with A, B or both A & B. Which scientist …

A
Isaac Newton (1642–1727) had a profound impact on astronomy, physics and mathematics. He was raised by his grandparents and it was thanks to an uncle that he went to university to study mathematics. He made the first modern telescope, and developed a branch of mathematics known as calculus. He is also famous for developing the scientific laws of motion and the law of gravity, which formed the basis of all models of the cosmos.

B
James Lovelock (1919–) first graduated as a chemist, and then obtained degrees in medicine and biophysics. He has produced a range of technical instruments, many of which are now used by NASA in space exploration. He is most famous for the 'Gaia Theory', which considers the planet Earth as a living being, capable of changing and restoring itself. He has brought his concern about climate change to the attention of both the public and the scientific world.

1 obtained a degree in chemistry? .....B.....
2 invented scientific instruments? ....
3 was worried about the future of the Earth? ....
4 developed theories of global importance? ....
5 was keenly interested in green issues? ....
6 showed a talent for mathematics? ....

Ⓥ *Vocabulary note*
科学家们做实验（an experiment）、测试（a test）或研究（research）用动词**do**，但是他们有所发现（a discovery）用动词**make**。

The environment

2.1 COMMON EXPRESSIONS There are currently many problems with the environment. Match the two halves of the sentences.

1 Global warming means that
2 Heavy traffic and exhaust fumes
3 The emissions produced by factories
4 The pesticides used on crops in the countryside
5 Heavy rain and rising water levels in rivers
6 Most households produce large amounts of waste

A pollute the air in most cities.
B which is taken to landfill sites.
C have caused serious flooding.
D create acid rain which destroys crops.
E the weather is becoming hotter and drier.
F are dangerous to birds and other wildlife.

2.2 Put a tick against the problems which exist in your country.

3.1 Schools are teaching their pupils about pollution and the need to live in sustainable buildings which cause no damage to the environment. Read the newspaper article below and answer the questions.

THE SUSTAINABLE SCHOOL

Cassop village primary school

Within 30 years, most scientists expect us to be living in a much harsher world, where droughts, storms and floods are stronger and more frequent, where extremes of heat and cold are greater, and where oil and coal are nearly used up. It is therefore vitally important that schools teach their pupils this, and are located in buildings which are environmentally sustainable.

Cassop village primary school near Durham is one such school. It has a wind turbine and solar panels. It got rid of its oil-fired boiler years ago. It can generate all of its own electricity, so its running costs are low.

Contrast this with a certain city school where the head teacher knows only too well that he is throwing away money and resources trying to heat, light and ventilate a building that is a furnace in summer and an icebox in winter. As he says, 'It was built in the 1970s and it should be pulled down'.

the article, find words for

three types of extreme weather ....

two resources that may be in short supply in 30 years' time ....

two alternative forms of energy ....

three ways that power is used to make a building more comfortable ....

three phrasal verbs ....

2 Look at these expressions. Which would you use to describe the two schools above?

wasteful   environmentally friendly   expensive to maintain   efficient   cheap to run

Village school: ....
City school: ....

3 How would you describe your school, college or place of work? Is it environmentally friendly? Write two or three sentences about it in your notebook.

3.4 We can all do something to help the environment. Mark the sentences below true (T) or false (F) for you.

How Green Are You?

1 I recycle as much of my rubbish as I can.

2 I switch off electrical equipment once I've used it to avoid wasting power.

3 I never sleep with the air conditioning on.

4 I buy organic food which is produced in my local area.

5 I put an extra sweater on rather than turn up the heating.

6 I walk or use public transport rather than drive.

Which of the things in 1–6 is easiest for you personally to do? Which do you think has the most benefit for the environment?

4 Read the speech below from a local council meeting about pollution and choose the correct answer: A, B, C or D

It is now widely accepted that pollution (1) ..D.. humans, the environment, and buildings. Some pollution spreads across local and national boundaries and lasts for many generations. Many chemicals do not biodegrade and gradually (2) ..... in the food chain. So, if the crops in our fields are sprayed carelessly, the pesticide has an immediate effect on local wildlife and can ultimately (3) ..... in our food.

Burning fossil fuels – oil, gas and coal – also (4) ..... pollution, in particular carbon dioxide, which is a major contributor to global (5) ..... . In our region eight out of the ten hottest years on (6) ..... have occurred during the last decade. We should therefore (7) ..... the use of renewable energy resources such as wind and solar energy, because these do not (8) ..... carbon dioxide.

However, the biggest single cause of pollution in our city is traffic. Poorly maintained, older vehicles and bad driving techniques (9) ..... the problem worse, and this pollution has been directly (10) ..... to the rising number of asthma sufferers in our region. We should be aiming to gradually (11) ..... vehicle use in the city on high pollution days and educate the public on the importance of purchasing (12) ..... friendly vehicles and maintaining them to a high (13) ..... .

1	**A** injures	**B** hurts	**C** wounds	**D** harms
2	**A** build up	**B** get on	**C** grow up	**D** break through
3	**A** turn out	**B** end up	**C** put across	**D** keep back
4	**A** gives	**B** leads	**C** begins	**D** causes
5	**A** heating	**B** melting	**C** warming	**D** thawing
6	**A** account	**B** record	**C** document	**D** report
7	**A** encourage	**B** advance	**C** help	**D** forward
8	**A** bring	**B** design	**C** create	**D** invent
9	**A** increase	**B** make	**C** do	**D** grow
10	**A** joined	**B** combined	**C** associated	**D** linked
11	**A** keep out	**B** put by	**C** cut down	**D** drop out
12	**A** universally	**B** atmospherically	**C** globally	**D** environmentally
13	**A** degree	**B** grade	**C** mark	**D** standard

Exam practice

USE OF ENGLISH Part 3

Read the text below. Use the word in capitals to form a word that fits in each space.
There is an example at the beginning.

CENTRE FOR ALTERNATIVE TECHNOLOGY (CAT)

We offer practical **(0)** ....*solutions*......... to some of the most serious challenges   SOLVE
facing the human race, such as climate change, **(1)** .... and   POLLUTE
the waste of resources. Living by example, we aim to show that living more
(2) .... is easy and can provide a better quality of life. We have a   SUSTAIN
particular interest in renewable energy, energy **(3)** .... and growing   EFFICIENT
fruit and vegetables **(4)** .... We promote our ideas in a   ORGANIC
(5) .... of ways. Our Visitor Centre, which has interactive displays   VARY
showing **(6)** .... issues, is open seven days a week. CAT also   GLOBE
provides a free **(7)** .... service, answering inquiries on a   INFORM
(8) .... range of topics.   MASS
We also run a range of **(9)** .... courses, lasting from a weekend to a   RESIDENT
year, and can offer six-month **(10)** .... for people willing to work as   PLACE
volunteers at our centre.

LISTENING Part 4

🎧 19 **You will hear an interview with an Australian sheep farmer called Gina Ellis, who is talking about her work and plans for the future. Choose the best answer (A, B or C).**

1 What does Gina say about sheep farming in Australia?
   A It is the main source of employment.
   B It takes place all over the country.
   C It is restricted to cooler areas.

2 What is the main challenge facing farmers who produce wool?
   A competition from manmade products
   B falling production levels
   C increasingly dry weather

3 Gina says that in future, wool will have most potential in
   A manufacturing carpets.
   B insulating houses.
   C making clothes.

4 What alternative form of energy is Gina investigating?
   A solar power
   B tidal power
   C wind power

🎧 **Listen again.**

5 What made Gina become interested in a new source of energy?
   A It will make her farm self-sufficient.
   B It fits in with her 'green' view of life.
   C She'll be able to earn money from it.

6 What does Gina say about the advice she has received in England?
   A It has encouraged her to lead a more sustainable lifestyle.
   B It has taught her to analyse financial issues.
   C It has convinced her that she has to give up farming.

7 How does Gina feel about her project?
   A She's worried about high costs.
   B She's aware that her plans need adapting.
   C She's confident that she can succeed.

> **Exam Tip**
> 这些问题是按照考生所听到的信息的先后顺序给出的。

20 My judgement
Crime, opinions

Crime

1.1 **Read this review of a crime novel. Then answer the questions.**

Burglars Can't Be Choosers is the first novel about Bernie Rhodenbarr, a surprisingly charming and very talented professional burglar in New York. The opening of the novel finds Bernie expertly breaking into an expensive apartment, commissioned to locate a mysterious blue leather box. The burglary goes smoothly until Bernie realises that the box is not there, the police are at the door and the owner of the apartment is lying dead on the bedroom rug. Bernie makes a rapid escape, and spends the rest of the novel employing all his investigative (not to mention criminal) skills trying to find out who set him up, and clear himself of the murder charge.

Are these statements true or false? Underline the words in the text which give you the answer.

1 Bernie makes a living from stealing. .....*True*.....

2 Bernie has been given the key to an expensive apartment. ....

3 The police catch Bernie with a blue leather box in his hand. ....

4 Bernie has murdered someone. ....

5 Someone has tried to make sure that Bernie is arrested. ....

1.2 **WORD BUILDING Complete the chart below.**

CRIME	CRIMINAL	VERB
burglary	burglar	
robbery		
theft		steal
		shoplift
murder		

1.3 **Now complete the sentences below with an appropriate word from the box above. Put the verbs in the correct tense.**

1 Most stores will prosecute people who ....*shoplift*........ .

2 Five men in masks .... a bank in the main street.

3 The cashier .... £100 from the till in the supermarket.

4 The gang admitted they had committed four recent bank ....

5 The .... admitted killing two people, and the judge sentenced him to life imprisonment.

6 When I came back from holiday I found that my car had been .... while I was away.

2 🎧 **20a** Listen to a man talking about his favourite crime novels. How would he answer the questionnaire below?

CRIME NOVELS

1 Do you enjoy reading crime novels and detectives stories?

Yes. I quite like them / I like them a lot / I love them

No. I dislike them/ I can't stand them

Give a reason for your answer: *because* ....

2 What is the name of your favourite writer? ....

3 What is special about his/her novels? ....

....

....

Look at the recording script for 20a and underline phrases that might be useful to talk about your own reading habits.

3 Look at the vocabulary below about crime. Which is the odd one out in each group?

burglar   robber   arsonist   thief

shoplifting   vandalism   kidnapping   speeding

3   evidence   proof   fact   clue

4   judge   barrister   detective   solicitor

Opinions

4.1 Read the text below about a woman judge.

Judge Anne Rafferty's ideas about the law are an unusual mix of the **traditional** and the very **radical**. She has strong opinions on the criminal justice system in England, but is convinced that it is **effective**. She is in favour of criminals meeting their victims face to face and trying to come to understand the effects of their crime, whether they are murderers or burglars. She is also **enthusiastic** about a scheme which is trying to identify whether an offender has drug or alcohol-related problems as soon as he or she is arrested, as this enables problems to be treated at the earliest possible stage. She also supports the idea of weekend jails, which as the name suggests, allows offenders to keep their job and thus provide for their family, but lose their leisure time.

However, while she approves of these **innovative** and **significant** changes to the justice system, she is totally against the idea of televising cases and believes that judges and lawyers should continue to wear old-fashioned wigs and gowns in court as they have always done.

Match the words in bold to their definitions below.

new   3   keen   5   important   ....

revolutionary   4   gets results   6   conservative   ....

4.2 Divide Anne Rafferty's ideas into two columns.

no TV in court
identifying drug and alcohol problems
judges wearing wigs and gowns
~~weekend jails~~
criminals meeting their victims

RADICAL	TRADITIONAL
weekend jails	

4.3 Read the text again and underline all the expressions used to show Anne's opinions. Then divide them into three groups and put them into the columns below

Used positively (agrees with)	Used negatively (disagrees with)	Could be used for either
in favour of		

4.4 Now write two or three sentences in your notebook giving your own views about the issues in the text. Remember you can make the expressions in 4.3 negative as well.

I'm not in favour of criminals meeting their victims, but I support the idea of televising court cases.

5.1 COMMON EXPRESSIONS Correct these sentences.

1 We're thinking ~~to go~~ to France on holiday.   *of going*
2 What did you think the concert last night?
3 I thought my answers before writing anything down.
4 I'm thinking leaving early to avoid the rush hour.
5 What do you think my new dress?
6 I was thinking my grandmother, who's been rather unwell.

> **Vocabulary note**
>
> **to think about something / someone**指脑中想着或关心某人或某事：*I was thinking about my sister.*（我正想着我的姐姐。）*I thought carefully about what I was going to say at the meeting.*（我认真地考虑在会议上要讲什么。）用**What do you think of / about...?**来询问某人的观点：*What did you think about the film?*（你觉得这部电影怎么样？）**think of doing**意思是考虑做某事的可能性：*I'm thinking of taking up karate.*（我正在考虑是否要学习空手道。）

5.2 IDIOMS There are lots of idioms and expressions in English using the verb *think*. The meaning is often very clear from the context. Match the two halves of the sentences.

1 If I were you I'd think long and hard
2 You've really got to think for yourself –
3 You weren't thinking straight
4 If you think back to this time last year,
5 I was really just thinking aloud
6 It's a good job you can think on your feet

A when you said you'd finish everything by Monday.
B because you had no time to consider your answer.
C you'll realise how much progress we've made.
D before you accept a job involving a lot of travel.
E no one is going to make the decision for you.
F when I said Alison deserved promotion.

Exam practice

SPEAKING Part 3

Imagine that the students in your English class are choosing a book to read. Here are the different types of books they can choose.
First decide what type of book each picture shows, and what the story is going to be about. Then decide which book you think would be the best choice for everyone in your class to read together. You can hear an example of two students doing this task on the CD 20b .

SPEAKING Part 4

Practise your answers to these questions.
Do you prefer reading or watching television?
Do people learn more from books or television?
What kind of books are popular in your country?

What is your favourite type of book?
What was the last book you read?
Will people still read books in the next century?

WRITING Part 2: essay

You have had a discussion in your English class and now your teacher has asked you to write an essay giving your opinions on the following statement:

Young people in my country today commit more crimes and behave far worse than young people did in the past.

Write 120–180 words.

> ***Exam Tip*** (also see writing checklist on p. 100)
> 考生不是一定要同意所给出的论述。可以同意或者不同意，也可以给出两方面的观点。举例子是很好的论证方式。另外，在文章结尾处应该得出明确的结论。

LISTENING Part 1

20c **Listen to the recording and choose the best answer (A, B or C).**
You hear the beginning of a radio programme. What is the programme going to be about?
A teenage criminals
B teenage volunteers
C teenage journalists

Listen again.

Test Four (Units 16–20)

Choose the correct letter: A, B, C or D.

1 In court, the .... stated that she had seen the man leave the house at 6.00 pm.
 A watcher **B** spectator **C** viewer **D** witness

2 My cousin wants to study .... because he cares passionately about the environment.
 A mathematics **B** astronomy **C** ecology **D** physics

3 Sweatshirts are often made out of manmade materials like .... rather than natural ones.
 A cotton **B** silk **C** wool **D** polyester

4 The radiator in the living room is leaking, so I'll have to get a .... to come round.
 A plumber **B** electrician **C** decorator **D** builder

5 Most people in the town .... the idea of tougher penalties for vandalism.
 A agree **B** approve **C** support **D** believe

6 If you have .... outside your windows, you don't really need curtains inside as well.
 A shutters **B** fences **C** hedges **D** gates

7 In many countries, education is .... until the age of sixteen.
 A necessary **B** essential **C** compulsory **D** legal

8 The .... fumes created by cars cause huge problems in cities.
 A pollution **B** acid **C** exhaust **D** waste

9 My brother went out and .... all his birthday money on an expensive pair of trainers.
 A paid **B** made **C** put **D** spent

10 Students who have successfully completed a degree course are known as ....
 A undergraduates **B** doctors **C** postgraduates **D** graduates

11 In most countries, fishermen's boats are built of .... cut from local trees.
 A bricks **B** wood **C** cement **D** cotton

12 Many people who are worried about eating chemicals buy .... food.
 A green **B** organic **C** recycled **D** environmental

13 My boss was .... on his way home last night and the thieves took his wallet.
 A stolen **B** burgled **C** shoplifted **D** robbed

14 I really liked the jacket, but I didn't buy it because it didn't .... the dress I'd already bought.
 A suit **B** fit **C** match **D** go

15 When I was a teenager my parents always expected me to .... chores around the house.
 A make **B** get **C** have **D** do

16 My cousin is .... a baby in September and the whole family is really excited about it.
   A waiting   **B** expecting   **C** hoping   **D** getting

17 We have a small .... room where we keep the drier, fridge freezer and so on.
   A utility   **B** kitchen   **C** machine   **D** shower

18 I've .... very carefully about how we can get everyone to agree to our plan.
   A realised   **B** thought   **C** supported   **D** approved

19 You should read the information in the university .... if you are thinking of studying there.
   A prospectus   **B** brochure   **C** leaflet   **D** report

20 They were .... free samples of cheese in the supermarket yesterday.
   A handing back   **B** giving in   **C** handing out   **D** giving up

21 Modern universities are usually located on a .... , where there is accommodation and all sorts of facilities for the students.
   A faculty   **B** campus   **C** department   **D** hall

22 It's best not to leave your computer on standby but to .... it off when you've finished with it.
   A switch   **B** close   **C** hold   **D** push

23 Older people often choose to live in a .... because there are no stairs for them to worry about.
   A villa   **B** cottage   **C** detached house   **D** bungalow

24 It's always a good idea to .... clothes on before you buy them.
   A put   **B** hang   **C** take   **D** try

25 Most household rubbish is disposed of in landfill ....
   A places   **B** locations   **C** sites   **D** factories

26 A lot of people wear .... in bed when it's cold at night.
   A sleeves   **B** tights   **C** pyjamas   **D** laces

27 The .... decides what the sentence will be if the accused is found guilty.
   A barrister   **B** warder   **C** judge   **D** solicitor

28 That .... you liked is one of the pieces of jewellery I inherited from my grandmother.
   A buckle   **B** bracelet   **C** collar   **D** tie

29 The police eventually dropped the case because they had insufficient .... to prosecute.
   A evidence   **B** proof   **C** clue   **D** fact

30 Global warming is likely to result in more .... because an increase in rainfall will cause rivers to burst their banks.
   A droughts   **B** floods   **C** storms   **D** waves

Appendix 1

Phrasal verbs

get

1.1 Read the sentences below. Try to work out the meaning of the phrasal verbs in bold.

1   We thought it would be a difficult problem to solve, but in the end we **got (a)round** it.

2   I had almost no money when I was a student, but I managed to **get by** on very little.

3   After Peter had made several unsuccessful attempts to **get through**, he asked the operator to connect him.

4   I managed to **get away from** the office just before the rush hour started.

5   I was really ill with flu last month, but I've **got over** it now.

6   This grey, wet weather really **gets me down**.

7   Tamsin is a good speaker who always **gets her message across**.

8   Nobody saw who smashed the window, so the boys **got away with** it.

9   I've been meaning to tidy the garage for some time, but I'm busy and I never seem to **get (a)round to** it.

10 If I can think of a reason to **get out of** the meeting tonight I will.

1.2 Complete the table below, using one of the meanings in the box. Look back at the sentences again.

avoid	contact by phone	depress	escape unpunished	~~explain clearly~~
overcome	have time for	leave	recover from	survive

	particle	use	meaning
GET	**across**	get a message across	explain clearly
	(a)round	get (a)round a problem	
	away from	get away from a place	
	away with	get away with a crime	
	by	get by (on little money)	
	down	bad weather gets me down	
	out of	get out of a commitment	
	over	get over an illness	
	(a)round to	get round to doing something	
	through	get through to someone on the phone	

1.3 Now make four sentences in your notebook about yourself using four of the phrasal verbs with GET.

come

2.1 Match the two halves of the sentence.

1	He came across some very old letters	A	when the Russian ballerina came on.
2	When the DVD of the concert came out	B	which means global supplies are good.
3	I'll come by your office one day this week	C	was the most difficult problem they came up against.
4	There was great applause from the audience	D	it sold millions of copies.
5	The racing driver was unconscious after the accident	E	but our plan didn't come off.
6	We hoped to visit our friends in Canada last year	F	but to everyone's relief he soon came round.
7	Oil prices have come down recently	G	while he was cleaning out the attic.
8	Getting permission to cross the border	H	so we can discuss it.

2.2 Underline the phrasal verbs with *come* in the sentences above. Then match them to their definitions.

.........*come across*......... find by chance   .... visit   .... fall

.... succeed   .... be released   .... appear on stage

.... face (a problem)   .... regain consciousness

2.3 Use one of the phrasal verbs above to complete these sentences.

1 I'll .... on my way into town and have a coffee.

2 The new children's film will .... before the start of the school holidays.

3 The mechanic .... a lot of difficulties when he tried to fix the old car.

4 I think our plan to build an extension on the house is going to ....

5 It was so hot in the shops I fainted and it took me a minute or two to ....

6 It was an hour before the main singer .... to perform.

7 I .... a beautiful old vase on one of the stalls in the market.

8 The price of electrical goods has .... considerably this year.

go

3.1 Answer these questions. Write your answer, using the phrasal verb:

1 When did you last **go down with** a cold? I *last went down with a cold a week ago.*

2 Have you ever **gone in for** a race?

3 Does food ever **go off** in your fridge?

4 What does most of your money **go on**?

5 Do your shoes **go with** your clothes?

6 Could you **go without** chocolate for a week?

3.2 Replace each of the phrasal verbs in the sentences with one of these words or phrases.

go bad   manage without   catch   match   spent on   entered

Appendix 2

Word building

Verbs to nouns

1.1 For each sentence, change the verb at the end in capitals into a noun using one of the suffixes in the box.

-sion   -tion   -ation   -ion

1   There are lots of organisations whose aim is the ......protection.......... of wildlife. PROTECT
2   The .... of the company meant I was offered promotion. EXPAND
3   The .... to the crossword will be in tomorrow's newspaper. SOLVE
4   If you don't give your homework in on time, I will need an .... EXPLAIN
5   After the children went to school, Elinor was free to work without any .... INTERRUPT
6   Don't forget to put a .... at the end of your essay. CONCLUDE
7   The winner of the .... was announced on the radio. COMPETE
8   There was a long queue at the hotel .... desk when I tried to check out. RECEIVE
9   The newspaper said there were 6,000 people at the festival but I think that was an ....
    EXAGGERATE
10 There is less demand for large cars so the factory lowered .... rates of some models. PRODUCT

1.2 Use the same suffixes to change these verbs into nouns.

1	reduce	......reduction......	6	divide	....
2	publish	....	7	impress	....
3	oblige	....	8	investigate	....
4	satisfy	....	9	destroy	....
5	predict	....	10	persuade	....

Verbs to nouns and nouns to adjectives

2 Read the following extract from a newspaper article. Decide if a noun or an adjective is required in each space. Then choose one word from the box below to go in each space. Change it to a noun (singular or plural) or adjective to fit the meaning. Use the suffix –al.

approve   propose   ~~globe~~   refuse   practice   survive

Now that we are living in a time of (1) ....global......... warming and climate change, it is important for everyone to take an interest in the (2) .... of the planet. The government has put forward (3) .... which, if they get (4) .... , will begin to help. However, some people have shown a (5) .... to accept that there are (6) .... things they can do such as drive smaller cars.

Adjectives to nouns

3.1 Using the suffixes in the box below, change the word given in capitals at the end of some of the lines to form a word that fits the gap in the same line.

-ity   -ety   -ness   -iness   -ence   -ance

Schools give great (1) ......*importance*...... to making sure children feel   **IMPORTANT**
comfortable when they first start school. The (2) .... of   **MAJOR**
children settle and do not show any (3) .... after the   **ANXIOUS**
first few days. Some children, however, are not ready for this essential
stage of (4) .... in their lives and show signs of   **INDEPENDENT**
(5) .... They need to be treated with great   **NAUGHTY**
(6) .... and given plenty of time to gain   **KIND**
(7) .... After a while they will be willing to join in a   **CONFIDENT**
(8) .... of (9) .... with the other children,   **VARIOUS/ACTIVE**
their early (10) .... completely forgotten.   **SHY**

3.2 Use the same suffixes to change these adjectives into nouns.

intelligent   ......*intelligence*......

popular   ....

necessary   ....

happy   ....

ill   ....

Nouns to verbs

Change these nouns to verbs.

When I was young, My uncle ......*encouraged*...... me to become an engineer. COURAGE

My friend says nothing .... her. FRIGHT

Never .... what Jamie says. BELIEF

The police could not arrest the woman because they could not .... she had committed the crime.
PROOF

The bridge was .... by replacing some of the old wood with cement. STRENGTH

Can you .... the man you saw steal the car? IDENTITY

Appendix 3

Spelling

Common errors

There are some spelling mistakes that are frequently made by FCE candidates in their written work. These sentences contain the correct spelling of the word and the way it is often spelled wrongly. Read the sentences. **Circle** the **correct** spelling and **underline** the spelling **error**.

Example:

0   *Accomodation/Accommodation* is often very expensive in big cities.

1   I saw an *advertisment/advertisement* for a very unusual holiday cottage yesterday.

2   I *believe/belive* you wanted to speak to Mr. Brown?

3   My daughter arrived with a *beatiful/beautiful* bunch of flowers in her hand.

4   It's no good ignoring your homework simply *becouse/because* it's difficult!

5   The *begining/beginning* of the month was cold and showery.

6   Susanna rode her *bycicle/bicycle* into town and locked it to the bike rack.

7   I think we should make the photo *biger/bigger* so you can see more detail.

8   The old armchair in the corner is *comfortable/confortable* if you want to curl up and read a book.

9   We live near the shops, which is very *convinient/convenient*.

10   I'm *definitly/definitely* going to buy a CD so I can practise my Spanish.

11   The way we live now is very *diferent/different* from fifty years ago.

12   I didn't get into the hockey team, which was very *disappointing/disapointing*.

13   A lot of what you read in the press these days concerns the *enviroment/environment*.

14   His sister was always giggling and making faces, which could be very *embarassing/embarrassing*.

15   Anna was very *greatful/grateful* for the help her friend gave her.

16   You sometimes begin a business letter with 'Dear Sir/ *Madam/Madame*'.

17   Very few people walk to work *nowdays/nowadays*.

18   I'd like to have the *opportunity/oportunity* to go to Canada.

19   Cars and lorries create a vast amount of *polution/pollution* on our roads.

20   Personally, I'd have *preferred/prefered* to leave later, but everyone else wanted an early start.

21   I *realy/really* like your new hairstyle – it suits you!

21   I *recommend/recomend* the shop on Green Street if you want to buy some good cheese.

22   I try to go *runing/running* every Saturday morning.

23   I hate going *shoping/shopping*, but my sister loves it.

24   I always stay up *untill/until* after midnight at New Year.

25   Let me know *wich/which* of the two designs you prefer.

Appendix 4

Speaking checklist

This is a list of things you should check **every time** you do a speaking task. There are also exam tips in the units which have speaking tasks in the Exam practice section.

- Use a variety of vocabulary. Look back through the unit and choose the vocabulary you can use in your answers.

- Some speaking exercises have a sample recording. After you have listened, look at the recording script and underline any useful words or phrases you can use.

- Check the pronunciation of the vocabulary you want to use. Look at the wordlist or check in a dictionary.

- If you don't know a word, explain what you want to say in another way:

> *I can't remember the word in English but it's a bit like a … / it's a sort of… / it looks like a … / it's shaped like a …*

- Don't answer questions with just *yes* or *no*. Say a bit more or give an example:

> *I like living in Milan because there's lots to do and it's near the mountains and the lakes.*

- Speak clearly and try not to leave long pauses. Practise your answer aloud, then record yourself. Play the recording and listen for the following:
  - Do I speak clearly?
  - Are there too many pauses?
  - Do I use a variety of vocabulary?
  - Do I give enough information?
  - Do I answer the question?

- For **Part 1**, make sure you can talk about your own life. You will be asked a few questions on one or two of the following subjects: where you live, your likes and dislikes, your personal experiences, your school or work, your free time, the media, travel and holidays.

- For **Part 2**, make sure you know how to say where things are in a photo:

> *In the background / On one side / On the left / On the right / Behind the … , In front of … , there's …*

- Describe what is happening even if you're not sure:

> *There's a man who might/could be …*
> *I think the woman is …*
> *They're probably …*

- Compare and contrast the two photos:

> *The people in photo A seem much happier probably because the sun is shining and they're enjoying themselves.*
> *The two places look very similar/different but …*
> *Photo A looks … whereas photo B is ….*

- Be ready to answer a quick question on your partner's photo, e.g. *Would you like to do this?*

- For **Part 3**, make sure you know how to give your opinion:

> *I think X is a bad idea.*
> *The best thing to do is…*
> *X is important because…*
> *In my opinion/view, X would be best because ….*
> *I think/feel/reckon X would be the best choice ….*
> *I like X, but most people prefer Y.*
> *I'd rather do X because ….*

  agree and disagree:

> *You're right. / I don't agree. / I'm not sure.*

  ask for an opinion:

> *What do you think? / Do you agree?*

  come to a conclusion:

> *So we've decided that X would be the most successful.*

- For **Part 4**, make sure you can give your opinion and give reasons for it:

> *In my opinion, X is not true/better/easier because …*
> *In my country, most people …*
> *I'd prefer … / I'd rather … because …*
> *My reason for choosing X is because ….*

Appendix 5

Writing checklist

This is a list of things you should check **every time** you do a writing task. There are also exam tips in the units which have writing tasks in the Exam Practice section.

Before you start writing
- Read the question carefully and identify the information you have to give/include.
- Think about what kind of task you have to do and who you are writing for, e.g. part one: letter/email, part two: article, essay, letter, story, report, review.
- Plan what you're going to write: think about using a mind map or word tree as well as a list.
- Look through the unit for key vocabulary, idioms and expressions you can use and make a note of them on your plan.

When you are writing
- Include as much varied vocabulary as you can.
- Remember to use paragraphs and proper punctuation.

When you have finished writing
- Check you have written the correct number of words part one: 120–150 words; part two: 120–180 words.
- Read what you have written and correct grammar and spelling errors.
- If you can improve your writing by adding or changing vocabulary, then do so.
- Read through your work once more and make sure it makes sense.
- Compare your answer with the model answer at the back of the book.

Things to remember when you do the FCE exam

Part one
- Make sure you understand the whole situation.
- Read the rubric and the input email or letter to get a general impression.
- Then read the notes **very** carefully.
- Plan what you are going to say in each of the points.
- Be aware of who you are writing to and how formal or informal you need to be (this will vary; it depends on whether you know the target reader, what his/her position is, how old he/she is and whether you know him/her – follow the style and tone of the email or letter you are given).
- Write in correct grammatical English in both the email and the letter.
- Open and close your email or letter in an appropriate way.
- Try to expand on two of the points.
- Keep to the word limit of 120–150 words (you will probably need to write 150 words if you expand on two of the points).

Part two
- Always choose a question you feel confident you can write about.
- Make sure you understand the question and know the relevant vocabulary.
- Avoid a question if you are uncertain of what it means or don't know the vocabulary to express your ideas.

Answer key

Unit 1

1.1
Meal A is high in fat, salt, sugar and calories and low in vitamins and fibre.
Meal B is high in vitamins, protein and fibre and low in salt, fat and sugar.

1.2
G *fruit* B *salt* G *vegetables* B sugar G exercise B *stress*
G *salad* B *smoking* B *chocolate* B *alcohol* G *water*
B *junk food* G *fish* G cutting out fat B putting on weight
G *joining a gym* G going on a diet G *getting enough sleep*

1.3
The things the sportsman mentions are in italics above.

1.4
2 F 3 T 4 T 5 T 6 T 7 T 8 F 9 T 10 F

1.6
2 cut down on 3 putting on 4 cut out
5 get 6 joining 7 going for

2.1
2 D 3 G 4 E 5 A 6 B 7 C 8 F

2.2
2 stitches 3 antihistamines
4 prescription 5 plaster 6 vaccinations
7 thermometer 8 scales 9 stretcher

2.3

Person	Problem	Where they got help	Treatment
1	Sore throat (red with spots)	Local surgery (doctor)	(Prescription for) antibiotics
2	Hit his thumb with a hammer	Casualty department	X-ray Bandage
3	Fell over someone and broke his arm	A and E*	Left arm in plaster Physiotherapy

*Accident and Emergency, another name for the Casualty Dept.

3.1
1 ✗ 2 ✓ 3 ✗ 4 ✓ 5 ✗

4
2 suggestion 3 decision 4 mistake 5 changes
6 speech 7 effort 8 arrangements 9 phone call

5
2 A 3 B 4 E 5 C

Exam practice
Use of English Part 1
1 a 2 make 3 for 4 enough 5 it 6 into
7 any 8 what 9 when(ever) 10 as 11 at 12 do

Use of English Part 4
1 cutting down on 2 made a helpful suggestion
3 about going on a

Writing Part 2
Model answer
Dear Annie
Well, everyone seems to have something to say about health and fitness at the moment. Every time I turn on the television or open a newspaper there's something about it! You asked what I do to be fit and healthy. Well, I think my family has always had a healthy diet. We just have a light breakfast, some cereal and fruit. Then for lunch I have a sandwich or a salad, and then we eat a big meal in the evening. We usually have chicken or fish and vegetables again. Sometimes we have pasta, or in the summer we have perhaps a steak from the barbecue, or a hamburger. We eat fruit again for dessert or a yoghurt, although at the weekend my mother often makes some really nice cakes. As you know, I don't do a lot of sport, because I don't really like it, but I think I'm quite fit because I haven't got a car, and I walk and cycle everywhere. And I do like dancing, so on a Saturday night I go out and dance till the early hours. It's enough I think!!
Hope that's the information you need.
Love
Susan

Unit 2

1.2

2 forests 3 streams 4 slopes 5 flowers
6 orchards 7 paths 8 valleys
The description matches Picture A. Picture B is of the Brazilian rainforest.

1.3

clear – muddy gentle – steep narrow – wide
wild – cultivated high – low winding – straight

1.4

Model answer

There is a thick forest with a narrow, winding path through it. Some of the trees are very tall and it is quite dark.

2.1

1 stream; canal; flood
2 forest; wood; rainforest; timber
3 mountain; hill; cliff; cave
4 sea; ocean; lake; waterfall
5 banks; shores; beach; coast
6 soil; mud; sand; dust

2.2

2 C 3 C 4 A 5 D 6 B 7 C

3.1

2 A 3 B 4 B 5 A 6 B 7 A 8 B
9 A 10 A 11 B 12 A

3.2

Picture A

Summers are mild and wet. In winter the temperature drops to below 0°C and the area is often cut off because of snow. The heavy snowfall in winter attracts skiers and tourists. It can rain heavily in July and August during the monsoon and skies are often cloudy in the mountains, whether it is summer or winter.

Picture B

It is always hot and humid and, as it is near the Equator, there is little difference in temperature between the warmest and the coolest months. Rain falls nearly every day and there is no dry season. In the rainforest, the morning of almost every day begins with a clear blue sky but by mid-afternoon there are sudden hard downpours and thunderstorms are common. The temperature at night is 20°C–25°C but during the day it rises to above 30°C.

3.3

In the Arctic (the person is talking about Greenland).

4.1

2 wind 3 sun 4 rain 5 sun 6 snow/ice 7 rain
8 snow/ice 9 wind 10 rain 11 snow/ice
12 snow/ice

5

stormy cloudy windy rainy dusty sunny foggy
icy

Exam practice
Reading Part 2

1 F 2 B 3 C 4 A 5 E

Unit 3

1.2

1 Yes 2 Yes 3 Yes, I play the flute (and piano)
4 No, never 5 Yes, frequently 6 As often as I can

2.1

rock 3 pop 2 classical 4 world music 1

2.2

2 harmonies 3 album 4 composer 5 band
6 tracks 7 cover version 8 distinctive style
9 old favourites 10 fans 11 lyrics 12 catchy tunes

2.4

2 fans 3 band 4 old favourites 5 lyrics
6 duets 7 distinctive style 8 cover version

3

1 rock 'n' roll 2 jazz 3 country and western 4 folk

4

2 group 3 concert 4 charts 5 cello 6 composer
7 guitar 8 opera 9 piano
The circled word is: orchestra

5.1

1 croak 2 whistle 3 creak 4 hiss 5 roar 6 hum
7 splash 8 grunt 9 howl 10 crash 11 bark
12 bang

5.2

2 E 3 G 4 I 5 J 6 A 7 B 8 C 9 D 10 F

5.3

2 hum 3 whistling 4 bang 5 creaking
6 hissed 7 grunted 8 crash 9 howl

Exam practice
Use of English Part 2

1 in 2 had 3 to 4 so 5 any 6 up 7 with
8 were 9 no 10 as 11 my 12 at

Writing Part 1: email
Model Answer

Hi Sam,
Yes, of course I'll give you the info you need. I'm really looking forward to the festival.
Our band plays blues, some traditional, some very modern, and we've got a really great singer – she's American.
We usually start with some really lively numbers to get everybody going and then Maria does some really cool songs.
We'd like to play on the first night if possible. We always get nervous, so that'll mean less waiting! We can just arrive and start playing straight away. The audience is usually enthusiastic at the start of a festival too, so the atmosphere's great then.
But I definitely don't want to camp because I get terrible hay fever and I hate insects. Is there a youth hostel or anything nearby? Something fairly cheap please!
Look forward to seeing you
Love Anneke   [135 words]

Unit 4

1.1

1 A coach from the national team to choose the three best players.   2 He broke his leg.   3 His brother.

1.2

positive: confident, excited, proud, relaxed
negative: ashamed, disappointed, embarrassed, guilty, jealous, upset

1.3

1 excited, confident, proud   2 disappointed, upset, jealous

1.4

ashamed, embarrassed, guilty

2.1 / 2.2

amazed	annoyed	depressed	frightened	pleased	worried
surprised astonished	cross furious	fed up miserable	scared afraid terrified	glad delighted	anxious concerned

3.2

1 that they phoned   2 to have   3 of going on
4 with   5 about   6 to realise

3.3

Student's own answers.

4

STRONG:	very extremely really terribly so
LESS STRONG:	quite fairly a bit

Note: Quite sometimes has a different, stronger meaning when used with words like impossible. It can mean 'completely': The crossword was quite impossible.

5

2 sad 3 happy 4 sad 5 happy 6 happy

6.1

2 disappointing 3 surprised 4 excited
5 worried 6 terrifying 7 relaxing

6.2

Adjectives ending in -ed describe a feeling.
Adjectives ending in -ing describe what caused the feeling.

6.3

Noun	fear	amazement	embarrassment
Verb	frighten	amaze	embarrass
Adjective	frightening frightened	amazing amazed	embarrassing embarrassed
Noun	pleasure	annoyance	excitement
Verb	please	annoy	excite
Adjective	pleased pleasing	annoying annoyed	exciting excited

Noun	depression	anger	pride
Adjective	depressing depressed	angry	proud
Noun	anxiety	misery	jealousy
Adjective	anxious	miserable	jealous

Exam practice
Listening
1 C   2 B

Use of English Part 3
1 unexpected   2 variety   3 disappointed
4 championship   5 congratulations   6 personal
7 annoyance   8 really   9 embarrassing   10 apologise

Writing Part 2
Model answers
Jakob was absolutely furious when he saw what was going on outside his window. There were two men with a huge machine and they were cutting down trees. Jakob lived on the fourth floor of a block of flats which looked out over a lovely park. When he realised what the men were doing, he ran out of his flat and shouted at them. They didn't take any notice and just carried on with their work. So Jakob rushed over to one of the trees which was still there, sat down in front of it and put his arms round it. He was so angry he decided he would stay there all day. He wasn't scared of the men and their machine because he knew they wouldn't hurt him. When some other people came by, he called to them to do the same with the other trees. In the end the men had to go away. Jakob felt very proud that he'd managed to save the rest of the trees but he knew the men would come back again.   [179 words]

Unit 5

1
2 F   3 E   4 A   5 B   6 G   7 H   8 D

2.2
2 cave paintings/wall   3 2,000 years ago
4 in prehistoric times   5 China/France

2.3
The Great Pyramid of Ghiza
About four and a half thousand years ago.

3.1
2 records   3 population   4 figures
5 inhabitants   6 tribes   7 ancestors   8 hunting
9 settled   10 produce   11 tools   12 beliefs
13 stories   14 invaded

3.2
prehistory – prehistoric   **archaeology** – archaeologist, archaeological   **evidence** – evident
civilise – civilisation, civilian   **invade** – invasion, invader
reside – residence, resident   **inhabit** – inhabitant
descend – descent, descendant   **believe** – belief, believer
survive – survival, survivor
discovery – discover   **abolition** – abolish   **cause** – cause
invention – invent   **colonisation** – colonise
introduction – introduce

4.1
2 last   3 takes   4 went on for   5 spent

4.2   Model answers
1 It takes (me) two hours to fly from Spain to London.
2 In my country, summer lasts about 4 months.
3 Several years have passed since I left primary school.
4 I've spent 30 minutes studying English today.
5 It takes me 20 minutes to walk from home to college.
6 The longest film I've ever seen was *Gladiator*. It went on for three hours.

5
1 A on time = to be punctual
  B in time = early enough
2 A have a lot of time for = have a lot of patience with her.
  B have no time for = have no patience with her.
3 A time flew = time went quickly
  B kill time = deliberately waste time

6
2 E   3 D   4 B   5 F   6 A

Exam practice
Use of English Part 1
1 A   2 B   3 C   4 A   5 C   6 D   7 A   8 B   9 D
10 A   11 C   12 B

Writing Part 2
Model answer
STONEHENGE : not just a stone circle.
Stonehenge is a giant circle of stones in Somerset in England. It's absolutely fascinating and it was built about 5,000 years ago, in prehistoric times. Lots of people come to see it from all over the world and there are still ceremonies there on Midsummer's Day.
It was built at a time when there were no modern tools and machines, so people wonder how it was built, because the stone blocks are huge. Archaeologists think that the stone came from Wales, and that people used rafts to move it by

water, and logs to roll it across land because wheels hadn't been invented then!

No one knows why Stonehenge is there. Some people think it was used for religious ceremonies, others that it's a giant astronomical clock that shows the movement of the sun, moon and stars. The sun shines on one of the most important stones on Midsummer's Day. That can't be coincidence, can it?

I went there early one morning last summer when it was very misty. It's very beautiful and has a fantastic atmosphere.

[177 words]

Test one

(Unit numbers in brackets show the unit where the vocabulary tested can be found.)

1 D (Unit 4)	11 A (Unit 1)	21 B (Unit 3)
2 C (Unit 2)	12 D (Unit 2)	22 A (Unit 5)
3 A (Unit 4)	13 B (Unit 3)	23 C (Unit 5)
4 C (Unit 3)	14 B (Unit 2)	24 D (Unit 1)
5 D (Unit 4)	15 B (Unit 1)	25 B (Unit 5)
6 D (Unit 5)	16 A (Unit 3)	26 A (Unit 4)
7 C (Unit 1)	17 B (Unit 5)	27 A (Unit 3)
8 B (Unit 2)	18 B (Unit 4)	28 D (Unit 2)
9 D (Unit 1)	19 A (Unit 1)	29 A (Unit 2)
10 B (Unit 4)	20 C (Unit 3)	30 B (Unit 5)

Unit 6

1

1 B   2 E   3 D   4 C   5 A

A slogan can be spoken or written.

2.1

An island with something for everyone is the best slogan. There is nothing about the future in the adverts.

2.2

A

Come to Sicily and experience its <u>amazing</u> colours, <u>stunning</u> landscapes and <u>delicious, healthy</u> food.

Visit the city of Catania which is a <u>perfect</u> combination of <u>spectacular</u> 17th century architecture, <u>lively</u> nightlife and <u>musical</u> traditions.

Relax on <u>fine, golden, sandy</u> beaches watched over by <u>Europe's biggest active</u> volcano, Mount Etna.

Last but not least, enjoy the <u>wonderful</u> flavours of <u>top-quality</u> products such as olives, pistachio nuts, honey, vegetables and dried fruit.

B

Come to Sicily and experience the <u>bright</u> colours, <u>beautiful</u> landscapes and <u>tasty</u> food.

Visit the city of Catania which is a combination of 17th century architecture, <u>busy</u> nightlife and traditions.

Relax on the <u>nice</u> beaches watched over by the volcano, Mount Etna.

Last but not least, enjoy the <u>good</u> flavours of products such as olives, pistachio nuts, honey, vegetables and dried fruit.

2.3

	Advert A	Advert B
Colours:	amazing	bright
Landscapes:	stunning	beautiful
Food:	delicious, healthy	tasty
Architecture:	spectacular, 17th century	17th century
Nightlife:	lively	busy
Traditions:	musical	
Volcano:	Europe's biggest active	
Beach:	fine, golden, sandy	nice
Flavours:	wonderful	good
Products:	top-quality	

Advert A makes you want to visit Sicily because it uses lots of adjectives. The adjectives in B are not very strong or convincing.

3.1

You should tick: extraordinary, fantastic, magical, remarkable, unique

agreeable, *nice* and *pleasant* aren't very strong. The other adjectives are much stronger.

3.2

1 only   2 ✓   3 only   4 ✓

4.1

2 C   3 A   4 B   5 C   6 A   7 B   8 A   9 C
10 B   11 A

5

2 home page   3 keyword   4 bestsellers
5 secure   6 sign   7 password   8 basket   9 click
10 online   11 enter   12 support

6.1

2 phone   3 visit   4 phone   5 visit

6.2

2 out   3 off   4 away   5 over

7.1

1 F   2 E   3 C   4 A   5 D   6 B

7.2

2 get   3 ring   4 cut   5 pick   6 call/ring

Exam practice

1

The main advantage of computers is that <u>it's easy to find out information</u> like how to travel somewhere. This means that people don't need to look in books or newspapers. However, <u>there is sometimes too much information available</u>. Also, when we read facts, we don't always know what is true. A further disadvantage is that <u>people throw their computers away after a few years.</u> This results in a lot of waste. There are a number of advantages for children such as being able to play games. In addition, <u>they make learning more fun.</u> But this leads to <u>children spending too much time on the computer.</u>

It is <u>easier to stay in touch with friends by email and another advantage is that you can send photos.</u> But people <u>send emails rather than talk to each other.</u> I sometimes think people rely on computers too much and <u>if a computer goes wrong</u>, for instance in a hospital, <u>it might be dangerous.</u>

In conclusion, I think computers improve our lives in lots of ways and the advantages are more important than the disadvantages.

2.2

to explain something C
to give an opposite opinion B
to introduce the next argument D
to give examples A

3   Model answer

The main advantage of mobile phones is that it's easy to get in touch with people so you can tell someone you're going to be late or change where to meet. However, this means that people can also contact you when you don't want them to or when it's not convenient. This leads to people never being able to relax. Also, a lot of people forget to turn their phones off in the cinema, for example, and that's very annoying.

A further disadvantage is that they are very easy to steal. This results in an increase in crime because everyone wants the latest phone.

Another advantage is that you can use them to do other things apart from phone people, such as play games, use the internet, take photos. In addition, they are essential in an emergency as they can be used almost anywhere for instance on a motorway or a mountain.

In conclusion, mobile phones have made our lives much easier so I think there are more advantages than disadvantages to having one. [174 words]

▮ Unit 7

1

Construction – electrician
Customer service – call centre manager
Emergency services – firefighter, police officer
Health – optician, psychologist
Hotel and catering – chef, kitchen assistant
Information technology – software engineer
Legal – solicitor
Leisure and sport – lifeguard
Scientific – lab assistant

2.1

A receptionist   B cleaner   C nursery assistant

2.2

2 A permanent   3 C possible promotion   4 B shift work
5 A good communication skills   6 B overtime

2.3

1 a salary   2 wages   3 a rate of pay

2.4

2 application   3 catering   4 qualifications
5 reliable   6 training   7 enthusiastic   8 ambitious

3.1

A efficient, well-organised, self-motivated, able to work without supervision, good communication skills
B reliable, flexible, honest, hard-working
C enthusiastic, dynamic, creative

3.2

Speaker 1 is a hairdresser.
Speaker 2 is a carpenter.

4

→ Phone or email for an application form → Fill in the application form → Email or post the application form → Have an interview → Receive a job offer → Accept the job offer

5.1
1 ✗ 2 ✓ 3 ✗ 4 ✗ 5 ✓ 6 ✓ 7 ✗ 8 ✓

5.2
Speaker 1 says he resigned and Speaker 7 says he gave up his job.
Speaker 3 says she was made redundant.

5.3
2 work 3 job 4 career 5 work 6 work
7 job 8 work 9 work 10 career

5.4
1 job 2 career 3 work

Reading Part 3
1 B 2 B 3 A 4 C 5 C 6 A 7 C 8 A
9 B 10 B

Writing Part 2
Sample answer

Dear Mr Pitt
I saw your advertisement in the local newspaper last week and I would like to apply for the job in your computer shop. At present I'm working in a sports shop where I enjoy helping people to find what they want. I have also worked as a waiter in hotels and restaurants so I am used to dealing with people.
My hobby is playing computer games. I have more than 200 games and I read computer magazines so I know all the latest developments.
I have completed several computer courses and do all the ordering in my present job. I am at present doing a training course in accounting.
I have good communication skills. I am reliable and happy to be flexible if I am required to work extra hours.
I look forward to hearing from you.
Yours sincerely

Ghang Lee

Unit 8

1.1
A is Sam and B is Toby.

1.2
Sam's dad has a <u>thin pointed face</u> and <u>freckles</u>. He's got <u>straight</u> brown <u>hair</u> but he's going bald. He's got <u>pale blue eyes</u> and a <u>long straight nose</u>. He doesn't wear glasses.

1.3
Toby's mum has got <u>a round face</u>. She's got long wavy hair which was <u>dark</u> but it's going grey now. She's got <u>a small turned-up nose</u>, <u>large</u> green <u>eyes</u> and <u>quite full lips</u>.

Toby looks like his mum. They've both got a round face. Their hair is similar but Toby's is darker and curlier. Toby's nose is just like his mum's but he has dark eyes. They have the same lips. They're very alike.

1.4/1.5
other possible words in italics
face: round, thin, pointed
hair: straight, curly, wavy, dark, blond, brown, fair, long, short, *red/ginger*
eyes: pale blue, large, green, *brown*

2.1
2 A 3 B 4 A 5 B 6 A 7 C 8 C

3.1
generous – mean gentle – aggressive hard-working – lazy
modest – big-headed polite – rude self-confident – shy

3.2
2 generous 3 rude 4 lazy 5 funny 6 aggressive

4.1
2 nosey 3 moody 4 bad-tempered 5 dishonest

5.1

im-	un-	in-	dis-	ir-
polite patient possible	popular kind imaginative sociable	considerate convenient expensive	honest satisfied	relevant responsible regular

im- is added to some adjectives beginning with *p-*
ir- is added to some adjectives beginning with *r-*

5.2
2 careless 3 colourless 4 powerful 5 painful
6 harmless 7 graceful

Exam practice
Reading Part 1
1 C 2 A 3 D

Use of English Part 4
1 takes after her
2 is so imaginative
3 don't look like

Unit 9

1.1
FAST run dash rush stride sprint
SLOW walk stroll creep crawl wander

1.2
an athlete sprint run dash **a tourist** stroll walk wander
a baby crawl **traffic** creep crawl run
a burglar creep crawl **someone late for work** run dash rush sprint stride

1.3
2 ran/dashed/sprinted 3 Walking 4 sprinted
5 striding 6 wandered/strolled/walked
7 dashed/rushed/ran/sprinted

2.2
2 D 3 F 4 B 5 E 6 A

2.3
1 run them down (to *run over* someone or something means to hit and drive over: *I dropped my hat in the road and a car ran over it.*)
2 run up against (to *run through* means to say or practise the details of something: *Before the meeting I ran through what I was going to say.*)
3 run across (see 1 for *run over*)
4 run through (to *run out of* means not to have any more: *I've run out of sugar – I'll go and buy some.*)
5 run out of (see 2 for *run up against*)
6 running around (see 1 for *run down*)

2.4 Model answers
1 … I think it's unkind.
2 … try to solve it as quickly as I can.
3 … stop for a chat.
4 … don't understand the first time.
5 … try to fix my computer.
6 … my sister visits with her children.

3.1
GO running skating cycling jogging walking swimming climbing skateboarding skiing diving snorkelling sailing snowboarding hiking surfing
TIP: These all end in **ing**

PLAY volleyball squash rugby badminton football table tennis baseball ice hockey hockey
TIP: These are all **played with a ball** (apart from ice hockey and badminton)

DO judo yoga aerobics athletics gymnastics martial arts

3.2
1 **F** Golf is played with clubs on a course.
2 **F** You play squash with a racket.
3 **F** You play hockey on a pitch using a stick.
4 **F** You go skating at a rink, and take your blades with you.
5 **T**
6 **T**
7 **F** Baseball is played with a bat.
8 **T**

3.3
ER runner skater jogger walker swimmer climber skateboarder skier diver snorkeller footballer   **NB sailor**
-PLAYER volleyball squash rugby badminton football (table) tennis baseball hockey
IRREGULAR cyclist gymnast athlete
NB There is no word in English for someone who does judo, yoga or aerobics

4.1
1 yoga 2 squash 3 hockey

5.1
1 beat/win 2 beat/won 3 won/beating
4 win/beating 5 beat/win

5.2
2 D 3 B 4 C 5 A

	IDIOM	MEANING
WIN	to win someone round	to convince someone of something
BEAT	if you can't beat them, join them	if you can't be as successful as someone else, then do the same as they do
	she beat me to it	she did it before I could
	to beat the rush	to do something before everyone else

Exam practice
Use of English Part 4
1 to run through 2 beat me to 3 ran into a lot
4 runs in Susie's

Writing Part 2
Model answer

Dear Michael,

Thanks for your letter. I'm writing to tell you something about sport in my country. I think football is probably the most popular sport in England, but tennis, golf and cricket are all popular as well.

People love football because they can play it as well as watch it, and most schools and colleges have football teams. Some boys spend all their time out of school playing football too. They dream about becoming stars and earning lots of money like Wayne Rooney does.

I like playing tennis, and I play nearly all year. It's a bit cold in winter, but I love it. It keeps me fit and I meet friends. We often go out to eat together or round to someone's house after we've played. I actually prefer doing sports to watching them, but if there are big matches on, I like watching them with my friends. I watch tennis, cricket, football, rugby – anything really.

I hope that tells you what you need to know. Good luck with the project!

Best wishes

Tim

[168 words]

Unit 10

1.1
2 colleagues   3 step-sisters   4 a married couple
5 sisters-in-law   6 flatmates   7 classmates
8 neighbours   9 nephew   10 penfriends

1.2
The people in 1, 3, 4, 5 and 9 are related.

2.1
1 reception   2 rings   3 cake   4 anniversary
5 guests   6 (across) priest   6 (down) photos   7 suit
8 invitation   9 present   10 (across) dress
10 (down) day   11 ceremony

2.2.
A is in Korea, and B is in France.

2.3
Dear Bill,
I'm glad you got the invitation to my brother's wedding and you're able to come. It will be a traditional wedding and (1) will take place in the garden of the bride's family. (2) The wedding day will begin with the groom arriving there on a horse. (3) The ceremony starts with the couple bowing to each other and to the priest. You will have to be patient as there are no chairs! (4) The bride and groom will both wear colourful, traditional clothes and all my relatives will probably wear traditional clothes too but the other guests just dress smartly. Don't dress too informally or wear black. After the wedding (5) we'll go to a restaurant to have a traditional lunch. (6) You can give the couple any kind of present but we usually give money. If you want to take photos of the couple, you can but you shouldn't go too close.

Dear Satya
I'm so pleased you're coming to my sister's wedding (1) in our village. She's getting married on the same day as my parents' silver wedding anniversary – they've been married for 25 years. (2) So first of all everybody goes to the Town Hall for a civil ceremony and (3) then we'll go to the village church where the bride and groom will exchange gold rings. In the church the bride's family sit on one side and the groom's on the other. (4) My sister is going to wear a long white dress and the groom will wear a suit. Most people dress formally and some women wear hats. On the way out of the church everyone throws rice or flower petals over the couple for good luck. Then we'll go to the (5) reception which will be in a hotel nearby. There'll be lots to eat and drink and a cake which is cut by the bride and groom. (6) If you want to bring a present, most people buy something for the couple's new home.

3.1
1 A   2 C   3 A   4 B

3.2
2 spoken   3 get   4 make   5 told   6 fell   7 got
8 get   9 lost   10 enjoy   11 keep   12 make   13 had

3.3
close   best   old   good

4.1
get in touch   get on well together   get to know someone

4.2
1 X   2 is getting   3 got   4 X

5
2 meet   3 couples   4 traditional   5 made
6 become   7 get   8 neighbour   9 in   10 best
11 each   12 on   13 out   14 to

Exam practice
Writing Part 2
Model answer
Dear Kim

I'm going to tell you about a big family party we had for my uncle, aunt and cousins who were on holiday here. They live in Canada now so we don't see them very often. In fact, I'd only met my cousins once before at a wedding when I was very small. We decided to have a party for them and invite the whole family. There were about 65 people altogether and we had the party outside in the garden. We put lights in the trees and we had a live band so people could dance. We invited my uncle, aunt and cousins for a meal but they didn't know there was a party. We told them to put their best clothes on because everyone wanted to dress smartly. We made a traditional meal as they live abroad now. When they arrived they couldn't believe it. There was lots of food for everyone and a big cake with icing. The party lasted nearly all night.

Hope to hear from you soon.

Love Alexander [175 words]

Listening Part 3
1 F   2 A   3 E   4 D   5 B

Test Two
Unit numbers in brackets refer to the unit where the vocabulary can be found.

1 B (Unit 7)	11 A (Unit 8)	21 C (Unit 6)
2 A (Unit 9)	12 A (Unit 6)	22 A (Unit 8)
3 D (Unit 7)	13 D (Unit 7)	23 C (Unit 6)
4 B (Unit 6)	14 B (Unit 10)	24 D (Unit 10)
5 B (Unit 8)	15 D (Unit 8)	25 C (Unit 10)
6 A (Unit 9)	16 C (Unit 6)	26 A (Unit 8)
7 D (Unit 9)	17 B (Unit 10)	27 D (Unit 6)
8 A (Unit 7)	18 A (Unit 9)	28 B (Unit 9)
9 D (Unit 10)	19 B (Unit 8)	29 A (Unit 7)
10 B (Unit 7)	20 C (Unit 10)	30 C (Unit 9)

Unit 11

1.1
2 check in   3 conveyor   4 pass   5 departure
6 control   7 security   8 board   9 gate   10 crew
11 seat   12 belt   13 refreshments   14 headset

1.3
1 train   2 bus   3 underground   4 taxi

1.4
Bus driver   fare   destination   single-decker   double-decker
Underground escalator   platform   train   rail   seat   sliding doors
Train commute   rush-hour   platform   carriage   seat   fare   season ticket
Taxi rank   fare   tip   driver   meter   cab

2.1
1 luggage/suitcase   2 accommodation/hotel
3 weather/storm   4 equipment/camera   5 money/coin
6 travel/journey   7 information/guidebook
8 transport/car

2.2.
Countable hotel   storm   camera   car   suitcase   journey   guidebook   coin
Uncountable travel   weather   equipment   information   transport   money   accommodation   luggage

3.2
Man   1 B   2 C   3 C   4 A   5 A   6 B
Woman   1 C   2 C   3 B   4 C   5 C   6 A

3.3   Model answers
1 I think it's better to book a holiday well in advance because then you can look forward to it.
2 I'd always prefer to travel independently because then you can see what you want when you want.
3 I'd rather stay in a five-star hotel because I love comfort

4
2 journey   3 journey   4 trip   5 travel   6 trip
7 travel   8 journey

5.1
2 C   3 A   4 D

5.2
1 B   2 A   3 C   4 D

Exam practice
Use of English Part 4
1 did/made the journey
2 on a short trip to
3 to set about fixing
4 to book (some/any) accommodation

Writing Part 2
Model answer
The Longest Journey
Have you ever been on a journey that you thought would never end? I have! It was when I went to San Francisco three years ago. We were going to visit friends we hadn't seen for several years. We took a taxi to the airport, but the traffic on the motorway was crawling along, so the driver decided to take another route. That meant going round lots of winding country roads. After a few miles we all felt as sick as parrots …

We made it to the airport just in time and joined a long queue to check in. I think we got the last few seats on the plane. We went into the departure lounge and discovered there was a delay on our flight, so it was three hours later that we boarded the plane. It was hot and crowded and everyone was grumpy, including us. The flight took ten hours, and we just got hotter and more fed up all the time. But, eventually we got there, and saw our friends waiting for us. We were so happy and excited.

The sun was shining and they drove us across the famous Golden Gate Bridge. It looked fantastic, and I knew then that it was going to be a great visit …

Unit 12

1.1
1 staying in   2 going out

1.3
STAYING IN
to have   a party, a drink, a barbecue, a quiet night in, friends round
to watch   TV, a DVD, a film, a match, a play
to play   cards, games, a match
GOING OUT
to go   swimming, surfing, shopping, clubbing
to go to   the cinema, a concert, a party, a restaurant, the theatre, a film, a barbecue, the beach, a play, a club, a match
to go for   a drink, a drive, a walk

1.4   Model answer
When I have some free time, I prefer to go out with friends and do something active, like go surfing or go clubbing. I also enjoy going to a film and going out for a meal. But I don't really like staying in and watching television or reading.

2.1
1 G   2 F   3 C   4 D   5 E   6 B   7 A   8 H

2.3
2 collects   3 do   4 do   5 play   6 play

3.1
take in information: hear and remember
take off your hat: remove
take on work: accept
take over a business: gain control of
take to a new friend: develop a liking for
take up space: fill up

3.2
2 take in   3 takes up   4 take off   5 takes after
6 take on   7 taken over

4.1
audience B   box office B   cartoon C   cast B
costumes B   comedy B   critic B   director B
documentary C   drama B   dressing room T
location C   musical B   performance B   plot B
rehearsal T   reviews B   science fiction C   screen C
soundtrack C   special effects B   stage T   studio C
subtitles C   thriller B   trailer C

4.2
The woman prefers going to the theatre because there's more atmosphere and every performance is special.
The man prefers going to the cinema because of the darkness in the cinema, the film music and the locations in the films.

5
1 documentary   2 cartoon   3 drama   4 western
5 thriller   6 romantic comedy

6.1
unimpressive N   stunning P   uninteresting N   tedious N
brilliant P   imaginative P   uninspired N
fascinating P   wooden N

6.2
brilliant   uninteresting   uninspired   tedious

Exam practice
Writing Part 1
Model answer
Dear Mr Johnstone,
I love the film club and most of the films you show, so I am writing to give my opinion.

If you want to choose films that students enjoy, you should always show the latest movies with big stars, but also some classics and lots of films about music. There are lots of films of famous bands in concert, and I think this would be popular. You could also show some famous foreign language films, with subtitles in English of course!

I think it would be an excellent idea to have a café, as we could meet our friends there before we went to see a film, or chat about it after we had seen it.

However, I do not think it would be sensible to have a film club on Thursday afternoon because most people are either at work or studying then. Friday evening is perfect for me.

Yours sincerely

Junko Takihiko   [151 words]

Reading Part 3
1 A   2 C   3 C   4 B   5 B   6 A

Unit 13

1.2
1 B   2 A   3 B   4 A   5 B   6 A

1.3
A Sentences 6, 2, 4
B Sentences 3, 5, 1

2.1
B

2.2
2 F   3 F   4 F   5 T   6 F

2.3
1 housing, industrial, business
2 residential, outskirts, suburbs
3 office, tower   4 precinct   5 multi-storey
6 run down   7 lane

3.1
1 leisure centre   2 health centre   3 car park
4 art gallery   5 concert hall   6 taxi rank
7 football stadium   8 ice rink   9 bowling alley
10 shopping centre

3.2
recreation ground; play games

4.1

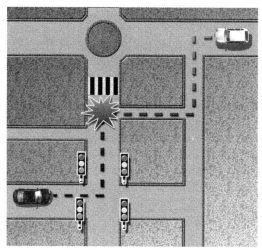

4.2
2 crossing   3 lights   4 overtook   5 per/an
6 slowing   7 side   8 one-way   9 way   10 cut
11 jam   12 bypass   13 broke

5.1
B slow down   C pull something down   D turn
something down   E break down (vehicle)   F write
something down

5.2
put down F   pull down C

6
2 underweight   3 overcrowded   4 underwater
5 overdue   6 overcooked   7 overcharged
8 overheard

Exam practice
Use of English Part 1
1 D   2 A   3 C   4 B   5 A   6 C   7 A   8 B
9 B   10 C   11 A   12 D

Writing Part 2
Model answer
I hope you'll enjoy your visit to my town. There are lots of things to see. It's divided into two main parts – the old city and the new city.

The old city

The old city is on a hill and has lots of medieval buildings. You should visit the church in the market square which has a beautiful ceiling. But most importantly, you mustn't miss the art gallery because there are some famous paintings in the exhibition. There's also a really nice café in the gallery which looks over the town.

There's a castle on the edge of the old town but that's now a ruin. There are lovely views from there and, if you go there in the evening, you can watch the sun set.

The new city

In the new city there's a shopping centre where you can also go to the cinema, go bowling or watch a band in the evening. It's a good place to spend time if the weather's bad. There's a little railway which takes you from the old town to the new town and that's quite fun to go on.

[188 words]

Unit 14

1.1

MEAT	**Cow:** beef, steak, burgers
	Pig: chop, ham, bacon, pork, sausages
	Sheep: lamb, chop
	Poultry: chicken, wing, breast, duck
FISH	**Fish:** trout, cod, plaice, tuna, salmon
	Shellfish: squid, mussels, prawns, lobster

2.1

Where you cook	How you cook	What you cook	What you use
Under the grill	grill	steak	a grillpan
On the hob	boil stew fry stir fry	an egg fruit fish vegetables	a saucepan a saucepan a frying pan a wok
In the oven	roast bake	beef a cake	a roasting tin a cake tin

2.2

1 Chinese   2 English   3 Italian

2.4

2 eggs   3 vegetables   4 banana
5 cheese   6 butter   7 cake   8 lemon   9 sauce

3.1

Everyday meals	Breakfast: cereal, juice, coffee
	Lunch: sandwich, salad, soup, roll
	Dinner: chicken, vegetables, potatoes, rice, pasta, fruit, yoghurt

What she doesn't eat: starter or dessert

Special meal	Day: Sunday
	Food: roast dinner e.g. roast beef and Yorkshire pudding, and a dessert like apple pie

3.3

2 NG   3 F   4 NG   5 T   6 T

3.4

2 G   3 F   4 C   5 A   6 B   7 E

3.5

1 tasteless   2 tasty   3 tasteful

4.1

1 drawings, water colours, oil paintings, prints
2 pottery, textiles, jewellery, sculptures
3 portrait, still life, landscape, abstract
4 exhibition, gallery, studio, collection

4.2

1 Very
2 painting, pottery
3 Yes, frequently
4 Likes portraits and landscapes
5 Favourite picture: Niagara Falls
6 Favourite artist: Albert Bierstadt

Exam practice

Use of English Part 3

1 hidden   2 thoroughly   3 friendly   4 tasty
5 celebration   6 seasonal   7 reasonable
8 popularity   9 selection   10 romantic

Listening Part 2

1 remote   2 plane   3 nature   4 realistic   5 desert
6 light   7 canvas   8 oils   9 companies
10 (magazine) articles

Unit 15

1.1

2 A   3 E   4 F   5 C   6 D

1.2

1 Reality TV   2 Comedy   3 Soap opera

1.4
TV: channel, screen, set
Radio: disc jockey, station
Both: aerial, highlights, remote control, repeats, studio

2.1
2 listened to   3 looked at   4 saw   5 heard
6 watched   7 read about

2.2
1 C   2 A   3 B

3
daily N   fashion M   glossy M   gossip M   local N
monthly M   morning N   tabloid N   today's N   travel M
women's M   N advertisement   NM article   M cover
NM editor   NM editorial   N headline   N report

4
2 A   3 B   4 C   5 B   6 A   7 C   8 C
9 B   10 A

5.1
Reference: atlas, cookery book, encyclopedia
Fiction: detective story, ghost story, poetry book, thriller,
science fiction novel
Non-fiction: biography, diary, guidebook, textbook

6.1
It's from a thriller or possibly a detective story

6.2
I had a brief glimpse of   I peered out   caught sight of
I made out

6.3
1 breathe   2 smell   3 sniff   4 stroke   5 overhear

In each group the other two words are connected with
seeing.

7.1
1 A, C, B, D   2 B, A   3 A, B   4 A, B

7.2
2 novelist   3 called   4 remember
5 fiction   6 characters   7 relationships   8 borrow
9 library   10 request   11 entertaining   12 chapter

Exam practice
Reading Part 1
1 B   2 D   3 B   4 C

Writing Part 2
Model answer
I've just read a novel called *Northern Lights* by Philip
Pullman. It starts off in England and moves to a fantasy
world of snow and northern lights.
The main character, Lyra, is a girl who overhears a
presentation by her uncle to his colleagues in Oxford
University. He is investigating the idea of another world
where everyone is born with an animal companion.
It's a magic world and Lyra goes there and has lots of
adventures.
The description of her journey is so well done that you feel
as though you're there with her. The book is thoroughly
entertaining and you won't be able to put it down until
you've finished the last chapter. The story is gripping and
quite frightening in places but that's what I enjoyed about
it. Although it is quite complicated, you really want to
know what happens so it isn't difficult to follow.
The book is extremely well-written and you could read it
several times and still find something new. I've since read
the next two books in the series and I'd highly recommend
them all. [180 words]

Test Three
*Unit numbers in brackets refer to the unit where the
vocabulary can be found.*

1 B (Unit 12)	11 A (Unit 11)	21 D (Unit 11)
2 C (Unit 15)	12 C (Unit 12)	22 A (Unit 15)
3 C (Unit 14)	13 B (Unit 13)	23 A (Unit 14)
4 D (Unit 12)	14 D (Unit 13)	24 D (Unit 12)
5 B (Unit 13)	15 A (Unit 15)	25 B (Unit 14)
6 B (Unit 11)	16 D (Unit 11)	26 C (Unit 13)
7 C (Unit 15)	17 A (Unit 12)	27 D (Unit 15)
8 A (Unit 14)	18 D (Unit 14)	28 B (Unit 11)
9 C (Unit 11)	19 C (Unit 14)	29 A (Unit 12)
10 A (Unit 13)	20 B (Unit 15)	30 B (Unit 13)

Unit 16

1.2
Martha is elderly   Rob is in his late twenties
Jessie is in her early thirties   Callum is in his early teens
Jim is middle-aged

1.3
2 As   3 three years old   4 gap year
5 pregnant   6 toddler   7 about my age
8 (very) childish   9 grown up   10 my age

2

2 tallish

3 reddish

4 eightish (change *about* to *at* – *eightish* = *about eight*)

5 longish (delete *quite* – *longish* = *quite long*)

6 newish

3

2 B 3 D 4 E 5 F 6 A

4.1

The text is aimed at people who are thinking of coming to the university as undergraduates.

4.2

1 terms, semesters, vacations

2 lectures, seminars, tutorials

3 lecturers, tutors

4 dissertation

5 undergraduates, graduates, postgraduate

6 campus

7 halls of residence, students' union

8 prospectus

9 departments, faculty

10 mature

5.1

1 term is used but we say school holidays not vacations

2 schools have lessons

3 schools have teachers not lecturers, they sometimes have tutors

4 schoolchildren do projects and essays or compositions

5 schools have pupils

8 schools and universities have prospectuses

9 schools have departments but not faculties

5.2

2 compulsory 3 age 4 start 5 age 6 attend

7 pupils 8 taught 9 miss 10 after 11 in

12 allowed 13 take 14 leave 15 study

16 opportunities

6.1

2 handed/given 3 handed 4 handed/gave 5 gave

6 handing/giving 7 give

6.2

meaning	hand	give	What you use
give to someone who will be alive after you have died	✓	✗	+ down
give to someone in authority	✓	✓	+ in
give to someone else	✓	✗	+ over
return something to someone	✓	✓	+ back
give to someone without asking for payment	✗	✓	+ away
give something to a large number of people	✓	✓	+ out
stop doing a regular activity	✗	✓	+up

Exam practice
Use of English Part 4

1 expecting/having / going to have a baby

2 give up eating

3 let me decide

Unit 17

1.1

2 buckle (a buckle is on a shoe or belt not on a shirt)

3 pyjamas (pyjamas are worn in bed not outside)

4 socks (socks are worn on your feet)

5 jacket (a jacket is worn on the top half of your body)

6 laces (laces are used to tie shoes)

7 belt (a belt is worn with trousers, etc., it is not jewellery)

8 nightdress (a nightdress is not worn on your feet)

1.2

Tights, pyjamas, jeans, shorts, trousers are always plural. We often say a pair of tights, trousers etc.

2.1

Jasmine: Picture C   Kariem: Picture A

2.2

2 baggy 3 pockets 4 belt 5 buckle 6 T-shirt

7 sweatshirt 8 hood 9 trainers 10 laces

11 short 12 long 13 neck 14 collar 15 bracelet

16 boots 17 flat

2.3

Pattern: checked, flowery, plain, spotted, striped

Material: cotton, leather, lycra, nylon, polyester, silk, wool

3

2 discount   3 sale   4 credit   5 trolley   6 Refunds, receipt

4.1

1 C   2 B   3 D   4 A

4.2

2 into   3 out of   4 on   5 back   6 off
7 into   8 up

4.3

2a) dress   2b) wear   3a) dressed   3b) wearing
4a) got   4b) took   5a) dressed   5b) wearing

5

B costs   C saved   D earned   E spent
F put   G paid for   H made   I paid   J donated
Correct order: D, C, I, F, H, G, A, E, J, B

Exam practice
Reading Part 2

1 B   2 F   3 E   4 C   5 A

Use of English Part 4

1 don't go with
2 have/'ve grown out of
3 take back the jacket / take the jacket back
4 doesn't suit Mary

Unit 18

1.1

She's describing C.

1.2

1 D   2 E   3 F   4 B   5 C   6 A

1.3

1 B, C, D, E, F   2 C   3 A, C   4 B, D   5 C, D
6 E   7 F

1.5   Model answer

The house we live in now is quite old and semi-detached, like a lot of houses in Britain. It was built in the 1930s. It's made of brick and there's a large garden at the back. The house isn't very spacious, but it's big enough for my family. Downstairs there's an open plan living and dining room and a large fitted kitchen, which is where we usually eat. Upstairs there are three bedrooms and a bathroom. We have central heating and a single garage for our car.

2.2

1 A   2 C   3 B   4 C   5 B   6 B

3

2 C   3 B   4 F   5 D   6 A

4

2 E   3 A   4 C   5 B   6 D

5.1

2 out   3 without   4 up

5.2

DO	someone in	out a room	up a building	without something
meaning	exhaust	decorate	renovate	manage without

5.3   Model answers

1 Yes, I did my room out recently. I painted it blue and yellow.
2 Yes, learning English sometimes does me in! But I like learning languages.
3 I can't do without a car because I live in the country. But I've got a bike too.
4 I've never done up a whole flat. I think it would take a very long time.

Exam practice
Use of English Part 2

1 to   2 and   3 for   4 one   5 because/as/since
6 where   7 In   8 of   9 were/are   10 This
11 due/owing   12 which

Use of English Part 3

1 perfectly   2 picturesque   3 historic   4 airy
5 combination   6 surrounding   7 wooden   8 fitted
9 appliances   10 additional

Unit 19

1.2

2 E   3 D   4 B   5 G   6 A   7 C

1.3

Answers in bold
astronomer   astronomy   **astronomical   biologist**
biology   biological   **chemist**   chemistry   **chemical**
ecologist   **ecology   ecological   geologist   geology**

geological **mathematician** mathematics
mathematical physicist physics physical

1.4
2 A/B 3 B 4 A/B 5 B 6 A

2.1
2 A 3 D 4 F 5 C 6 B

3.1
1 droughts, storms, floods
2 oil, coal
3 wind turbines, solar panels
4 heat, light, ventilate
5 use up, throw away, pull down (*get rid of* is a useful
   expression meaning throw away, but not a phrasal verb)

3.2
Village school: environmentally friendly, efficient, cheap to
run
City school: wasteful, expensive to maintain

3.3 Model answer
The place where I work has air conditioning and heating,
but it's still always too hot or too cold and it's not well
ventilated. I think it's probably quite expensive to maintain
as well. It's being refurbished at the moment, so I think
things may improve.

4
2 A 3 B 4 D 5 C 6 B 7 A 8 C 9 B 10 D
11 C 12 D 13 D

Exam practice
Use of English Part 3
1 pollution 2 sustainably 3 efficiency 4 organically
5 variety 6 global 7 information 8 massive
9 residential 10 placements

Listening Part 1
1 B 2 C 3 B 4 C 5 C 6 A 7 C

Unit 20

1.1
2 False 3 False 4 False 5 True

Burglars can't be Choosers is the first novel about Bernie
Rhodenbarr, a surprisingly charming and <u>very talented
professional burglar</u> (1) in New York. The opening of the
novel finds Bernie <u>expertly breaking into an expensive</u>

<u>apartment</u> (2), commissioned to locate a mysterious blue
leather box. The burglary goes smoothly until Bernie
<u>realises that the box is not there</u> (3), the police are at the
door and <u>the owner of the apartment is lying dead on the
bedroom rug</u> (4). Bernie makes a rapid escape, and spends
the rest of the novel employing all his investigative (not to
mention criminal) skills <u>trying to find out who set him up</u>
(5), and clear himself of the murder charge.

1.2

CRIME	CRIMINAL	VERB
burglary	burglar	burgle
robbery	robber	rob
theft	thief	steal
shoplifting	shoplifter	shoplift
murder	murderer	murder

1.3
2 robbed 3 stole 4 robberies 5 murderer 6 stolen

2
1 Yes, I love them because they make you think, like a
   crossword puzzle.
2 My favourite writer is PD James.
3 She writes fantastic descriptions of places and her
   characters are really interesting, especially the
   detective, Inspector Dalgliesh.

3
1 arsonist – They set fire to things, the others all steal.
2 kidnapping – It is a crime against a person.
3 clue – the others provide information which is certain.
4 detective – a detective does not usually work in a court.

4.1
1 innovative 2 radical 3 enthusiastic 4 effective
5 significant 6 traditional

4.2
RADICAL weekend jails, criminals meeting their victims,
identifying drug and alcohol problems
TRADITIONAL no TV in court, judges wearing wigs and gowns

4.3
Used positively: in favour of, is enthusiastic about,
supports the idea that, approves of
Used negatively: is totally against
Either: has strong opinions on, is convinced that, believes
that

5.1

1 We're thinking *of going* to France on holiday.
2 What did you think *of/about* the concert last night?
3 I thought *about* my answers before writing anything down.
4 I'm thinking *of* leaving early to avoid the rush hour.
5 What do you think *of/about* my new dress?
6 I was thinking *about* my grandmother, who's been rather unwell.

5.2

2 E   3 A   4 C   5 F   6 B

Exam practice
Writing Part 2
Model Answer

What you think about this statement depends quite a lot on where you live. I live in a village and there are lots of small crimes committed by young people. For example, there has been vandalism in the bus shelter, and small amounts of money and garden tools are stolen from houses and sheds. This is different from the past. Fifty years ago, lots of women spent the day at home and so there were always eyes watching! I am sure that it stopped people committing these crimes.

And if I go into the city, it is quite safe until late in the evening, when all the young people start to go home from the bars and clubs. Then there are sometimes fights, and people can get hurt. My grandparents say there have always been fights like this, but now there are more.

So in conclusion, I agree that young people do commit more crimes and behave worse. I think this is because today young people have more freedom and more money, and they don't always use them well.   [179 words]

Listening Part 1
B

Test Four

Unit numbers in brackets refer to the unit where the vocabulary can be found.

1 D (Unit 20)	11 B (Unit 18)	21 B (Unit 16)
2 C (Unit 19)	12 B (Unit 19)	22 A (Unit 19)
3 D (Unit 17)	13 D (Unit 20)	23 D (Unit 18)
4 A (Unit 18)	14 C (Unit 17)	24 D (Unit 17)
5 C (Unit 20)	15 D (Unit 18)	25 C (Unit 19)
6 A (Unit 18)	16 B (Unit 16)	26 C (Unit 17)
7 C (Unit 16)	17 A (Unit 18)	27 C (Unit 20)
8 C (Unit 19)	18 B (Unit 20)	28 B (Unit 17)
9 D (Unit 17)	19 A (Unit 16)	29 A (Unit 20)
10 D (Unit 16)	20 C (Unit 16)	30 B (Unit 19)

Appendix 1 Phrasal verbs

1.2

get across: explain clearly
get (a)round: overcome
get away from: leave
get away with: escape unpunished
get by: survive
get down: depress
get out of: avoid
get over: recover from
get (a)round to: have time for
get through: contact by phone

2.1

2 D   3 H   4 A   5 F   6 E   7 B   8 C

2.2

come by: visit
come down: fall
come off: succeed
come out: be released
come on: appear on stage
come up against: face (a problem)
come round: regain consciousness

2.3

1 come by   2 come out   3 came up against
4 come off   5 come round   6 came on
7 came across   8 come down

3.1   Model answers

2 Yes, I went in for the 100 metres.
3 Yes, salad sometimes goes off in my fridge.
4 Most of my money goes on rent and food.
5 Yes, my shoes go with my clothes very well.
6 No, I definitely couldn't go without chocolate for a week!

3.2

1 catch   2 entered   3 go bad   4 (is) spent on
5 match   6 manage without

Appendix 2 Word building

1.1

2 expansion   3 solution   4 explanation
5 interruption   6 conclusion   7 competition
8 reception   9 exaggeration   10 production

1.2

2 publication   3 obligation   4 satisfaction
5 prediction   6 division   7 impression
8 investigation   9 destruction   10 persuasion

2

2 survival   3 proposals   4 approval
5 refusal   6 practical

3.1

2 majority   3 anxiety   4 independence
5 naughtiness   6 kindness   7 confidence
8 variety   9 activities   10 shyness

3.2

2 popularity   3 necessity   4 happiness
5 illness

4

2 frightens   3 believe   4 prove
5 strengthened   6 identify

Appendix 3 Spelling

1 advertisment/advertisement   2 believe/belive
3 beatiful/beautiful   4 becouse/because
5 begining/beginning   6 bycicle/bicycle   7 biger/bigger
8 comfortable/confortable   9 convinient/convenient
10 definitly/definitely   11 diferent/different
12 disappointing/disapointing
13 enviroment/environment
14 embarassing/embarrassing   15 greatful/grateful
16 Madam/Madame   17 nowdays/nowadays
18 opportunity/oportunity   19 polution/pollution
20 preferred/prefered   21 realy/really
21 recommend/recomend   22 runing/running
23 shoping/shopping   24 untill/until   25 wich/which

Recording scripts

Recording 1a

Well, I'm a keen athlete, so I try to have a healthy diet. I eat a lot of protein, especially fish and lean meat, and plenty of fruit and veg. That's no problem, because I like those things and I love crunchy salads. But I also need quite a lot of carbohydrate to give me energy, so I tuck into pasta and baked potatoes. I can't resist chocolate either; I've cut down a bit, but I don't think I'd want to cut it out of my diet completely! Anyway, because I do so much exercise I don't ever put on weight. I have reduced my salt intake though – I never put it on food and I normally avoid junk food, which is full of salt and fat. I go to a training session two evenings a week with my local team. I also belong to a gym and I go there three times a week. I've never smoked and don't drink much alcohol. What I do drink is lots of water – you really need it if you do a lot of exercise. And I also try and get eight hours sleep a night – I find it makes a big difference. I think I'm fit, and being fit helps me deal with stress, at work and at home.

Recording 1b

Speaker 1: I got home from work on Thursday with a really awful sore throat, and when I looked in the mirror on Friday I realised it was bright red and covered in spots. So I made an appointment at the local surgery. My doctor gave me a prescription for antibiotics. It cleared up quickly once I started taking them.

Speaker 2: Well, I felt really stupid the other day. I was trying to put up some bookshelves in my study. I had the hammer and nails out ... and well, I suppose I just stopped concentrating for a minute and the next thing I knew I hit my thumb with a hammer! It really hurt. My wife took me up to the casualty department and they sent me for an X-ray. It wasn't broken, so they just put a bandage on it.

Speaker 3: I was out playing hockey. I'm in the college team. Anyway, I went for this ball at the same time as someone on the opposition. I fell over and there was this awful crack. I knew I'd broken something. I couldn't move: it hurt too much. They called an ambulance, put me on a stretcher and took me up to A and E. My left arm will be in plaster for another two weeks, and then I have to start physiotherapy.

Recording 1c

Speaker 1: I'm really out of sorts at the moment – I've been feeling tired and headachy all week.

Speaker 2: Me? I'm feeling as fit as a fiddle. I've been in good shape since I took up running on a regular basis.

Speaker 3: I've felt a bit off colour since yesterday. I think I'm going down with a cold.

Speaker 4: I'm fine thanks. I've got loads of energy now. I always come back from a holiday feeling refreshed and ready for anything!

Speaker 5: I'm a bit under the weather at the moment. Too many late nights and not enough sleep I think, so it serves me right!

Recording 2

People often associate my country with cold and darkness and it can, of course, get very cold. In winter there isn't much light and in some places the sun doesn't rise for a whole three months. We have more hours of summer than other countries further south, but the weather is nowhere near as warm, even though the light is much more intense. The climate is generally dry, which makes it feel warmer. –10°C, for instance, seems a very pleasant temperature to us. The temperature is mostly below freezing except for short periods in the summer.

Recording 3a

Yes, I'd definitely describe myself as musical. All the women in my family are, and we all play a musical instrument of some kind. I learnt to play the piano and the flute when I was at school, and I still play the flute in a local orchestra. My two sisters both sing in a choir, but that's something I've never done. I go to concerts a lot, mostly classical ones. But I like all kinds of music, and when I'm at home, I'm always listening to something. It's often pop or jazz though rather than classical. Music's an important part of my life really.

Recording 3b

Speaker 1: I've loved it ever since I first heard Buddy Holly and Elvis Presley. It's just great to dance to because the rhythm's so strong and your feet just go with it. I think the electric guitars you got then were great, and I love the clothes from that era, the full skirts and tight jeans. The fifties had a great influence on all the music that follows.

Speaker 2: My friends think it's really strange that it's my favourite kind of music, but I love it, especially played on a saxophone. It always creates such an atmosphere, and the voices of some of the singers are so rich. It all goes back to the black American traditions of New Orleans, but there're a lot of good artists in Britain today and they're getting into the pop charts too.

Speaker 3: When I hear it I always think Texas! The songs all tell a story – something everyone can relate to. There are things about love, and splitting up and having a hard life. Johnny Cash is probably the most famous singer, but a lot of the others are women. The chorus is always important so everyone can sing along. I enjoy singing to it when I'm driving!

Speaker 4: Well, my parents go along to a club once a month to listen to it. It's mostly just one or two people with a guitar singing, although you do get groups too. They seem to play a lot of very traditional songs from different regions that the audience know well and join in with. Sometimes you get quite old-fashioned instruments like accordions and harmonicas, and a few unusual things I don't know the name of!

Recording 3c

[Sounds.]

Recording 4a

I've played football since I was eight years old and I'm now fifteen. I play in one of the best football teams in my region. My brother who's fourteen is also in the team. My aim is to play in the national team – the under-sixteens of course. Last week we were told that a coach was coming from the national team to watch us play so that he could choose the three best players to play in a match against another country. The big moment arrived on Tuesday and we played our match. Just before the final whistle, I scored a goal and I knew we'd won the match. I looked over at the coach and he nodded to me. The whistle blew. I knew I'd played really well and I was sure I would be chosen. I couldn't wait to hear my name called. I ran over to the other players but I was so excited I wasn't looking where I was going and bumped into someone. I fell badly and I broke my leg. I was taken to the hospital and I found out that the coach had chosen me but now I can't play and my brother will take my place. The match is on Saturday.

Recording 4b

On Saturday I went to watch the match in a wheelchair. My brother played well and our team won but I refused to clap and say well done to him. When we got home that evening he gave me a big parcel. It was a football signed by some of our national players that he'd met after the match. He wanted me to have it. All I could think of was how badly I'd behaved.

Recording 4c

1

Examiner: Listen to the recordings and choose the best answer: a, b or c.
You overhear a woman telling a friend about a conversation she had with her parents. How did her parents feel about her news, a furious b astonished c pleased?

Man: So what happened when you told your parents about Mark and you getting married?

Woman: Well, I was a bit nervous about it because I haven't known him that long. They've met him a few times but they didn't seem to get on all that well because Mark is really shy so he didn't say much. But I was surprised at their reaction. They said they were delighted and it was what they'd expected after they saw us together. In fact, I'd expected them to be really angry.

Man: Why?

Woman: Because we've decided to go and live in Canada and it means I won't be able to finish the course I'm doing.

2

Examiner: You hear a man talking about an activity holiday he went on. How did he feel at the end of it, a annoyed b relieved c upset?

Man: I've just got back from an activity holiday that my daughter persuaded me to go on. She'd been on one and she was convinced I'd really enjoy it. Well, I didn't have very high expectations as it's not really my kind of thing but I did enjoy some of it. I wasn't very good at most of the activities and I was just glad when it finished that I'd survived without having broken an arm or a leg. I think my daughter was a bit annoyed when I told her that as she'd really thought it was the perfect holiday for me.

Examiner: Now listen again.

Recording 5a

Student: I can see a very old wall in the first picture and some paintings in a cave in the second. I think the cave paintings are much older than the wall. The wall was built about 2,000 years ago and the paintings were done in prehistoric times, so they're really ancient. The Great Wall is in China – I've never been there but I recognise the picture. The cave paintings are in France, and they go back to prehistoric times. You can see some animals.

Recording 5b

Interlocutor: What is the oldest thing you can see in your country? What is it and when was it made?

Student: One of the oldest things you can see in my country, Egypt, is the Great Pyramid of Ghiza. People come from all over the world to see it. It was built about four and a half thousand years ago, for a king called Khufu. It's absolutely enormous, and for centuries it was the tallest building in the world. There are lots of ancient things in my country and many pyramids, but because of its size, this one is very famous.

Recording 6a

For the next two weeks Direct Books has a special offer just for you. We're giving you a unique opportunity. You can save up to 40% off selected books. So all you pay is the price of your books – postage and packing is absolutely FREE in the UK for orders over £15. And if you spend over £50 you'll receive a free mystery gift worth at least £5. To take advantage of this offer, put your order in now. Don't forget it's only for a limited period – the next two weeks. Your books will be promptly delivered, direct to your door. We also offer a guarantee allowing you to return any book within seven days and we will give you a full refund. If you're looking for a particular book please contact us and if it's available we'll get it to you.

Recording 6b

This is Tanya's answerphone. I can't answer my phone now. Please leave me a message.

Tanya, this is Lara. Thanks for the message. I was hoping you'd pick up. I'll text you instead.

Tanya this is mum. You promised you'd keep your phone switched on today but maybe it's on silent if you're at college. I'll ring later.

Hi Tanya it's Joe. I'm glad I dialled the right number this time. I got a strange man just now who hung up on me. We're all going into town tonight. Do you want to come? Ring me up if you do.

Hello Tanya, it's Sarah. You're still not there. Can you ring me please? I tried to phone you loads of times yesterday but I couldn't get through because your phone was engaged all the time. Talk to you soon.

Hello Tanya, this is Dad. I've had a great day walking. We've just got back. I tried to ring you from the top of the mountain but my phone wouldn't work up there. I wish you could have come with me.

Tanya, it's Peter, can you call me back please? I've nearly run out of credit so I can't talk for long. I'll get cut off. I'm going out at six so ring me soon.

Recording 7a

Speaker 1: It's important to be cheerful and friendly in my job. I get on well with people, which is lucky because I spend most of my day talking to people. I'm on my feet all day so the job is quite tiring but I'm very enthusiastic about my work and I'm quite ambitious – I'd like to own my own salon one day.

Speaker 2: I'm an energetic person and physically fit. I like to be doing things. I enjoy my job and don't mind working indoors or outdoors. I'm good with my hands and enjoy being creative – I sometimes design cupboards or shelves for people. I'm not really ambitious – I'm quite happy with what I'm doing.

Recording 7b

Speaker 1: I used to work for an oil company but I resigned because I hated travelling. I'm trying to change career and I'm looking for work as a teacher.

Speaker 2: I do shifts – some days and some nights.

Speaker 3: I was made redundant when the company closed down and I've been unemployed ever since although I've just applied for a job at the theatre.

Speaker 4: I had a long career in the police force. I retired when I was 55 and I'm getting a really good pension.

Speaker 5: I commute every day – the journey takes an hour each way so I don't have time to do much after work.

Speaker 6: I do four long days which is very hard work but then I get three days off every week.

Speaker 7: I gave up my job as a chef a year ago because it was too stressful and I'm still out of work. I'm interested in advertising and I'm going to do some unpaid work experience soon in an agency near here.

Speaker 8: I was promoted last week so that's very good for my career. The next step is manager.

Recording 8

Girl: It's great that you're coming to visit us at last Toby.

Boy: Yeah. After being penfriends for so long, it will be good to meet.

Girl: Sorry I can't come to the airport but Sam, my brother, will be there. He's quite tall and he's got straight blond hair – quite thick and long. He's got blue eyes and he wears glasses.

Boy: OK. Shouldn't be too difficult to spot him. Tell Sam I've got dark curly hair – it's quite short – and dark eyes. I'm quite slim and not very tall.

Girl: All right. You'll have your mobiles anyway – I'll give you his number ....

Recording 9a

Speaker 1: I find it's a really great thing to do if you really want to relax at the end of the day and de-stress. You don't need much equipment, just a mat and some old loose clothes. The exercises are very varied, and you stretch a lot and really improve your balance. Our teacher is very good – she tries to give everyone individual advice so you can do some practice at home every day.

Speaker 2: I've been playing it since I was 12 and it's really quite demanding. The court is small and the ball is very fast, so you have to have quick reactions. If you don't move rapidly, you can end up being hit by the ball or running into your opponent or his racket

– I've got a black eye several times. But I love it – I find it really exhilarating.

Speaker 3: I've always loved team sports, and this really is one of the best. There's a lot of running up and down involved, so you get fit. But it also needs a lot of skill to use your stick well when you pass the ball and to tackle your opponents. And it's a great feeling when you score a goal!

Recording 9b

Well, in the first picture I can see some runners at the end of a race and in the second picture I can see a hockey match. I think a runner has just won the race. The two hockey teams are in the middle of a match and I think one side is going to score a goal.

The runner is wearing a T-shirt without sleeves and some shorts and trainers. The hockey team are wearing short-sleeved T-shirts and shorts. You don't need special equipment for running – just yourself and lots of training! For hockey you need a sort of stick and a ball.

Running is for one person and hockey is a game for a team, that's the biggest difference. A running race can be very quick, unless it's a marathon – and a hockey game goes on for about an hour I think. In my opinion being a runner can be quite lonely, and playing in any team like hockey is more fun. I've never played hockey, but I have done some running – that's another difference for me!

Recording 10a

Speaker 1: I know it's silly but I fell out with Mike over money. I lent him some and he never gave it back. There was an argument and we haven't spoken to each other for three months. I know I should get in touch with him to make up because we were very close friends. In fact he was my best friend and we told each other everything.

Speaker 2: My cousin introduced me to Francesca. The moment I saw her I fell in love with her. I don't know how she feels about me. We spent the whole evening chatting and we got on well together but I haven't seen her since – that was three days and four hours ago. I'd really like to get to know her but she doesn't answer her phone.

Speaker 3: I have a good friendship with Jasmine. Our fathers worked together and were old friends so Jasmine and I became good friends and we used to play together. After we both got married we lost touch for a while but then my brother had a party and invited us both and we remembered how much we enjoyed each other's company so we make sure we keep in touch now. We phone each other every week.

Speaker 4: I don't make friends easily but when I do make a friend we usually become close. Petra was in the same class as me at college last year and we sometimes had lunch together. We discovered we had things in common like we both enjoy films. So we've been to the cinema together a few times.

Recording 10b

My family are the most important people in my life because I know they will always be there if I need them. We do all argue sometimes but mostly we get on well together and enjoy each other's company. My friends are also important. Most of my friends like doing the same things as me – shopping, watching TV and films. A few of my friends are in the swimming team with me so we have that in common. Most we have the same ideas about things but we sometimes fall out over something small. My best friend is Meena. I've known her since I was five years old. We live next door to each other and we tell each other everything. She's really good fun and very kind.

Recording 10c

Examiner: You will hear five different people talking about a family party. For questions one to five, choose from the list a to f what each speaker says about the party. Use the letters only once. There is one extra letter which you do not need to use.

Speaker 1: I arrived at the party late because I have to work on Saturdays and I also got lost because I'd forgotten to bring a map. My brother had rented a large room above a café for our mother's eightieth birthday and the café made all the food. It was really delicious. The room was great as it had windows looking over the river. It was very crowded because the whole family came and there were lots of children so it wasn't possible to dance or even move around much. I don't think Peter had expected everyone to turn up.

Speaker 2: I was really looking forward to Granny's birthday. I got there at about eight which is what the invitation said but the party had already started. Apparently most people got there earlier before Granny so she could have a surprise but not everyone had been told about that. Some other people arrived even later when nearly all the food had gone. That was the only problem really – there wasn't enough of it. The children ate most of it before the adults got near it.

Speaker 3: It was my birthday on Saturday and I had a lovely party organised by my son Peter. There were more than 80 people there. I didn't realise I had such a large family. There were so many children – I've got four great-grandchildren and of course great-nephews and nieces too – and they were so well-behaved. There were also lots of people from my generation but some of them struggled to get up the two flights of stairs to the room. Although it was a wonderful setting, a ground floor room would have been better. Everyone enjoyed it, especially the food, although I didn't manage to eat much.

Speaker 4: My sister had a lovely birthday party last Saturday. Everyone dressed up in their best clothes – well, most people did. Some of the young people didn't bother but I suppose they don't nowadays. And there were lots of children. In fact, I found them a bit annoying as they got bored and just rushed around making a lot of noise. They needed a quiet area with a TV or something. Anyway, they had a good time like everyone else. The best thing for me was that I didn't have to think about any of the arrangements because my son took me there and just told me when to be ready.

Speaker 5: My auntie was 80 last weekend and the whole family was invited to a party. It was down a little side street so not easy to find but I took a taxi there so it wasn't a problem for me. It had a large balcony so, although there were a lot of people, there was plenty of room out there when you needed a breath of air. The invitation didn't say what to wear so I put on a long dress and I felt a bit embarrassed. Some people looked as though they'd come straight from the beach. It didn't matter though and everything went off perfectly.

Recording 11a

Making your first flight

First of all, don't forget to pack your ticket and your passport in your hand luggage. When you arrive at the check-in desk, your bags will be weighed and put on a conveyor belt. You will be given a boarding pass, allocated a seat and told to go to the departure lounge. To get there, you will pass through passport control and a security check. Look at the departure board in the lounge so you know which gate number you must go to when it's time to board.

The cabin crew will direct you to your seat when you board, and you have to fasten your seat belt before take-off. You will be served refreshments and most companies provide an entertainment system with a headset.

Recording 11b

Speaker 1: Well I commute to London every day and unfortunately I travel in the rush hour. It all goes okay if everything's running on time! But it's cold waiting on the platform and sometimes the carriages are very crowded and there aren't enough seats. The fares are expensive too, but my company pays for a season ticket, so that really helps.

Speaker 2: The service in my area is quite good. There are always lots of people at the stop waiting to go into town and I see the same driver most mornings. You pay your fare when you get on and if you don't know where you're going, he'll call out when you reach your destination. We only get single-deckers around our way, no big double-deckers like you get in London.

Speaker 3: It's always packed in the morning and you have to go down several escalators to get to it. If the platform's empty when you get there, you know you've just missed your train. Once you're on, you have to hang on to the rail if you haven't got a seat. Oh, and you have to be careful not to stand too near the sliding doors!

Speaker 4: Well, there's a rank right outside the station that I use quite often. Of course it's quite pricey because you have to pay your fare and give the driver a tip, but there's a meter in every cab, so you know you're being charged the right amount. And if you share with other people, it can actually be quite an inexpensive way of travelling.

Recording 11c

Man: Well, we're not very organised and we usually make all the arrangements at the last minute. My wife hates flying, so that means we don't go anywhere by plane. Our favourite destination is France and we usually go by train. We take the Eurostar which goes under the Channel – it's an excellent service, fast and comfortable. Then we just travel around various cities looking at places of interest. We really enjoy cultural activities, so we'll go to art exhibitions, stroll around historic buildings, that sort of thing. We usually stay in small family-run hotels, nothing big and luxurious. What do I like best about holidays? Well, seeing places I've never been to before and really having time to explore them I suppose. I just love it! I really look forward to it.

Woman: Well, I like to do things the easy way now I'm working! My sister and I usually go away with a couple of friends. We haven't got a lot of money, but if you book well in advance, you can get some very cheap flights. We often go to Italy – we love the seaside places and the beaches. And we often stay on a campsite – there are some you can go to where the tents are put up for you. There are proper beds and even a fridge – it's really luxurious! We don't do very much – I just like being out of the office and in the fresh air, swimming and sunbathing.

Recording 11d

Well, I really like camping and sleeping in a tent. My parents always took me for camping holidays when I was young. It's great, you meet lots of other families on the campsite, and there's usually a beach and a swimming pool. The disadvantages – well, on one holiday I got bitten by hundreds of mosquitoes, and it's terrible being in a tent if the weather's bad.

If you like cycling, then the second holiday is great. You get fit and you're in the open air all the time. But it's very energetic and not very relaxing for me.

Beach holiday, well that's great. I love swimming and snorkelling and chatting with friends, and having a barbecue on the beach at night. But I like to do a bit of sightseeing too, so I think the last picture is quite a good holiday. If I go to a new country, I like to visit the famous places and do some sightseeing. But a sightseeing holiday can be very tiring and young people don't always like that sort of thing. They often find it boring. So, I prefer to go on a beach holiday and have fun and relax with my friends. I'm studying very hard at the moment and I also have a job at the weekends, so I need time to just relax and enjoy myself.

For my last holiday I actually went to visit my cousins who live in Sicily. We went to the beach a lot and I had a great time. They also have a boat, so we went fishing and had picnics and barbecues on the sand.

Recording 12a

Speaker 1: Well I always like going for a meal with friends. And I'll go to a party if I'm invited. But to be honest, I'm happiest at home. I get in from work quite late, so I just put some music on and cook myself something to eat. I don't watch much television because I've got several hobbies. I paint and draw, which is really relaxing, and I also collect china and porcelain. I go to antique fairs and look in old junk shops and places like that when I get the chance! And I love catching up on recent films too – I've got a big collection of DVDs, so I often watch one of those. I'm certainly never bored!

Speaker 2: What do I do after work? Well I get together with friends mostly. We sometimes go round to someone's flat if there's a big match on, and we cook together or get a take-away and then sit down and watch the match. After that we sometimes play cards too. But we'd rather go out if we get the chance. We go clubbing once a week, we go to the cinema, that sort of thing. And in the summer we get outside – we go to the beach, go swimming and surfing, have a barbecue. I don't spend a lot of time in, but when I am at home I tend to read a book rather than watch TV – well, unless there's sport on….

Recording 12b

Woman: Well to be honest I like both. I loved the cinema from the moment my parents first took me to see a cartoon, and the special effects you get in science fiction films today are amazing. But for me, there's far more atmosphere in the theatre, and every performance the actors give is special, and that's why I like it better. I went to see a fantastic musical the other night at the theatre. It was funny and fast-moving – the audience loved it …..

Man: The theatre's great of course. I've done some acting myself, and being on stage is quite an experience. Giving a performance in front of an audience is amazing. But what I love most is escaping from the world and going into the cinema. I love the darkness and hearing the soundtrack at full volume – film music is fantastic these days. You see exotic locations on the screen and your imagination takes off ….

Recording 12c

Review 1: …offering the audience a lively view of the origins of skateboard culture in early 1970s Los Angeles, director Stacy Peralta's film 'Dogtown and the Z-boys' offers a surprisingly *moving* and *dramatic* view of recent history. The film is narrated by actor Sean Penn, who grew up in the neighbourhood between Santa Monica and Venice Beach which was nicknamed Dogtown …

Review 2: …a star-studded cast provides the voices for the cutely drawn prehistoric creatures in this *entertaining* computer-animated story called 'Ice Age', which is set 20,000 years ago …

Review 3: Richard Gere pairs up with Jennifer Lopez in 'Shall We Dance?' a convincing film about a lawyer whose interest in life is unexpectedly restored by a dance teacher. He first glimpses her from a train window as he travels home from work and then …

Review 4: … a beautifully shot and very *stylish* film, 'The Last Wagon' stars Richard Widmark as a white man brought up by Comanche Indians. When the wagon train he is riding with is attacked, he must lead the survivors to safety through the desert …

Review 5: …Fabian Bielinsky's excellent film 'Nine Queens' is a complicated tale of cops and robbers. The plot is *gripping* and, with its constant twists and turns, it keeps the viewer guessing until the very last minute …

Review 6: … this gently *amusing* film, written by Marc Norman and Tom Stoppard, 'Shakespeare in Love' tells the story of England's most famous playwright, William Shakespeare, as he tries to win fame in London and gain the love of would-be stage star Viola. It's an extremely *funny* and very clever blend of fact and fiction.

Recording 13a

I only moved to this city recently and I think I'm going to like it. I live on a housing estate in a residential area which is on the outskirts. It's a mixture of houses and flats but there's lots of space around the buildings and some lovely parks. I work in an office block on a small industrial estate which is in a business district only about ten minutes' drive from where I live. The city centre is about three kilometres from my house in the other direction. There's a huge pedestrian precinct there with every shop you'd ever want. I usually cycle to the city centre because there are cycle lanes everywhere so it's a really pleasant ride. But it's also easy to drive because there are several multi-storey car parks in the centre. I used to live in a city with a historic centre which meant it was almost impossible to drive there. Also because it's surrounded by hills there isn't much space and most people live in tower blocks in the suburbs on the edge of the city. My flat had a great view but you live with other people's noise all the time and I got tired of that so I decided to have a change. And the area was a bit run down – it hadn't had any money spent on it for years. My life is easier here.

Recording 13b

Woman: I came along Regent Street and turned left at the traffic lights – you know at the big crossroads on the High Street and I was driving along the High Street towards the roundabout on the bypass. I could see someone standing at the pedestrian crossing ahead so I started to slow down. It was rush hour so I wasn't driving fast – only about 20 kilometres per hour. You couldn't go any faster. Suddenly the van in front of me stopped outside a shop – I suppose to deliver something so I pulled out and overtook him. Just as I got round him a white Fiat appeared from a side road on the right and went straight into the side of me. It was definitely his fault.

Man: I was driving along the bypass by the river coming up to the big roundabout on the High Street but there was a terrible traffic jam because a lorry had broken down so I thought I'd take a short cut. I turned left just before I got to the roundabout then I took the first turning on the right so I would come out onto the High Street. When I was halfway down I realised it was a one-way street and I was going the wrong way. I stopped at the junction and I was trying to get out onto the High Street. The traffic was moving slowly and a van driver stopped to let me in. Then suddenly a black Renault appeared from nowhere and I went into the side of it. It was going so fast the driver didn't see me.

Recording 13c

Interlocutor: What is special about your capital city?

Student: I come from Mexico and I grew up in Mexico City. My family live in the suburbs but I go into the centre a lot. I love it – there's lots of nightlife and it's a really exciting place to be. It's a very special place. It's huge and very busy and that's a disadvantage of course. I suppose some people get tired of the pollution and traffic but there are also beautiful parks. The centre is really old and there are some very impressive buildings. We get a lot of tourists because of that. The estate I live on is modern and it's a bit more peaceful than in the centre.

Interlocutor: Is there a city you'd like to visit in the future?

Student: I haven't been to Asia and I hear that Thailand is very beautiful. Bangkok is maybe a bit like Mexico City – very noisy and busy but exciting so I'd like to go there. But I'd also like to go to the beach and visit the islands.

Recording 14a

Speaker 1: My favourite kind of food? Well, I love vegetables and seafood, you know, prawns and scallops and things like that, and I like food that's lightly cooked and has a lot of flavour. I also like ginger and spices and a bit of soy sauce, so of course I love stir fries. And I've never been keen on potatoes, so rice and noodles suit me fine.

Speaker 2: Well, I'm quite traditional in my tastes. I love meat, but I really like it just roasted or grilled – I'm not keen on fancy sauces. I like everything quite plain really, I'm a meat and two veg man – I like cauliflower and cabbage, peas, that sort of thing, and I absolutely adore roast potatoes. And I like desserts too, things like apple pie, or strawberries and cream.

Speaker 3: Me? Well, I love fish and chicken cooked in the oven with nice sauces made with herbs and some cheese or tomatoes. And I absolutely adore all kinds of pasta, and salad and fruit. And one of my favourite things is olives – I like the green ones best, stuffed with red peppers.

Recording 14b

Well I do the typical English thing and have three meals a day. When I'm at home, I'll have a light breakfast of juice and cereal and a cup of coffee. For lunch I'll usually just have a salad or a sandwich in the summer, and some soup and a roll in the winter. We have our main meal in the evening – usually just a main course, some chicken and vegetables, usually potatoes, although we eat quite a lot of rice and pasta too. And then we have some fruit and a yoghurt, or sometimes some cheese. We don't have a starter or a proper dessert unless we go out to eat in a restaurant. But we often have a special Sunday lunch – a traditional roast 'dinner' with something like roast beef, Yorkshire pudding, roast potatoes, parsnips, carrots, cabbage. It's great. And then I will make a special dessert like apple pie ... the children love that meal.

Recording 14c

So what do you want to know? Right, well I'd say I was definitely artistic. I do some painting, but my big interest is pottery – I make a lot of vases and ornaments and sell some of them. And I go to art exhibitions quite a lot, small ones mostly in the local area. I don't get the chance to go to big galleries very much these days. I don't like abstracts very much, and I hate all this stuff with real objects in it. It's a bit of a joke isn't it? I really like landscapes, but I find portraits interesting too. You can learn a lot about a person by looking carefully at their face and body language. But my favourite picture is Niagara Falls, by an American artist called Albert Bierstadt. That's B-I-E-R-S-T-A-D-T. Not many people have heard of him, but in fact he's my favourite artist. The picture is a landscape, a picture of the waterfall that's so realistic you can almost touch it. When I look at it I can hear the waterfall and feel the water vapour on my face. The colours are fantastic and it's absolutely huge, which is what makes it so impressive.

Recording 14d

Examiner: You will hear an interview with an Australian artist called Anna Roberts. For questions 1–10, complete the sentences.

Interviewer: ....and continuing our series of features on Australian artists, today I'm very pleased to welcome Anna Roberts to the studio. She was born in Hobart, Tasmania and is already one of Australia's best known young artists, so we're delighted to have her with us. Welcome to the studio Anna.

Anna: Thank you, it's a pleasure to be here.

Interviewer: Now Anna, from what I've seen, your pictures all have one very important thing in common. Would you like to tell us about what you paint?

Anna: Well, I've established a reputation for painting pictures of very remote locations ...

Interviewer: Yes – many of them are a long way from towns and roads aren't they?

Anna: Absolutely – so getting to them can be very challenging. I sometimes trek to them on foot, but if that's impossible I'll travel by plane – provided there's somewhere to land, of course.

Interviewer: So that means you've had a few narrow escapes over the years, does it?

Anna: (laughs) Oh yes, but it's been worth it. You see the subject of all my paintings is nature. I want to show just how beautiful it is. So of course I have to experience it myself.

Interviewer: Right, and I've been to several of your exhibitions, and there's certainly nothing abstract about the landscape paintings you do ....

Anna: Oh no, one art critic told me recently that many of my pictures could be mistaken for photographs because they're so realistic.

Interviewer: I think that's certainly true of the paintings you do of beaches. I love those.

Anna: Oh yes. I've painted lots of beaches with the surf beating down on them ...

Interviewer: But just recently you've done a new series of pictures using different shades of yellow and orange.

Anna: Yes, I wanted to do something completely different, so I've done some paintings of the desert. I've tried to give an impression of the lines in the sand and the heat.

Interviewer: So what is it that makes your pictures unique do you think?

Anna: I'd say it's the way I portray the light. It's not something many other artists do.

Interviewer: And your paintings are very large aren't they – that's unusual too ....

Anna: Yes, they're big and I work on canvas – I find it very hard to use any other surface, like board, though other artists have been very successful with it.

Interviewer: I see. And what type of paint do you use?

Anna: Well, I've tried painting in acrylic and water colours, but I now paint exclusively in oils – personally I think it suits my style.

Interviewer: Well, other people obviously think so as well – your paintings sell well, don't they?

Anna: They certainly do, and not just to private individuals. A lot of my pictures are now bought by companies because they consider them to be a good investment.

Interviewer: That's great.

Anna: It certainly is.

Interviewer: And your talents don't stop at painting, do they? I believe you also write?

Anna: Mmm ... I've written some short stories for children, which I did illustrations for, and a number of my articles about painting have appeared in different magazines ....

Interviewer: Do you have plans for any other commercial ventures?

Anna: I do! I'm planning to launch a series of cards and calendars this year ...

Interviewer: Fantastic. Well, Anna, we wish you every success with that, and thanks for talking to us today. It's been most interesting.

Anna: Thank you for asking me, I've really enjoyed it.

Examiner: Now listen to the interview a second time.

Recording 15

Speaker 1: My favourite programme is *Big Brother*. It's so entertaining to watch a group of strangers being thrown together in a house. I find it quite compelling. I've watched every series.

Speaker 2: My favourite programme is *The Office*. I watch all the repeats and I've got all the DVDs and they still make me laugh. The acting is absolutely brilliant.

Speaker 3: I really love *Neighbours*. It's on every day during the week at lunchtime but it's repeated in the evenings. The characters become like your family or good friends because you get to know them so well and you want to know what happens to them. The plots have been really good recently.

Recording 16a

Martha: My name is Martha and I've been a widow for twenty years. As a child, I always wanted to have six children. I actually had two but I have six grandchildren and a great-granddaughter who is three years old.

Rob: My name is Rob and before I'm thirty in a couple of years' time, I want to do some travelling because I didn't have a gap year between school and university.

Jessie: My name is Jessie and I've just stopped working because I'm pregnant. The baby's due in March – the day after my thirty-second birthday. I've already got a toddler so it will be hard work.

Callum: I'm Callum. I'm an only child and I've got a cousin who's about my age so we spend quite a lot of time together. But I find him very childish – he still plays with his train set like a kid and he's going to be fourteen soon.

Jim: I'm Jim and my children are grown up. I'll retire in ten years' time. I don't feel my age though and I don't think I look it either.

Recording 16b

Student: The photos show two different classrooms. In the top one the children are doing a practical lesson. I think they are probably making things out of wood and they're wearing something to cover their clothes. Each person is doing something different. At the back a girl's doing something by a machine but I'm not sure what exactly. In the bottom picture, the students are sitting at desks in rows and the teacher is standing at the front. He's pointing at someone, probably asking them a question. This classroom is more formal and the students aren't finding things out for themselves. Both classes have a teacher but in the top picture the teacher looks like he is helping the students with their questions. In both pictures, the students look interested in what they're learning but I think it's better to learn by doing things yourself instead of just sitting and listening.

Recording 17a

Conversation 1

Girl 1: What do you think of this top, Rachel? I want something to wear with this skirt.

Girl 2: Have they got any others but in a different shade of red? I don't think it goes with that skirt.

Girl 1: No, they're all this shade. But I think you're right. Let's look somewhere else.

Conversation 2

Assistant: Can I help you?

Simon: Yes, I've just tried this jacket on but it's a bit big. Have you got any smaller ones?

Assistant: What size is it?

Simon: It's a medium.

Assistant: I'm afraid we've sold all the small ones.

Conversation 3

Assistant: How did you get on?

Woman: I like the style of the dress but I think this colour makes me look very pale. I never wear cream. Have you got it in black or pink?

Assistant: No, it only comes in that colour. I'm sorry.

Conversation 4

Man: This shirt is in the sale, isn't it?

Assistant: Let me see the label. Oh, I'm sorry, no. It's new stock so it isn't.

Man: So how much is it?

Assistant: It's £80. Our sale rail is over here.

Man: Well, I like it but it's not worth £80. I'll wait until it's in the sale next year.

Recording 17b

Simon: Mum. I got trousers, a jacket and a shirt to wear to Jason's wedding. I've put them on so you can see.

Mum: Good. You need to dress smartly. I'm sorry I couldn't come shopping with you.

Simon: So, what do you think?

Mum: Well, the jacket's a bit big but you might grow into it I suppose.

Simon: I've stopped growing, Mum. I couldn't find a smaller one. Anyway I like it and I've grown out of my other one. I've had it since I was twelve. The trousers are good though, aren't they?

Mum: Mmm, well I'm not sure.

Simon: I went to loads of shops and tried lots of things on.

Mum: Can you take the trousers back?

Simon: I can but I think they're OK.

Mum: Well, OK but take them off now. Go and change into your jeans again before you get them dirty.

Simon: I'll hang them up and I'll decide tomorrow.

Recording 19

Examiner: You will hear an interview with an Australian sheep farmer called Gina Ellis, who is talking about her work and plans for the future. Listen and choose the best answer for each question: a, b or c.

Interviewer: And on today's Green Magazine programme, we have Gina Ellis, an Australian sheep farmer. Welcome, Gina.

Gina: Thank you.

Interviewer: So Gina, tell our listeners something about sheep farming in your country.

Gina: Well, I'm from New South Wales, where over 30% of sheep farming takes place. But in fact, although it's concentrated in one area, there are large sheep farms right across the country, and it doesn't only go on in the coolest places.

Interviewer: I see. And I believe sheep farmers are experiencing problems at the moment?

Gina: Yeah, that's right. There are two, one to do with markets and the other environmental. There's a good market for meat, but the wool industry is struggling. Although Australia still produces about 10% of the world's wool, including nearly half of the top quality merino wool, demand is falling – consumers often prefer synthetic clothing, like fleeces, which are cheaper than woollen jumpers and equally warm. But the biggest issue for all us farmers is climate change – drought is causing major water shortages in farming areas, so it's becoming harder to find enough for our animals and crops.

Interviewer: Let's talk about the market problems a bit more. Are you looking for new uses for your wool?

Gina: Well yes. It is very versatile and has been put to so many uses over the centuries. Of course carpet manufacture still absorbs a high percentage of our product as it always has, and now we're looking for other domestic uses. The most promising seems to be the idea of using it in buildings as a form of insulation. Companies developing it have found it very effective. And there's also interest in eco-clothing, you know, clothing made from all natural products, and produced organically. But it's a specialised market and may turn out to be uneconomic in the end....

Interviewer: So why are you over here in the UK at the moment? Are you looking for solutions to your business problems?

Gina: Well, yes. I'm working in co-operation with ten other large farms to see if we could develop an alternative energy system producing enough electricity to sell as well as meeting our own needs. Clearly hydro-electricity isn't for us, and, er, tidal power is out, so I've been looking into ideas for harnessing wind power, using large turbines. Britain has a lot of expertise in that area, so that's why I'm here. Of course, we have potential for solar power, but I don't think we could produce a surplus with that.

Interviewer: That's interesting. What made you consider these options?

Gina: Well, if the predictions about global warming are correct, farmers in Australia will have to diversify, and look for other sources of income. That's my reason for looking into wind power. Of course, since then I've begun to realise that being self-sufficient and not having to rely entirely on other power sources is attractive and I'm starting to think in a greener way.

Interviewer: I see. And what do you feel about the advice you've been given?

Gina: Well, it's given me a lot of food for thought and, er, taught me the advantages of a more ecologically aware approach to life and work. And now that I have the information I've worked out that the investment involved is manageable. We should be able to scale down on the amount of animals we raise and still make a living.

Interviewer: Great, so how would you sum up your feelings about your project?

Gina: Well to my delight our basic plans are viable and we can press on very optimistically, without making any major alterations. And the costs involved do seem to be lower than we'd feared...

Interviewer: Gina, we wish you luck, and thanks for coming in today.

Gina: Thank you ....

Examiner: Now listen again.

Recording 20a

Well, I'm mad about crime novels and I read a lot of them, especially when I'm on a long flight. It makes me think when I read those stories, so it's like doing a crossword. I feel you have to read carefully so you don't miss the clues. I used to like the American writer Charlotte Centrone, but now I feel that all the detail she goes into about dead bodies is really horrible, so I avoid her books now. I'd rather read something by PD James – in my opinion she's a brilliant writer. She does fantastic descriptions of places, and I reckon her characters are realistic – you can sort of get inside their heads. And Inspector Dalgliesh is my favourite detective. He's a quiet man, but incredibly clever and I'm sure he really understands people.

Recording 20b

Interlocutor: Now I'd like you to talk about something together for about three minutes. I'm just going to listen.

The students in your class are choosing a book to read. Here are the different types of books they can choose.

First talk to each other about what type of book each picture shows, and what the story is going to be about. Then decide which book would be the best choice for everyone in your class to read together. You only have about three minutes for this. So, once again, don't worry if I stop you, and please speak so that we can hear you. All right?

Student A: Okay. Well, I know this first one, it's an old-fashioned story about Sherlock Holmes, a murder story I think ... crime.

Student B: Oh yes, I saw a film with Sherlock Holmes. And the next one is a science fiction story ... You know, space, rockets and things. And this one, well it has to be a love story I think ..... very romantic.

Student A: Mmm and I don't know the word for this, but I think it's a story about a phantom ...

Student B: Yes, a ghost story I think .... and this one is what? A thriller or adventure story? Who are these people running away?

Student A: They could be thieves I suppose, or even the good guys .... And there's a plane, so it could be exciting.

Student B: Yes, and this last picture is about history – a historical novel. It's set in the past. That's why they're wearing these strange clothes. And there's going to be a fight with swords.

Student A: Okay, so we know what the books are. What shall we choose for our class? It has to be something everyone will like.

Student B: Well, I like ghost stories, but I think most people prefer adventure stories, thrillers.

Student A: Yeah, maybe ... I'd rather read the science fiction story because I like that sort of thing. But do you think the others will like that?

Student B: Probably not!! And I don't think most people will want to read the love story, do you?

Student A: Definitely not! They're always so sentimental and you always know there's going to be a happy ending.

Student B: Okay. So what are we left with? The thriller and the crime novel, the one we think is Sherlock Holmes, and the historical novel .... What do you reckon?

Student A: In my opinion the thriller would be best, because most people will like it and it's modern. But I think the crime novel would be my second choice.

Student B: Yes, exactly, I agree with you. I think the thriller is the best choice.

Student A: So we can say we have agreed on this?

Student B: Definitely! We have decided that the thriller is the best choice for our class. We think nearly everyone will like it.

Recording 20c

Examiner: Listen to the recording and choose the best answer: a, b or c. You hear the beginning of a radio programme. What is the programme going to be about, a teenage criminals, b teenage volunteers, c teenage journalists?

Radio presenter: As anyone who reads a newspaper knows, young people often get a very bad press these days, with sensational stories about drug and crime problems everywhere. So it's good to be able to present a series of shows with a different focus and look at the positive contribution of young people in our very own area. We'll be looking at a whole range of voluntary work being done by our local youth from working in the region's hosptals to environmental work. So, let's turn first to the health service and ....

Examiner: Now listen again.

Wordlist

UNIT 1

HEALTH AND FITNESS

Nouns
alcohol /ˈælkəhɒl/
calories /ˈkæləriz/
carbohydrate /ˌkɑːbəˈhaɪdreɪt/
diet /ˈdaɪət/
exercise /ˈeksəsaɪz/
fat /fæt/
fibre /ˈfaɪbə/
fish /fɪʃ/
fruit /fruːt/
gym /dʒɪm/
junk food /dʒʌŋk fuːd/
salad /ˈsæləd/
salt /sɒlt/
sleep /sliːp/
smoking /ˈsməʊkɪŋ/
stress /stres/
sugar /ˈʃʊgə/
vegetables /ˈvedʒtəbəlz/
vitamins /ˈvɪtəmɪnz/

Adjectives
(un)healthy /ʌnˈhelθi/
high in (fat) /haɪ ɪn/
low in (salt) /ləʊ ɪn/

Verb phrases
cut down on (salt)
cut out (fat)
go on (a diet)
go for (a run)
join (a gym)
make sure
put on (weight)

ILLNESS AND TREATMENT

Nouns
A&E (Accident and Emergency) /ˈeɪənˈiː/
antibiotics /ˌæntɪbaɪˈɒtɪks/
antihistamines /ˌæntɪˈhɪstə miːnz/
bandage /ˈbændɪdʒ/
blister /ˈblɪstə/

casualty /ˈkæʒjuəlti/
cold /kəʊld/
flu /fluː/
jet lag /dʒet læg/
operating theatre /ˈɒpəreɪtɪŋ ˈθɪətə/
plaster /ˈplɑːstə/
prescription /prɪˈskrɪpʃən/
scales /skeɪlz/
scar /skɑː/
sore throat /sɔː θrəʊt/
splinter /ˈsplɪntə/
stethoscope /ˈsteθəskəʊp/
stitches /ˈstɪtʃɪz/
stomach upset /ˈstʌmək ˈʌpset/
stretcher /ˈstretʃə/
surgery /ˈsɜːdʒəri/
syringe /sɪˈrɪndʒ/
thermometer /θəˈmɒmɪtər/
vaccinations /ˌvæksɪˈneɪʃənz/
wheelchair /ˈwiːltʃeə/
X ray /eks reɪ/

Adjectives
jet lagged /dʒet lægd/
run down /rʌn daʊn/
sunburnt /ˈsʌnbɜːnt/

Verb phrases
be sunburnt
get a blister
get a splinter
have a headache
have a sore throat
have a stomach upset
make a decision
make a mistake
make a phone call
make a speech
make a suggestion
make an effort
make arrangements
make changes
make for (the centre of town)
make out (what sb is saying)
make sth into (sth else)
make up (an excuse)
make up for (lost time)

UNIT 2

GEOGRAPHY

Nouns
bank /bæŋk/
beach /biːtʃ/
canal /kəˈnæl/
cave /keɪv/
cliff /klɪf/
coast /kəʊst/
desert /ˈdezət/
dust /dʌst/
flood /flʌd/
flower /flaʊə/
forest /ˈfɒrɪst/
ground /graʊnd/
hill(side) /hɪl/
lake /leɪk/
land /lænd/
mountain /ˈmaʊntɪn/
mud /mʌd/
ocean /ˈəʊʃən/
orchard /ˈɔːtʃəd/
path /pɑːθ/
peak /piːk/
rainforest /ˈreɪnˌfɒrɪst/
river /ˈrɪvə/
sand /sænd/
sea /siː/
shade /ʃeɪd/
shore /ʃɔː/
slope /sləʊp/
soil /sɔɪl/
stone /stəʊn/
stream /striːm/
timber /ˈtɪmbə/
valley /ˈvæli/
waterfall /ˈwɔːtəfɔːl/
wood /wʊd/

Adjectives
cultivated /ˈkʌltɪveɪtɪd/
deep /diːp/
dry /draɪ/
fertile /ˈfɜːtaɪl/
gentle /ˈdʒentəl/
high /haɪ/
low /ləʊ/
muddy /ˈmʌdi/
narrow /ˈnærəʊ/

pine /paɪn/
shallow /ˈʃæləʊ/
snow-capped /snəʊ kæpt/
steep /stiːp/
straight /streɪt/
thick /θɪk/
towering /ˈtaʊərɪŋ/
wide /waɪd/
wild /waɪld/
winding /ˈwaɪndɪŋ/
wooded /ˈwʊdɪd/

Verbs
flow /fləʊ/
grow /grəʊ/

CLIMATE AND WEATHER

Nouns
blizzard /ˈblɪzəd/
breeze /briːz/
downpour /ˈdaʊnpɔː/
fog /fɒg/
frost /frɒst/
gale /geɪl/
hailstone /ˈheɪlstəʊn/
heatwave /ˈhiːtˌweɪv/
ice /aɪs/
monsoon /mɒnˈsuːn/
mud /mʌd/
puddle /ˈpʌdəl/
rain /reɪn/
season /ˈsiːzən/
shower /ˈʃaʊə/
snow(fall) /snəʊ/
storm /stɔːm/
sun /sʌn/
temperature /ˈtemprətʃə/
thunderstorm /ˈθʌndəstɔːm/
wind /wɪnd/

Adjectives
clear /klɪə/
cloudy /ˈklaʊdi/
common /ˈkɒmən/
cool /kuːl/
dry /draɪ/
fine /faɪn/
frozen /ˈfrəʊzən/
hard /hɑːd/
heavy /ˈhevi/

humid /ˈhjuːmɪd/
mild /maɪld/
slippery /ˈslɪpəri/
soaked /səʊkt/
strong /strɒŋ/
sudden /ˈsʌdən/
warm /wɔːm/
wet /wet/

Verb phrases
blow down
be cut off
drop/rise (used for temperature)
pour (= rain heavily) /pɔː/

UNIT 3

MUSIC

Nouns
album /ˈælbəm/
band /bænd/
cello /ˈtʃeləʊ/
charts /tʃɑːts/
choir /kwaɪə/
composer /kəmˈpəʊzə/
concert /ˈkɒnsət/
country and western /ˈkʌntri
    ənd ˈwestən/
cover version /ˈkʌvə ˈvɜːʃən/
duet /djuˈet/
fan /fæn/
folk /fəʊk/
guitar /gɪˈtɑː/
harmony /ˈhɑːməni/
hit /hɪt/
instrument /ˈɪnstrəmənt/
jazz /dʒæz/
lyrics /ˈlɪrɪks/
orchestra /ˈɔːkɪstrə/
piano /piˈænəʊ/
review /rɪˈvjuː/
rock n'roll /rɒk ənˈrəʊl/
saxophone /ˈsæksəfəʊn/
single /ˈsɪŋgəl/
solo /ˈsəʊləʊ/
style /staɪl/
track /træk/
tune /tjuːn/

Adjectives
catchy (tune) /ˈkætʃi/
classical (music) /ˈklæsɪkəl/
distinctive (style) /dɪˈstɪŋtɪv/
musical /ˈmjuːzɪkəl/
original (song/number/version)
    /əˈrɪdʒənəl/
pop (music) /pɒp/
rock (music) /rɒk/

world (music) /wɜːld/

Verb phrases
be musical
go to a concert

SOUNDS

Nouns and regular verbs.
bang /bæŋ/
bark /bɑːk/
crash /kræʃ/
creak /kriːk/
croak /krəʊk/
grunt /grʌnt/
hiss /hɪs/
howl /haʊl/
hum /hʌm/
roar /rɔː/
splash /splæʃ/
whistle /ˈwɪsəl/

UNIT 4

FEELINGS

Nouns
anger /ˈæŋgə/
amazement /əˈmeɪzmənt/
annoyance /əˈnɔɪəns/
anxiety /æŋˈzaɪəti/
depression /dɪˈpreʃən/
embarrassment
    /ɪmˈbærəsmənt/
excitement /ɪkˈsaɪtmənt/
fear /fɪə/
jealousy /ˈdʒeləsi/
misery /ˈmɪzəri/
pleasure /ˈpleʒə/
pride /praɪd/

Adjectives
afraid /əˈfreɪd/
amazed /əˈmeɪzd/
amazing /əˈmeɪzɪŋ/
angry /ˈæŋgri/
annoyed /əˈnɔɪd/
annoying /əˈnɔɪɪŋ/
anxious /ˈæŋʃəs/
ashamed /əˈʃeɪmd/
astonished /əˈstɒnɪʃt/
bored /bɔːd/
boring /ˈbɔːrɪŋ/
concerned /kənˈsɜːnd/
confident /ˈkɒnfɪdənt/
cross /krɒs/
delighted /dɪˈlaɪtɪd/
depressed /dɪˈprest/

depressing /dɪˈpresɪŋ/
disappointed /ˌdɪsəˈpɔɪntɪd/
disappointing /ˌdɪsəˈpɔɪntɪŋ/
embarrassed /ɪmˈbærəst/
embarrassing /ɪmˈbærəsɪŋ/
excited /ɪkˈsaɪtɪd/
exciting /ɪkˈsaɪtɪŋ/
fed up /ˌfedˈʌp/
frightened /ˈfraɪtənd/
frightening /ˈfraɪtənɪŋ/
furious /ˈfjʊəriəs/
glad /glæd/
guilty /ˈgɪlti/
jealous /ˈdʒeləs/
miserable /ˈmɪzərəbəl/
pleased /pliːzd/
pleasing /ˈpliːzɪŋ/
proud /praʊd/
relaxed /rɪˈlækst/
relaxing /rɪˈlæksɪŋ/
relieved /rɪˈliːvd/
scared /skeəd/
surprised /səˈpraɪzd/
surprising /səˈpraɪzɪŋ/
terrified /ˈterəfaɪd/
terrifying /ˈterəfaɪɪŋ/
upset /ʌpset/
worried /ˈwʌrid/
worrying /ˈwʌriɪŋ/

Verb phrases
amaze /əˈmeɪz/
annoy /əˈnɔɪ/
be full of the joys of spring
be thrilled to bits
be walking on air
burst into tears
embarrass /ɪmˈbærəs/
excite /ɪkˈsaɪt/
feel on top of the world
feel sorry for yourself
frighten /ˈfraɪtən/
look /lʊk/
seem /siːm/

Adverbs
a bit
extremely /ɪkˈstriːmli/
fairly /ˈfeəli/
quite /kwaɪt/
really /ˈrɪəli/
terribly /ˈterəbli/
very /ˈveri/

UNIT 5

HISTORY

Nouns
abolition /ˌæbəˈlɪʃən/
ancestor /ˈænsestə/
ancient /ˈeɪnʃənt/
antique /ænˈtiːk/
archaeologist /ˌɑːkiˈɒlədʒɪst/
archaeology /ˌɑːkiˈɒlədʒi/
battle /ˈbætəl/
belief /bɪˈliːf/
cause /kɔːz/
cave /keɪv/
century /ˈsenʃəri/
civilisation /ˌsɪvəlaɪˈzeɪʃən/
descendant /dɪˈsendənt/
dinosaur /ˈdaɪnəsɔː/
discovery /dɪˈskʌvəri/
dynasty /ˈdɪnəsti/
evidence /ˈevɪdəns/
fact /fækt/
figure /ˈfɪgə/
goods /gʊdz/
helicopter /ˈhelɪkɒptə/
historian /hɪˈstɔːriən/
history /ˈhɪstəri/
inhabitant /ɪnˈhæbɪtənt/
introduction /ˌɪntrəˈdʌkʃən/
invasion /ɪnˈveɪʒən/
invention /ɪnˈvenʃən/
machine /məˈʃiːn/
prehistory /ˌpriːˈhɪstəri/
population /ˌpɒpjəˈleɪʃən/
president /ˈprezɪdənt/
record /ˈrekɔːd/
rocket /ˈrɒkɪt/
site /saɪt/
story /ˈstɔːri/
space /speɪs/
survivor /səˈvaɪvə/
survival /səˈvaɪvəl/
tool /tuːl/
tribe /traɪb/

Adjectives
archaeological /ˌɑːkiəˈlɒdʒɪkəl/
historic /hɪˈstɒrɪk/
historical /hɪˈstɒrɪkəl/
prehistoric /ˌpriːɪˈstɒrɪk/

Verb phrases
abolish /əˈbɒlɪʃ/
attack /əˈtæk/
believe /bɪˈliːv/
cause /kɔːz/
hunt /hʌnt/
inhabit /ɪnˈhæbɪt/

invade /ɪn'veɪd/
invent /ɪn'vent/
last /lɑːst/
pass /pɑːs/
settle /'setəl/
survive /sə'vaɪv/

TIME

Verb phrases

go on for several days
have time / no time / a lot of
    time for sb or sth
kill time /kɪl taɪm/
last /lɑːst/
pass /pɑːs/
spend /spend/
take /teɪk/
waste time /weɪst taɪm/

UNIT 6

ADVERTISING

Nouns

advertisement /əd'vɜːtɪsmənt/
advertising /'ædvətaɪzɪŋ/
catalogue /'kætəlɒg/
commercial break
    /kə'mɜːʃəl breɪk/
guarantee /ˌgærən'tiː/
mailshot /'meɪlʃɒt/
offer /'ɒfə/
opportunity /ˌɒpə'tjuːnəti/
poster /'pəustə/
publicity /pʌb'lɪsəti/
slogan /'sləugən/

Adjectives

agreeable /ə'griːəbəl/
extraordinary /ɪk'strɔːdənəri/
fantastic /fæn'tæstɪk/
free /friː/
limited /'lɪmɪtɪd/
magical /'mædʒɪkəl/
nice /naɪs/
particular /pə'tɪkjələ/
pleasant /'plezənt/
remarkable /rɪ'mɑːkəbəl/
unique /juː'niːk/

COMPUTERS

Nouns

basket /'bɑːskɪt/
home page /həum peɪdʒ/
keyword /'kiːwɜːd/

password /'pɑːswɜːd/
support /sə'pɔːt/

Adjectives

online /ˌɒn'laɪn/
secure /sɪ'kjuə/

Verb phrases

browse (for sth) /brauz/
click /klɪk/
enter /'entə/
sign in /saɪn ɪn/
telephoning /'telɪfəunɪŋ/

Verb phrases

be called away on business
call back
call for sb
call out sth
call sb over
call sth off
get cut off
get through
hang up /hæŋ ʌp/
make a phone call
pick up /pɪk ʌp/
ring up /rɪŋ ʌp/

UNIT 7

JOBS

Nouns

accountant /ə'kauntənt/
administration
    /ədˌmɪnɪ'streɪʃən/
application /ˌæplɪ'keɪʃən/
architect /'ɑːkɪtekt/
assistant /ə'sɪstənt/
builder /'bɪldə/
call centre manager
candidate /'kændɪdət/
career /kə'rɪə/
chef /ʃef/
cleaner /'kliːnə/
communication skills /kəˌmjuː
    nɪ'keɪʃən skɪlz/
construction /kən'strʌkʃən/
customer service /'kʌstəmə
    'sɜːvɪs/
electrician /ˌelɪk'trɪʃən/
emergency services /ɪ'mɜːdʒə
    nsi 'sɜːvɪsɪz/
experience /ɪk'spɪəriəns/
firefighter /'faɪəfaɪtə/
health /helθ/
hotel and catering /hə'tel ənd
    'keɪtərɪŋ/

information technology
    /ˌɪnfə'meɪʃən tek'nɒlədʒi/
kitchen/nursery assistant
lab assistant /læb ə'sɪstənt/
leisure and sport /'leʒə ənd
    spɔːt/
lifeguard /'laɪfgɑːd/
mechanic /mɪ'kænɪk/
optician /ɒp'tɪʃən/
overtime /'əuvətaɪm/
plumber /'plʌmə/
police officer /pə'liːs 'ɒfɪsə/
promotion /prə'məuʃən/
psychologist /saɪ'kɒlədʒɪst/
qualifications
    /ˌkwɒlɪfɪ'keɪʃənz/
rate of pay
receptionist /rɪ'sepʃənɪst/
salary /'sæləri/
sales manager /seɪlz 'mænɪdʒə/
shift (work) /ʃɪft/
software engineer /'sɒfweə
    'endʒɪ'nɪə/
solicitor /sə'lɪsɪtə/
supervision /ˌsuːpə'vɪʒən/
training /'treɪnɪŋ/
vacancy /'veɪkənsi/
wage /weɪdʒ/

Adjectives

legal /'liːgəl/
permanent /'pɜːmənənt/
scientific /ˌsaɪən'tɪfɪk/
temporary /'tempərəri/

PERSONAL QUALITIES

Adjectives

ambitious /æm'bɪʃəs/
cheerful /'tʃɪəfəl/
creative /kri'eɪtɪv/
efficient /ɪ'fɪʃənt/
dynamic /daɪ'næmɪk/
energetic /ˌenə'dʒetɪk/
enthusiastic /ɪnˌθjuːzi'æstɪk/
flexible /'fleksɪbəl/
friendly /'frendli/
hard-working /ˌhɑːd'wɜːkɪŋ/
honest /'ɒnɪst/
physically fit /'fɪzɪkəli fɪt/
reliable /rɪ'laɪəbəl/
self-motivated /self
    'məutɪveɪtɪd/
well-organised /wel 'ɔːgənaɪzd/

EMPLOYMENT AND UNEMPLOYMENT

Nouns

agency /'eɪdʒənsi/
career /kə'rɪə/
job /dʒɒb/
occupation /ˌɒkjə'peɪʃən/
pension /'penʃən/
work /wɜːk/

Adjectives

unemployed /ˌʌnɪm'plɔɪd/

Verb phrases

be made redundant
be out of work
be promoted
commute /kə'mjuːt/
give up /gɪv ʌp/
have three days off
retire /rɪ'taɪə/
resign /rɪ'zaɪn/

UNIT 8

PHYSICAL APPEARANCE

Nouns

face /feɪs/
freckles /'frekəlz/
glasses /'glɑːsɪz/
lips /lɪps/

Adjectives

alike /ə'laɪk/
curly /'kɜːli/
dark /dɑːk/
fair /feə/
full (lips) /ful/
pale /peɪl/
pointed (face) /'pɔɪntɪd/
round (face) /raund/
short /ʃɔːt/
similar /'sɪmɪlə/
slim /slɪm/
straight /streɪt/
tall /tɔːl/
thick /θɪk/
thin /θɪn/
turned-up (nose) /tɜːnd ʌp/
wavy (hair) /'weɪvi/

Verb phrases

go bald
go grey
look like
take after

PERSONALITY /

Adjectives

aggressive /ə'gresɪv/
bad-tempered /ˌbæd'tempəd/
big-headed /bɪg 'hedɪd/
bossy /'bɒsi/
cheerful /'tʃɪəfəl/
(in)considerate /kən'sɪdərət/
(dis)honest /'ɒnɪst/
easy-going /'iːzi 'gəʊɪŋ/
fun /fʌn/
funny /'fʌni/
generous /'dʒenərəs/
gentle /'dʒentəl/
hard-working /ˌhɑːd'wɜːkɪŋ/
(un)imaginative /ɪ'mædʒɪnətɪv/
(im)patient /'peɪʃənt/
(un)kind /kaɪnd/
lazy /'leɪzi/
lively /'laɪvli/
mean /miːn/
modest /'mɒdɪst/
moody /'muːdi/
nosey /'nəʊzi/
outgoing /ˌaʊt'gəʊɪŋ/
(im)polite /pə'laɪt/
(un)popular /'pɒpjələ/
rude /ruːd/
selfish /'selfɪʃ/
sensitive /'sensɪtɪv/
sensible /'sensɪbəl/
serious /'sɪəriəs/
shy /ʃaɪ/
(un)sociable /'səʊʃəbəl/
sympathetic /ˌsɪmpə'θetɪk/
talkative /'tɔːkətɪv/
thoughtful /'θɔːtfəl/
thoughtless /'θɔːtləs/
relaxed /rɪ'lækst/
unkind /ʌn'kaɪnd/
unreliable /ˌʌnrɪ'laɪəbəl/

UNIT 9

MOVEMENT

Verb phrases

(feelings) run high
be on the run
beat the rush
crawl /krɔːl/
creep /kriːp/
dash /dæʃ/
run /rʌn/
run across sb
run around
run in the family

run out of patience
run round in circles
run sb down
run through details
run up against a problem
run wild
run yourself into the ground
rush /rʌʃ/
sprint /sprɪnt/
stride /straɪd/ ˌ
stroll /strəʊl/
walk /wɔːk/
wander /'wɒndə/
win /wɪn/

SPORT

Nouns

aerobics /eə'rəʊbɪks/
athlete /'æθliːt/
athletics /æθ'letɪks/
badminton /'bædmɪntən/
baseball /'beɪsbɔːl/
bat /bæt/
boots /buːts/
climbing /'klaɪmɪŋ/
club /klʌb/
cycling /'saɪkəlɪŋ/
cyclist /'saɪklɪst/
diving /'daɪvɪŋ/
football /'fʊtbɔːl/
golf /gɒlf/
gymnast /'dʒɪmnæst/
gymnastics /dʒɪm'næstɪks/
hiking /'haɪkɪŋ/
hockey /'hɒki/
ice hockey /aɪs 'hɒki/
jogging /'dʒɒgɪŋ/
judo /'dʒuːdəʊ/
martial arts /'mɑːʃəl ɑːts/
player /pleɪə/
racket /'rækɪt/
rugby /'rʌgbi/
runner /'rʌnə/
running /'rʌnɪŋ/
sailing /'seɪlɪŋ/
skateboard /'skeɪtbɔːd/
skates /'skeɪtz/
skis /'skiːz/
snorkelling /'snɔːkəlɪŋ/
snowboard /'snəʊbɔːd/
squash /skwɒʃ/
stick /stɪk/
swimming /'swɪmɪŋ/
table tennis /'teɪbəl 'tenɪs/
volleyball /'vɒlibɔːl/
walking /'wɔːkɪŋ/
winner /'wɪnə/
yoga /'jəʊgə/

Verb phrases

be a winner
beat sb to sth
beat the rush
If you can't beat them, join them
win sb round

UNIT 10

FAMILY AND RELATIONSHIPS

Nouns

classmate /'klɑːsmeɪt/
colleague /'kɒliːg/
couple /'kʌpəl/
cousin /'kʌzən/
flatmate /'flætmeɪt/
neighbour /'neɪbə/
nephew /'nefjuː/
niece /niːs/
penfriend /'pen,frend/
relative /'relətɪv/
step-sister /step 'sɪstə/
sister-in-law /'sɪstərɪnlɔː/

Celebrations

Nouns

(silver) wedding anniversary
　/'wedɪŋ ˌænɪ'vɜːsəri/
bride /braɪd/
ceremony /'serɪməni/
gift /gɪft/
groom /gruːm/
guest /gest/
outdoors /ˌaʊt'dɔːz/
present /'prezənt/
priest /priːst/
reception /rɪ'sepʃən/
ring /rɪŋ/
suit /suːt/

Adjectives

civil /'sɪvəl/
colourful /'kʌləfəl/
traditional /trə'dɪʃənəl/

Verb phrases

dress smartly/informally/formally
get/be married to sb
get/be engaged to sb
get/be divorced from sb

FRIENDS

Adjectives

close/best/old (friends)

Verb phrases

fall in love (with sb)
fall out (with sb)
get in touch (with sb)
get on well (with sb)
get to know sb
have things in common (with sb)
keep in touch (with sb)
lose touch (with sb)
make friends (with sb)
make up with sb

UNIT 11

Transport

Nouns

boarding pass /'bɔːdɪŋ pɑːs/
bus /bʌs/
cab /kæb/
cabin crew /'kæbɪn kruː/
carriage /'kærɪdʒ/
conveyor belt /kən'veɪə belt/
departures board/lounge
destination /ˌdestɪ'neɪʃən/
driver /'draɪvə/
escalator /'eskəleɪtə/
fare /feə/
headset /'hedset/
hand luggage /hænd 'lʌgɪdʒ/
meter /'miːtə/
passport control /'pɑːspɔːt kə
　n'trəʊl/
platform /'plætfɔːm/
rail /reɪl/
refreshments /rɪ'freʃmənts/
seat belt /siːt belt/
season ticket /'siːzən 'tɪkɪt/
security check /sɪ'kjʊərəti
　tʃek/
sliding doors /'slaɪdɪŋ dɔːz/
taxi rank /'tæksi ræŋk/
tip /tɪp/
train /treɪn/
underground /'ʌndəgraʊnd/

Verb phrases

board /bɔːd/
commute /kə'mjuːt/
land /lænd/
pack /pæk/
take off /teɪk ɒf/
weigh (a bag) /weɪ/

TRAVEL

Nouns

activity holiday /æk'tɪvəti
  'hɒlədeɪ/
accommodation
  /ə,kɒmə'deɪʃən/
coin /kɔɪn/
guidebook /'gaɪdbʊk/
journey /'dʒɜːni/
luggage /'lʌgɪdʒ/
sightseeing /'saɪtsiːɪŋ/
suitcase /'suːtkeɪs/
storm /stɔːm/
travel /'trævəl/
trip /trɪp/
trolley /'trɒli/

HOLIDAYS

Nouns

beach /biːtʃ/
campsite /'kæmpsaɪt/
hotel /hə'tel/
towel /taʊəl/
(sun) umbrella /ʌm'brelə/

Adjectives

five-star /faɪv stɑː/
luxurious /lʌg'ʒʊəriəs/

Verb phrases

get away from (routine)
get to know (a new place)
get together with (friends)
relax /rɪ'læks/
set about sth
set in
set sth off
set out
set sth up
take it easy
travel independently

UNIT 12

LEISURE ACTIVITIES

Verb phrases

go clubbing
go for a drink
go for a drive
go for a walk
go shopping
go surfing
go swimming
go to the theatre
go to a barbecue

go to a club
go to a concert
go to a play
go to a restaurant
go to the beach
go to the cinema
have a barbecue
have a drink
have a party
have a quiet night in
have friends round
play cards
play games
watch a DVD
watch a film
watch a match
watch TV

HOBBIES AND GAMES

Nouns

backgammon /'bækgæmən/
cards /kɑːdz/
chess /tʃes/
dominoes /'dɒmɪnəʊz/
jigsaw puzzle /'dʒɪgsɔː 'pʌzəl/
snakes and ladders /sneɪks ənd
  'lædəz/
stamps /stæmps/
su doku /su'dəʊkuː/

Verb phrases

collect stamps /kə'lekt
  stæmps/
do a crossword
play chess /pleɪ tʃes/
take after sb (in the family)
take sth in
take sth off
take on work
take over a business
take to (a person/a hobby)
take up space

CINEMA AND THEATRE

Nouns

actor /'æktə/
audience /'ɔːdiəns/
box office /bɒks 'ɒfɪs/
cartoon /kɑː'tuːn/
cast /kɑːst/
costume /'kɒstjuːm/
comedy /'kɒmədi/
critic /'krɪtɪk/
director /dɪ'rektə/
documentary /,dɒkjə'mentəri/
drama /'drɑːmə/
dressing room /'dresɪŋ ruːm/

location /lə'keɪʃən/
musical /'mjuːzɪkəl/
performance /pə'fɔːməns/
plot /plɒt/
rehearsal /rɪ'hɜːsəl/
reviews /rɪ'vjuːz/
science fiction /saɪəns 'fɪkʃən/
screen /skriːn/
soundtrack /'saʊntræk/
special effect /'speʃəl ɪ'fekt/
stage /steɪdʒ/
studio /'stjuːdiəʊ/
subtitle /'sʌb,taɪtəl/
thriller /'θrɪlə/
trailer /'treɪlə/

Adjectives

brilliant /'brɪliənt/
fascinating /'fæsɪneɪtɪŋ/
gripping /'grɪpɪŋ/
imaginative /ɪ'mædʒɪnətɪv/
stunning /'stʌnɪŋ/
tedious /'tiːdiəs/
unimpressive /,ʌnɪm'presɪv/
uninteresting /ʌn'ɪntrəstɪŋ/
wooden /'wʊdən/

Unit 13

CITIES AND TOWNS

Nouns

(rural/residential) area /'eəriə/
atmosphere /'ætməsfɪə/
attraction /ə'trækʃən/
(office/tower) block /blɒk/
(multi-storey) car park /kɑː pɑːk/
church /tʃɜːtʃ/
(capital/industrial/historic) city
  /'sɪti/
(business) district /'dɪstrɪkt/
(housing/industrial) estate
  /ɪ'steɪt/
(leisure) facilities /fə'sɪlətiz/
(bus/cycle) lane /leɪn/
market square /'mɑːkɪt skweə/
mosque /mɒsk/
nightlife /'naɪtlaɪf/
outskirts /'aʊtskɜːts/
pedestrian precinct /pɪ'destriən
  'priːsɪŋt/
(wide open) spaces /'speɪsɪz/
suburbs /'sʌbɜːbz/
(market/seaside) town /taʊn/
temple /'tempəl/

Adjectives

ancient /'eɪnʃənt/

cobbled /'kɒbəld/
cosmopolitan /,kɒzmə'pɒlɪtən/
delightful /dɪ'laɪtfəl/
famous /'feɪməs/
huge /hjuːdʒ/
impressive /ɪm'presɪv/
lively /'laɪvli/
medieval /,medi'iːvəl/
narrow /'nærəʊ/
peaceful /'piːsfəl/
picturesque /,pɪktʃər'esk/
ruined /'ruːɪnd/
up-to-date /ʌptə'deɪt/

Verb phrases

ban /bæn/
be run down

FACILITIES

Nouns

art gallery /ɑːt 'gæləri/
bowling alley /'bəʊlɪŋ 'æli/
concert hall /'kɒnsət hɔːl/
football stadium /'fʊtbɔːl
  'steɪdiəm/
health centre /helθ 'sentə/
ice rink /aɪs rɪŋk/
leisure centre /'leʒə 'sentə/
recreation ground /,rekri'eɪʃən
  graʊnd/
shopping centre /'ʃɒpɪŋ 'sentə/
taxi rank /'tæksi ræŋk/

TRAFFIC

Nouns

bypass /'baɪpɑːs/
kilometres per hour
one-way street /wʌn weɪ striːt/
pedestrian crossing
  /pɪ'destriən 'krɒsɪŋ/
roundabout /'raʊndə,baʊt/
rush hour /rʌʃ aʊə/
short cut /ʃɔːt kʌt/
side road /saɪd rəʊd/
traffic jam /'træfɪk dʒæm/
traffic lights /'træfɪk laɪts/

Verb phrases

overtake
break down
knock sth down
let sb down
put sth down
slow down
turn sth down
write sth down

UNIT 14

FOOD AND DRINK

Nouns
apple /'æpəl/
bacon /'beɪkən/
banana /bə'nɑːnə/
breast /brest/
burgers /'bɜːgəz/
butter /'bʌtə/
cake /keɪk/
chicken /'tʃɪkɪn/
chop /tʃɒp/
cod /kɒd/
coffee /'kɒfi/
cream /kriːm/
duck /dʌk/
fish /fɪʃ/
flour /flaʊə/
fruit /fruːt/
eggs /egz/
ham /hæm/
lobster /'lɒbstə/
juice /dʒuːs/
lemon /'lemən/
meat /miːt/
milk /mɪlk/
mussels /'mʌsəlz/
noodles /'nuːdəlz/
onion /'ʌnjən/
plaice /pleɪs/
pork /pɔːk/
prawns /prɔːnz/
salad /'sæləd/
salmon /'sæmən/
sauce /sɔːs/
sausages /'sɒsɪdʒɪz/
squid /skwɪd/
steak /steɪk/
trout /traʊt/
tuna /'tjuːnə/
vegetables /'vedʒtəbəlz/
wing /wɪŋ/

COOKING

Nouns
cake tin /keɪk tɪn/
cook /kʊk/
cooker /'kʊkə/
frying pan /'fraɪɪŋ pæn/
grill /grɪl/
grillpan /'grɪlpæn/
hob /hɒb/
oven /'ʌvən/
saucepan /'sɔːspən/
wok /wɒk/

Verbs
bake /beɪk/
beat /biːt/
boil /bɔɪl/
chop /tʃɒp/
fry /fraɪ/
grate /greɪt/
grill /grɪl/
mix /mɪks/
peel /piːl/
pour /pɔː/
roast /rəʊst/
slice /slaɪs/
stew /stjuː/
stir /stɜː/
stir fry /stɜː fraɪ/
taste /teɪst/

Adjectives
tasteful /'teɪsfəl/
tasteless /'teɪsləs/
tasty /'teɪsti/

ART

Nouns
art gallery /ɑːt 'gæləri/
artist /'ɑːtɪst/
collection /kə'lekʃən/
drawing /drɔːɪŋ/
exhibition /,eksɪ'bɪʃən/
jewellery /'dʒuːəlri/
landscape /'lænskeɪp/
oil painting /ɔɪl 'peɪntɪŋ/
painter /'peɪntə/
portrait /'pɔːtrɪt/
pottery /'pɒtəri/
print /prɪnt/
sculpture /'skʌlptʃə/
still life /stɪl laɪf/
studio /'stjuːdiəʊ/
textiles /'tekstaɪlz/
watercolour /'wɔːtə,kʌlə/

Adjectives
abstract /'æbstrækt/
artistic /ɑː'tɪstɪk/

Verbs
draw /drɔː/
paint /peɪnt/

UNIT 15

TELEVISION AND RADIO

Nouns
aerial /'eəriəl/
awards /ə'wɔːdz/
celebrity /sə'lebrəti/
channel /'tʃænəl/
character /'kærəktə/
comedy /'kɒmədi/
current affairs /'kʌrənt ə'feəz/
disc jockey /dɪsk 'dʒɒki/
documentary /,dɒkjə'mentəri/
drama /'drɑːmə/
episodes /'epɪsəʊdz/
highlights /'haɪlaɪts/
programme /'prəʊgræm/
reality TV /ri'æləti ,tiː'viː/
remote control /rɪ'məʊt
    kən'trəʊl/
repeats /rɪ'piːts/
screen /skriːn/
script /skrɪpt/
series /'sɪəriːz/
TV set /,tiː'viː set/
show /ʃəʊ/
soap opera /'səʊp,ɒpərə/
radio station /'reɪdiəʊ 'steɪʃən/
storyline /'stɔːrilaɪn/
studio /'stjuːdiəʊ/

Adjectives
entertaining /,entə'teɪnɪŋ/
factual /'fæktʃuəl/
gripping /'grɪpɪŋ/
humorous /'hjuːmərəs/

Verbs
aim /eɪm/
broadcast /'brɔːdkɑːst/

NEWSPAPERS AND MAGAZINES

Nouns
comic /'kɒmɪk/
newspaper /'njuːs,peɪpə/
magazine /,mægə'ziːn/
advertisement /əd'vɜːtɪsmənt/
article /'ɑːtɪkəl/
cover /'kʌvə/
editor /'edɪtə/
editorial /,edɪ'tɔːriəl/
headline /'hedlaɪn/
report /rɪ'pɔːt/

Adjectives
daily /'deɪli/
fashion /'fæʃən/
glossy /'glɒsi/
gossip /'gɒsɪp/
in-flight /,ɪn'flaɪt/
local /'ləʊkəl/
monthly /'mʌnθli/
morning /'mɔːnɪŋ/
tabloid /'tæblɔɪd/
today's /tə'deɪz/
travel /'trævəl/
women's /wɪmɪnz/

Verbs
accuse /ə'kjuːz/
admit /əd'mɪt/
advise /əd'vaɪz/
announce /ə'naʊns/
apologise /ə'pɒlədʒaɪz/
appeal /ə'piːl/
believe /bɪ'liːv/
blame /bleɪm/
care /keə/
claim /kleɪm/
declare /dɪ'kleə/
demand /dɪ'mɑːnd/
deny /dɪ'naɪ/
describe /dɪ'skraɪb/
disapprove /,dɪsə'pruːv/
emphasise /'emfəsaɪz/
expect /ɪk'spekt/
express /ɪk'spres/
hope /həʊp/
offer /'ɒfə/
oppose /ə'pəʊz/
predict /prɪ'dɪkt/
prepare /prɪ'peə/
promise /'prɒmɪs/
propose /prə'pəʊz/
refuse /rɪ'fjuːs /
regret /rɪ'gret/
suggest /sə'dʒest/
threaten /'θretən/
warn /wɔːn/

BOOKS

Nouns
atlas /'ætləs/
author /'ɔːθə/
biography /baɪ'ɒgrəfi/
cookery book /'kʊkəri bʊk/
detective story /dɪ'tektɪv 'stɔːri/
diary /'daɪəri/
encyclopedia /ɪn,saɪklə'piːdiə/
fiction /'fɪkʃən/
ghost story /gəʊst 'stɔːri/
guidebook /'gaɪdbʊk/
journalist /'dʒɜːnəlɪst/
non-fiction /nɒn 'fɪkʃən/
novelist /'nɒvəlɪst/
poet /'pəʊɪt/
poetry book /'pəʊɪtri bʊk/
reference book /'refərəns bʊk/
science fiction novel

textbook /'teksbʊk/
thriller /'θrɪlə/

Verbs

breathe /briːð/
gaze /geɪz/
glance /glɑːns/
glimpse /glɪms/
notice /'nəʊtɪs/
observe /əb'zɜːv/
overhear /ˌəʊvə'hɪə/
smell /smel/
sniff /snɪf/
spot /spɒt/
stare /steə/
stroke /strəʊk/
view /vjuː/
wink /wɪŋk/
witness /'wɪtnəs/

UNIT 16

DIFFERENT AGES

Nouns

gap year /gæp jɪə/
toddler /'tɒdələ/
widow /'wɪdəʊ/

Adjectives

childish /'tʃaɪldɪʃ/
elderly /'eldəli/
grown up /grəʊn ʌp/
middle-aged /ˌmɪdəl'eɪdʒd/
pregnant /'pregnənt/
three-year-old (daughter) /θriː
jɪə əʊld/

Verb phrases

be full of life
be in his/her (early/late) teens
be in his/her (early/late) twenties
expect a baby

UNIVERSITY

Nouns

campus /'kæmpəs/
department /dɪ'pɑːtmənt/
dissertation /ˌdɪsə'teɪʃən/
faculty /'fækəlti/
graduate /'grædʒuət/
hall of residence /hɔːl ɒv
  'rezɪdəns/
lecture /'lektʃə/
lecturer /'lektʃərə/
mature student /mə'tjʊə
  'stjuːdənt/

open day /'əʊpən deɪ/
postgraduate /ˌpəʊs'grædʒuət/
prospectus /prə'spektəs/
school-leaver /skuːl 'liːvə/
seminar /'semɪnɑː/
students' union /'stjuːdənts
  'juːnjən/
term /tɜːm/
tutor /'tjuːtə/
tutorial /tjuː'tɔːriəl/
undergraduate
/ˌʌndə'grædʒuət/
vacation /və'keɪʃən/
school /skuːl/

Nouns

deadline /'dedlaɪn/
kindergarten /'kɪndəˌgɑːtən/
nursery school /'nɜːsəri skuːl/
primary school /'praɪməri skuːl/
pupil /'pjuːpəl/
secondary school /'sekəndəri
  skuːl/
state school /steɪt skuːl/
uniform /'juːnɪfɔːm/

Adjectives

compulsory /kəm'pʌlsəri/
vocational (courses)
/vəʊ'keɪʃənəl/

Verb phrases

attend a school
be at school
fail an exam
give sth away
give sth back
give sth in   fail an exam
give sth up
hand sth down to sb
hand sth in
hand sth over
pass an exam
start school
take an exam

UNIT 17

CLOTHES

Nouns

beads /biːdz/
belt /belt/
blouse /blaʊz/
boots /buːts/
bracelet /'breɪslət/
buckle /'bʌkəl/
button /'bʌtən/
cagoule /kə'guːl/

cap /kæp/
coat /kəʊt/
collar /'kɒlə/
cuff /kʌf/
dress /dres/
earrings /'ɪərɪŋz/
gloves /glʌvz/
hat /hæt/
(high) heels /hiːlz/
hood /hʊd/
jacket /'dʒækɪt/
jeans /dʒiːnz/
jumper /'dʒʌmpə/
laces /'leɪsɪz/
necklace /'nekləs/
nightdress /'naɪtdres/
outfit /'aʊtfɪt/
pocket /'pɒkɪt/
pullover /'pʊləʊvə/
pyjamas /pɪ'dʒɑːməz/
ring /rɪŋ/
sandals /'sændəlz/
scarf /skɑːf/
(flat) shoes /ʃuːz/
shorts /ʃɔːts/
skirt /skɜːt/
sleeve /sliːv/
slippers /'slɪpəz/
socks /sɒks/
sweatshirt /'swetʃɜːt/
T-shirt /'tiːʃɜːt/
tie /taɪ/
tights /taɪts/
trainers /'treɪnəz/
trousers /'traʊzəz/

Adjectives

baggy /'bægi/
bare (legs) /beə/
dark (blue) /dɑːk/
light (green) /laɪt/
checked /tʃekt/
cool /kuːl/
cotton /'kɒtən/
dark /dɑːk/
denim /'denɪm/
flowery /'flaʊəri/
knee-length /niː leŋθ/
leather /'leðə/
lycra /'laɪkrə/
nylon /'naɪlɒn/
open-toed /'əʊpən təʊd/
plain /pleɪn/
polyester /ˌpɒli'estə/
round /raʊnd/
short-sleeved /ʃɔːt sliːvd/
silk /sɪlk/
silver /'sɪlvə/
sleeveless /'sliːvləs/

spotted /'spɒtɪd/
straight (legs) /streɪt/
striped /straɪpt/
wool /wʊl/
V neck /viː nek/

Verb phrases

match /mætʃ/
feel/look good

SHOPPING AND MONEY

Nouns

basket /'bɑːskɪt/
cashback /'kæʃbæk/
cashier /kæʃ'ɪə/
checkout /'tʃekaʊt/
cheque /tʃek/
credit cards /'kredɪt kɑːdz/
discount /'dɪskaʊnt/
fortune /'fɔːtʃuːn/
gift voucher /gɪft 'vaʊtʃə/
label /'leɪbəl/
receipt /rɪ'siːt/
refund /'riːfʌnd/
sale /seɪl/
shade /ʃeɪd/
size /saɪz/
trolley /'trɒli/
waste (of money) /weɪst/

Adjectives

fully dressed /'fʊli drest/
over-priced /'əʊvə praɪst/
reduced /rɪ'djuːst/

Verb phrases

be dressed in
be in stock
bring/take sth back
change into sth
fit /fɪt/
get dressed/undressed
go with something
grow into/out of sth
hang sth up
put sth on
suit /suːt/
take sth off
try sth on
wear /weə/

MONEY

Verbs

cost /kɒst/
donate /dəʊ'neɪt/
earn /ɜːn/
inherit /ɪn'herɪt/

make a lot of money
pay for sth
pay sb
save /seɪv/
spend /spend/

UNIT 18

HOUSE AND HOME

Nouns
air conditioning /eə kən'dɪʃənɪŋ/
apartment (block) /ə'pɑːtmənt/
bedroom /'bedrʊm/
brick /brɪk/
bungalow /'bʌŋgələʊ/
central heating /ˌsentrəl 'hiːtɪŋ/
cottage /'kɒtɪdʒ/
deck /dek/
dining room /'daɪnɪŋ ruːm/
drier /'draɪə/
drive /draɪv/
fence /fens/
freezer /'friːzə/
garage /'gærɑːʒ/
gate /geɪt/
hedge /hedʒ/
home /həʊm/
kitchen /'kɪtʃɪn/
lighting /'laɪtɪŋ/
living room /'lɪvɪŋ ruːm/
sink /sɪŋk/
shutter /'ʃʌtə/
storey /'stɔːri/
tap /tæp/
utility room /juː'tɪləti ruːm/
villa /'vɪlə/
wood /wʊd/

Adjectives
detached (house) /dɪ'tætʃt/
fitted (kitchen) /'fɪtɪd/
modern /'mɒdən/
semi-detached (house) /'semi dɪ'tætʃt/
terraced (house) /'terɪst/

HOUSEHOLD PROBLEMS

Nouns
builder /'bɪldə/
decorator /'dekəreɪtə/
dry cleaner /draɪ 'kliːnə/
electrician /ˌelɪk'trɪʃən/
plumber /'plʌmə/
service agent /'sɜːvɪs 'eɪdʒənt/

Verb phrases
be home and dry

do chores (e.g. the washing, gardening)
do out a room
do sb in
do sth up
do without sth
drip /drɪp/
feel homesick /fiːl 'həʊmsɪk/
hammer sth home
hit the nail on the head
make sth (e.g. a cake)
make the bed
make yourself at home
put your own house in order

UNIT 19

SCIENCE

Nouns
astronomer /ə'strɒnəmə/
astronomy /ə'strɒnəmi/
biologist /baɪ'ɒlədʒɪst/
biology /baɪ'ɒlədʒi/
chemist /'kemɪst/
chemistry /'kemɪstri/
conference /'kɒnfərəns/
data /'deɪtə/
discovery /dɪ'skʌvəri/
ecology /ɪ'kɒlədʒi/
ecologist /ɪ'kɒlədʒɪst/
experiment /ɪk'sperɪmənt/
geologist /dʒi'ɒlədʒɪst/
geology /dʒi'ɒlədʒi/
invention /ɪn'venʃən/
instruments /'ɪnstrəmənts/
mathematics /ˌmæθəm'ætɪks/
mathematician /ˌmæθəmə'tɪʃən/
observation /ˌɒbzə'veɪʃən/
physicist /'fɪzɪsɪst/
physics /'fɪzɪks/
research /rɪ'sɜːtʃ/
scientist /'saɪəntɪst/
statistics /stə'tɪstɪks/
space /speɪs/
talent /'tælənt/
theory /'θɪəri/

Adjectives
global /'gləʊbəl/
outstanding /ˌaʊt'stændɪŋ/
scientific /ˌsaɪən'tɪfɪk/

Verb phrases
analyse statistics
attend a conference
carry out an experiment
do research
make a discovery

THE ENVIRONMENT

Nouns
acid rain /'æsɪd reɪn/
air conditioning /eə kən'dɪʃə nɪŋ/
climate /'klaɪmət/
drought /draʊt/
environment /ɪn'vaɪrəmənt/
exhaust fumes /ɪg'zɔːst fjuːmz/
emissions /ɪ'mɪʃənz/
flooding /'flʌdɪŋ/
global warming /'gləʊbəl 'wɔːmɪŋ/
impact /'ɪmpækt/
pesticide /'pestɪsaɪd/
resource /rɪ'zɔːs/
rubbish /'rʌbɪʃ/
solar panels /'səʊlə pænəlz/
storms /stɔːmz/
waste /weɪst/
wildlife /'waɪldlaɪf/

Adjectives
environmentally friendly /ɪnˌvaɪərə'mentəli 'frendli/
green /griːn/
local /'ləʊkəl/
major /'meɪdʒə/
organic /ɔː'gænɪk/
sustainable /sə'steɪnəbəl/
wasteful /'weɪsfəl/

Verbs
cause /kɔːz/
create /kri'eɪt/
pollute /pə'luːt/
heat /hiːt/
light /laɪt/
waste /weɪst/

UNIT 20

CRIME

Nouns
arsonist /'ɑːsənɪst/
barrister /'bærɪstə/
burglar /'bɜːglə/
burglary /'bɜːgləri/
burgle /'bɜːgəl/
crime /kraɪm/
criminal /'krɪmɪnəl/
detective /dɪ'tektɪv/
evidence /'evɪdəns/
fact /fækt/
hijacking /'haɪdʒækɪŋ/
lawyer /'lɔɪə/

kidnapping /'kɪdnæpɪŋz/
murder /'mɜːdə/
murderer /'mɜːdərə/
police officer /pə'liːs 'ɒfɪsə/
prison /'prɪzən/
proof /pruːf/
robber /'rɒbə/
robbery /'rɒbəri/
shoplifter /'ʃɒplɪftə/
shoplifting /'ʃɒplɪftɪŋ/
solicitor /sə'lɪsɪtə/
speeding /'spiːdɪŋ/
thief /θiːf/
theft /θeft/
vandalism /'vændəlɪzəm/
witness /'wɪtnəs/

Verb phrases
burgle a house
commit a crime
murder /'mɜːdə/
rob a bank
shoplift /'ʃɒplɪft/
steal /stiːl/

OPINIONS

Adjectives
conservative /kən'sɜːvətɪv/
effective /ɪ'fektɪv/
enthusiastic /ɪnˌθjuːzi'æstɪk/
innovative /'ɪnəvətɪv/
keen /kiːn/
radical /'rædɪkəl/
revolutionary /ˌrevəl'uːʃənəri/
significant /sɪg'nɪfɪkənt/

Verb phrases
approve of sth
be in favour of / against sth
have strong opinions on sth
support sth
think about/of
think aloud
think for yourself
think long and hard about sth
think on your feet
think straight

Tracklist